.NET MAUI Cookbook

Build a full-featured app swiftly with MVVM, CRUD, AI, authentication, real-time updates, and more

Alexander Russkov

.NET MAUI Cookbook

Copyright © 2024 Packt Publishing

The author acknowledges the use of cutting-edge AI, in this case ChatGPT, with the sole aim of enhancing the language and clarity within the book, thereby ensuring a smooth reading experience for readers. It's important to note that the content itself has been crafted by the author and edited by a professional publishing team.

Every effort has been made in the preparation of this book to ensure the accuracy of the information presented. However, the information contained in this book is sold without warranty, either express or implied. Neither the author, nor Packt Publishing or its dealers and distributors, will be held liable for any damages caused or alleged to have been caused directly or indirectly by this book.

Packt Publishing has endeavored to provide trademark information about all of the companies and products mentioned in this book by the appropriate use of capitals. However, Packt Publishing cannot guarantee the accuracy of this information.

Group Product Manager: Rohit Rajkumar
Publishing Product Manager: Tanisha Mehrotra
Book Project Manager: Arul Viveaun S
Senior Editor: Mark D'Souza
Technical Editor: K Bimala Singha
Copy Editor: Safis Editing
Proofreader: Mark D'Souza
Indexer: Manju Arasan
Production Designer: Prashant Ghare
Senior DevRel Marketing Executive: Nivedita Pandey

First published: December 2024
Production reference: 1141124

Published by Packt Publishing Ltd.
Grosvenor House
11 St Paul's Square
Birmingham
B3 1RB, UK.

ISBN 978-1-83546-112-9

www.packtpub.com

Contributors

About the author

Alexander Russkov is a seasoned software engineer and product manager with over 12 years of experience in the .NET domain and XAML-based technologies. Throughout his career at DevExpress, he has made significant contributions to the .NET MAUI, WPF, and WinForms teams. With a deep understanding of customer needs and project optimization, Alexander offers valuable insights for developers looking to sharpen their cross-platform application skills.

I want to thank my incredible team at DevExpress for inspiring me to push the limits and always aim higher. A heartfelt thanks to my family for their constant support and patience. And to the .NET community and all the developers I've learned from – with shared knowledge and collective efforts, we can achieve great things!

About the reviewers

Leela Vardhan Siramdasu is a software developer with experience in .NET technologies and machine learning. His work focuses on building efficient, scalable applications, leveraging advanced C#, Python, ASP.NET, MAUI and related frameworks. Passionate about clean code, he is committed to enhancing the user experience through intuitive and well-structured software solutions. Vardhan has a proven ability to collaborate with teams and deliver projects on time, while continuously seeking to expand his technical expertise and contribute to the tech community.

Lokesh Sehgal has 14 years of experience in the apps and backend development; he brings deep expertise in server-side and frontend technologies, including Azure, AWS, C#, ASP.NET, and microservices. He has got a strong background in frontend programming languages such as C#, Objective-C, SwiftUI, Swift, Java, and Kotlin. His focus is on creating scalable, efficient, and high-performing mobile solutions that integrate seamlessly with robust back-end systems, ensuring optimal user experiences and technical excellence across the full development stack. He is proficient in creating RESTful APIs, managing databases, and implementing efficient data processing workflows.

Table of Contents

2

Mastering the MVVM Design Pattern   35

3

Advanced XAML and UI Techniques   75

4

Connecting to a Database and Implementing CRUD Operations   111

5

Authentication and Authorization   169

6

Real-Life Scenarios: AI, SignalR, and More   231

7

Understanding Platform-Specific APIs and Custom Handlers   289

8

Optimizing Performance   309

Preface

Think about this: how many of challenges that you face during development of your app (or future app) would have already been overcome by other developers? How much time could you save by reusing the shared knowledge within the developer community? While every app is unique, most have similar core modules.

I wrote this book for you, .NET MAUI developers, to help you build cross-platform apps faster and with higher quality. It offers solutions and best practices for the tasks you'll likely face during development, along with common pitfalls to avoid. You'll also get insights into how things work under the hood, enabling you to tackle variations of these tasks with ease. This book is designed to save you time and guide you toward building modern .NET MAUI applications with expert-level quality.

It covers a wide range of essential topics, including UI best practices, MVVM, dependency injection, performance, and memory profiling. Since real-world apps go beyond frontend development, this book also explores backend integration for authentication, data processing, synchronization, and real-time updates. Plus, you'll learn how to integrate AI strategies – no prior machine learning experience is required.

The book is organized into step-by-step recipes, each focusing on a specific task. Each recipe includes detailed explanations to help you apply the knowledge to your unique projects.

By the end, you'll have the skills to create high-performance, interactive cross-platform apps with .NET MAUI, saving you valuable time on future projects.

Who this book is for

This book is primarily aimed at developers who are already familiar with the basics of .NET MAUI. Whether you're actively building a .NET MAUI app or just starting to plan one, this guide will help you develop more efficiently and with better quality. Inside, you'll discover advanced techniques and practical examples to enhance your skills and tackle real-world development challenges.

While a basic understanding of .NET MAUI and XAML is assumed, the recipes are presented in a simple, step-by-step format, making them easy to follow, even without prior experience. The only requirement is having your development environment set up, including Visual Studio or VS Code, .NET MAUI workloads, and an emulator or device for debugging.

What this book covers

Chapter 1, Crafting the Page Layout, dives into the most commonly used layouts in .NET MAUI, highlighting common misconceptions and pitfalls to avoid. You'll explore dynamic layouts that adapt based on platform, device, and orientation. This chapter also deepens your understanding of element measuring and arranging, while guiding you through creating a custom layout panel from scratch.

Chapter 2, Mastering the MVVM Design Pattern, shares best practices for working with the MVVM pattern. You'll learn how to decouple the UI from the view model, inject dependencies, and manage communication between view models. It also covers techniques to reduce boilerplate code and prevent UI freezes by leveraging asynchronous programming patterns.

Chapter 3, Advanced XAML and UI Techniques, explores advanced strategies for building responsive and reusable UI components. This chapter covers attached properties, behaviors, and views, while offering guidance on supporting themes and incorporating animations such as Lottie. You'll also learn how to create custom-drawn controls based on your own logic.

Chapter 4, Connecting to a Database and Implementing CRUD Operations, walks you through building apps that load data from both local and remote databases. You'll also learn how to modify data across different screens while adhering to mobile UX best practices. Each recipe builds on the previous one, introducing you to the **repository** and **unit of work** patterns, showing their power in real-world scenarios.

Chapter 5, Authentication and Authorization, focuses on user authentication, role-based access control, session management, Google OAuth, and biometric authentication. The chapter is centered around a self-hosted ASP.NET Core service, giving you complete control over your app's business logic.

Chapter 6, Real-Life Scenarios: AI, SignalR, and More, covers practical AI integration strategies – whether using cloud-based models, hosting them on your own server, or deploying them on end user devices. You'll also tackle real-time updates with SignalR, chunked file uploads, push notifications, and handling online/offline data synchronization to ensure your app works seamlessly even without an internet connection.

Chapter 7, Understanding Platform-Specific APIs and Custom Handlers, covers ways to tailor your app's behavior based on platform-specific requirements. This chapter explains conditional compilation with preprocessor directives, creating cross-platform APIs with platform-specific implementations, and customizing native controls through handlers.

Chapter 8, Optimizing Performance, focuses on techniques to boost your app's performance. You'll learn why certain approaches improve speed and how to measure their impact. The chapter also delves into performance and memory profiling, equipping you with the tools to fine-tune your app's performance on your own.

To get the most out of this book

To understand the code in this book, you'll need to have a basic understanding of C# and XAML.

Software/hardware covered in the book	OS requirements
Visual Studio	Windows
VS Code	Windows or macOS

Before diving into the first recipe, you'll need to set up your development environment. This includes installing Visual Studio and the .NET MAUI workloads and setting up an emulator or a device for debugging. If you're working with iOS, you'll also need a Mac, Xcode, and a paid Apple Developer account. For more details, check out the official .NET MAUI documentation at `https://learn.microsoft.com/en-us/dotnet/maui/get-started/installation?view=net-maui-8.0&tabs=vswin`.

If you are using the digital version of this book, we advise you to type the code yourself or access the code via the GitHub repository (link available in the next section). Doing so will help you avoid any potential errors related to the copying and pasting of code.

Download the example code files

You can download the example code files for this book from GitHub at `https://github.com/PacktPublishing/.NET-MAUI-Cookbook`. If there's an update to the code, it will be updated in the GitHub repository.

We also have other code bundles from our rich catalog of books and videos available at `https://github.com/PacktPublishing/`. Check them out!

Conventions used

There are a number of text conventions used throughout this book.

`Code in text`: Indicates code words in text, database table names, folder names, filenames, file extensions, pathnames, dummy URLs, user input, and Twitter handles. Here is an example: "By adding `BindableProperty`, you can configure your custom `ContentView` or pass data to it, as we did with the `Text` property."

A block of code is set as follows:

```
public string Text {
    get { return (string)GetValue(TextProperty); }
    set { SetValue(TextProperty, value); }
}
public static readonly BindableProperty TextProperty =
BindableProperty.Create("Text", typeof(string), typeof(EditableCard));
```

When we wish to draw your attention to a particular part of a code block, the relevant lines or items are set in bold:

```
<Grid ColumnDefinitions="*,*" RowDefinitions="*,*">
    <Label Grid.Row="1" Grid.Column="1"/>
</Grid>
exten => i,1,Voicemail(s0)
```

Any command-line input or output is written as follows:

```
$ mkdir css
$ cd css
```

Bold: Indicates a new term, an important word, or words that you see onscreen. For example, words in menus or dialog boxes appear in the text like this. Here is an example: "Type any text into the input field and press the **Send** button."

> **Tips or important notes**
> Appear like this.

Sections

In this book, you will find several headings that appear frequently (*Getting ready*, *How to do it...*, *How it works...*, and *There's more...*).

Getting ready

This section tells you what to expect in the recipe and describes how to set up any software or any preliminary settings required for the recipe.

How to do it...

This section contains the steps required to follow the recipe.

How it works...

This section usually consists of a detailed explanation of what happened in the previous section.

There's more...

This section consists of additional information about the recipe in order to make you more knowledgeable about the recipe.

Get in touch

Feedback from our readers is always welcome.

General feedback: If you have questions about any aspect of this book, mention the book title in the subject of your message and email us at customercare@packtpub.com.

Errata: Although we have taken every care to ensure the accuracy of our content, mistakes do happen. If you have found a mistake in this book, we would be grateful if you would report this to us. Please visit www.packtpub.com/support/errata, selecting your book, clicking on the Errata Submission Form link, and entering the details.

Piracy: If you come across any illegal copies of our works in any form on the Internet, we would be grateful if you would provide us with the location address or website name. Please contact us at copyright@packtpub.com with a link to the material.

If you are interested in becoming an author: If there is a topic that you have expertise in and you are interested in either writing or contributing to a book, please visit authors.packtpub.com.

Share Your Thoughts

Once you've read *.NET MAUI Cookbook*, we'd love to hear your thoughts! Scan the QR code below to go straight to the Amazon review page for this book and share your feedback.

https://packt.link/r/1-835-46112-3

Your review is important to us and the tech community and will help us make sure we're delivering excellent quality content.

Download a free PDF copy of this book

Thanks for purchasing this book!

Do you like to read on the go but are unable to carry your print books everywhere?

Is your eBook purchase not compatible with the device of your choice?

Don't worry, now with every Packt book you get a DRM-free PDF version of that book at no cost.

Read anywhere, any place, on any device. Search, copy, and paste code from your favorite technical books directly into your application.

The perks don't stop there, you can get exclusive access to discounts, newsletters, and great free content in your inbox daily

Follow these simple steps to get the benefits:

1. Scan the QR code or visit the link below

https://packt.link/free-ebook/978-1-83546-112-9

2. Submit your proof of purchase

3. That's it! We'll send your free PDF and other benefits to your email directly

1
Crafting the Page Layout

Great applications start with a good idea and a vision of what users will see on the screen. I won't be able to come up with an idea for your app, but I can help you avoid expending your energy when you get around to creating the user interface. While crafting the page layout may seem like a basic topic, many professional developers waste considerable time during this step or create views with performance/UX issues.

In this chapter, we'll create the main layout types you'll mostly need in **.NET MAUI** applications, learn how to avoid pitfalls, and delve into details of the algorithm for arranging UI elements.

By the end of this chapter, you will be able to create simple, advanced layouts with your custom arranging mechanism. We will create adaptive views for both desktop and mobile devices. You will get a deep understanding of how the .NET MAUI layout mechanism works, which will help you always make the right choice on what panel works best in your specific scenario.

In this chapter, we'll be covering the following recipes:

- Creating horizontal/vertical layouts
- Creating grid layouts
- Creating scrollable layouts
- Implementing device-specific layouts
- Implementing layouts with dynamic orientation
- Building a layout dynamically based on a collection
- Implementing a custom arranging algorithm

Technical requirements

I hope you've had the chance to create at least some basic .NET MAUI projects already, so your development environment should be all set up. If not, make sure to follow the tutorial provided by Microsoft: `https://learn.microsoft.com/en-us/dotnet/maui/get-started/installation`.

You can download all the projects created in this chapter from GitHub: `https://github.com/PacktPublishing/.NET-MAUI-Cookbook/tree/main/Chapter01`

Creating horizontal/vertical layouts

User experience experts constantly emphasize that simplicity is key to a well-designed application. Horizontally or vertically arranged elements are essential for creating clean and clear views. Mastering these layout techniques is crucial to avoid unexpected issues on a user's device.

Though this topic might seem straightforward, many developers run into issues due to the specific nuances of elements such as **HorizontalStackLayout/VerticalStackLayout**.

Let's create several horizontal/vertical layout types to get a basic understanding of how the .NET MAUI layout system works and how to avoid potential issues.

Getting ready

To follow the steps described in this recipe, we just need to create a blank .NET MAUI application. The default template includes sample code in the `MainPage.xaml` and `MainPage.xaml.cs` files, but you can remove this code and leave only a blank `ContentPage` in XAML and a constructor with the `InitializeComponent` method in the page class. When copying code snippets with namespaces, don't forget to replace them with the namespaces in your project.

The code for this recipe is available at `https://github.com/PacktPublishing/.NET-MAUI-Cookbook/tree/main/Chapter01/c1-HorizontalAndVerticalLayouts`.

How to do it...

We'll create four linear layouts with buttons using the following panels:

- `HorizontalStackLayout`
- `VerticalStackLayout`
- `Grid`
- `FlexLayout`

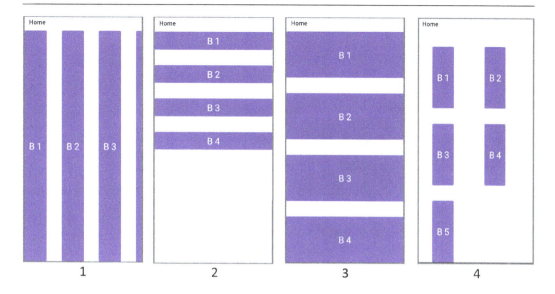

Figure 1.1 – Linear layouts

1.   Add `HorizontalStackLayout` with four buttons to arrange elements horizontally:

MainPage.xaml

```
<ContentPage
xmlns="http://schemas.microsoft.com/dotnet/2021/maui"
xmlns:x="http://schemas.microsoft.com/winfx/2009/xaml"
x:Class="c1_HorizontalAndVerticalLayouts.MainPage">

    <HorizontalStackLayout Spacing="50">
            <Button Text="B 1"/>
            <Button Text="B 2"/>
            <Button Text="B 3"/>
            <Button Text="B 4"/>
    </HorizontalStackLayout>
</ContentPage>
```

If you run the project, you should see the result shown on the left-hand side of *Figure 1.1.*

2. Replace HorizontalStackLayout with VerticalStackLayout:

```
<VerticalStackLayout Spacing="50">
    <Button Text="B 1"/>
    <Button Text="B 2"/>
    <Button Text="B 3"/>
    <Button Text="B 4"/>
</VerticalStackLayout >
```

Run the project to see the result.

3. Do the same as we did in the previous step, but now, replace VerticalStackLayout with Grid, with four rows. Assign the Grid.Row attached property to each button:

```
<Grid RowDefinitions="*,*,*,*" RowSpacing="50">
    <Button Text="B 1"/>
    <Button Text="B 2" Grid.Row="1"/>
    <Button Text="B 3" Grid.Row="2"/>
    <Button Text="B 4" Grid.Row="3"/>
</Grid>
```

Run the project to see the result.

4. Do the same as we did in the previous step, but now, replace Grid with FlexLayout. Add one more button to the panel:

```
<FlexLayout Wrap="Wrap">
    <Button Text="B 1" Margin="25"/>
    <Button Text="B 2" Margin="25"/>
    <Button Text="B 3" Margin="25"/>
    <Button Text="B 4" Margin="25"/>
    <Button Text="B 5" Margin="25"/>
</FlexLayout>
```

Run the project to see the result.

How it works...

All panels in .NET MAUI use the same algorithm to arrange elements. Here's a broad overview of how it works:

1. The panel asks its child elements how much space they need to display their content by calling the Measure method. This process is called **measuring**. During this, the panel informs the child elements about the available space, allowing them to return their optimal size based on these constraints. In other words, the panel communicates the size limits to its elements.

2.   Based on the measurements from the first step, the panel then calls `Arrange` for each child to position them. This process is called **arranging**. While the panel considers each element's **desired size**, it doesn't always give them as much space as they request. If all the child elements demand more space than the panel has available, the panel may reduce some of its children.

For a simple linear arrangement task, we used four panel types available in the standard .NET MAUI suite, and all of them have a unique measuring and arranging logic:

*   `HorizontalStackLayout`: When measuring its children, the `HorizontalStackLayout` does so without any horizontal constraints. Essentially, it asks each child, *"How wide would you like to be if you had infinite width available?"* The `height` constraint, however, is determined by a panel's height. In the scenario from the first step, buttons return the width needed to display their text. The panel then arranges the buttons horizontally in a single row, giving each button as much space as requested. Each button is separated by the distance specified in the `Spacing` property. If the panel doesn't have enough space to display an element, that element gets cut off (as seen in *Figure 1.1*, where the fourth button is not displayed in the first layout).

> **Key point**
> `HorizontalStackLayout` provides its child elements with as much width as they require to display all content.

*   `VerticalStackLayout`: This panel works exactly like `HorizontalStackLayout`, but all the logic is *rotated by 90 degrees*.

> **Key point**
> `VerticalStackLayout` provides its child elements with as much height as they require to display all content.

*   `Grid`: The grid panel has a more complex measuring/arranging logic since it may have multiple rows and columns, but in the scenario demonstrated in *step 3* in the *How to do it* section, it does the following:

    *   All the space available for the grid is divided into four equal parts because we defined four rows.
    *   When measuring the children, the grid provides each child with as much height as available in a corresponding row. Their width is limited by the width of the grid itself.
    *   When arranging, each element is placed in its row.

- FlexLayout: While this panel also has a complicated measuring/arranging logic because of various settings, in the configuration demonstrated previously, the panel moves elements to the next line when they don't fit the current row.

There's more...

What could go wrong in such straightforward scenarios? It might not be obvious at first, but let's consider the following code example, where CollectionView, displaying items vertically, is added to VerticalStackLayout:

```
<VerticalStackLayout>
    <CollectionView>
        <CollectionView.ItemsSource>
            <x:Array Type="{x:Type x:String}">
                <x:String>Item1</x:String>
                <x:String>Item2</x:String>
                <x:String>Item3</x:String>
                <!--...-->
                <x:String>Item100</x:String>
            </x:Array>
        </CollectionView.ItemsSource>
    </CollectionView>
    <Button Text="Some Button"/>
</VerticalStackLayout>
```

Many developers would expect to get the result demonstrated on the left of the following figure, but instead, they would get the output illustrated on the right:

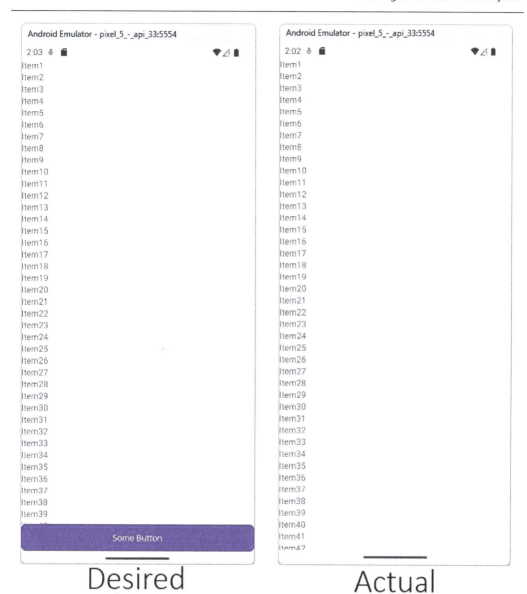

Figure 1.2 – An issue with CollectionView in VerticalStackLayout

The reason for this is that `VerticalStackLayout` provides infinite height to `CollectionView` during the measuring cycle and `CollectionView` arranges its elements based on the size required to display all items. Since `CollectionView` has 100 items, it returns a larger desired size than `VerticalStackLayout` has. But since `VerticalStackLayout` doesn't constrain its children, the button element is shifted by `CollectionView` beyond the screen. Besides this layout issue, this results in performance problems because `CollectionView` creates its elements even if they are not visible on the screen.

To achieve the result demonstrated on the left-hand side of *Figure 1.2*, use the `Grid` panel with two rows:

```xml
<Grid RowDefinitions="*,Auto">
    <CollectionView>
        <CollectionView.ItemsSource>
            <x:Array Type="{x:Type x:String}">
                <x:String>Item1</x:String>
                <x:String>Item2</x:String>
                <x:String>Item3</x:String>
                <!--more items here-->
                <x:String>Item100</x:String>
            </x:Array>
        </CollectionView.ItemsSource>
    </CollectionView>
    <Button Grid.Row="1" Text="Some Button"/>
</Grid>
```

Note that `RowDefinitions` is set to `"*, Auto"`, which means that the second row gets as much space as required by the button and the first row gets all the remaining space.

Creating grid layouts

Linear layouts address most scenarios, but what if you need to create something more complex? For example, what if we want to create a simple editing form with labels and editors, where the first column is resized based on the longest label in all rows?

We can use `Grid`, which is an extremely powerful panel with a simple concept, but as with any other control, it may pose unexpected challenges for those who don't fully understand its specifics.

Let's look at some common grid-related layouts/techniques and potential pitfalls you may encounter.

Getting ready

To follow the steps described in this recipe, we just need to create a blank .NET MAUI application. The default template includes sample code in the `MainPage.xaml` and `MainPage.xaml.cs` files, but you can remove it and leave only a blank `ContentPage` in XAML and a constructor with the `InitializeComponent` method in CS.

The code for this recipe is available at https://github.com/PacktPublishing/.NET-MAUI-Cookbook/tree/main/Chapter01/c1-GridLayouts.

How to do it...

In this recipe, we will create two simple layouts using the Grid panel, allowing us to use most of Grid's capabilities, which we will discuss in later sections on this topic:

Figure 1.3 – Grid row spanning and alignment

I used a non-transparent background for child elements in the Grid to demonstrate the space occupied by the elements in grid cells.

1. Create a two-column layout where the first column is increased based on the largest element. To automatically adjust the size of the first column based on its content, set the first column's width to Auto using the ColumnDefinitions property:

MainPage.xaml

```
<Grid RowDefinitions="40,80"
    ColumnDefinitions="Auto, *">
    <Label Text="Title"/>
    <Label Text="Description"
        Grid.Row="1"/>
    <Editor Grid.Column="1"/>
    <Editor Grid.Row="1"
        Grid.Column="1"/>
</Grid>
```

If you run the project, you should see the result shown on the left-hand side of *Figure 1.3*.

2. Now, let's create a layout with two columns and stretch a label in the second column across two rows. To do this, define two columns and two rows, and set Grid.RowSpan to span multiple lines with the label:

```
<Grid RowDefinitions="40,40"
    ColumnDefinitions="*, 60">
    <Label Text="Headline"/>
```

```
        <Label Text="Supporting text"
               TextColor="DarkGray"
               Grid.Row="1" />
        <Label Text="100+"
               VerticalOptions="Center"
               HorizontalOptions="End"
               Grid.RowSpan="2"
               Grid.Column="1" />
    </Grid>
```

Run the project to see the result.

How it works...

As you may know, the `Grid` panel uses the `RowDefinitions` and `ColumnDefinitions` properties to specify rows and columns, respectively. Both properties accept a collection of `RowDefinitions` and `ColumnDefinitions` classes that can be automatically converted to XAML from the following values:

- `Double`: A constant value
- `Auto`: The space required to display a child element without trimming
- `*` (star): All the remaining space after other rows or columns

Sometimes, developers are confused by `*` and `Auto` because both values calculate the width/height automatically, but there is a key difference between them:

When a row definition is set to `Auto`, `Grid` provides elements in the row with as much space as they need. In this mode, content in a row is measured similarly to elements in `VerticalStackLayout`. For example, if you add three rows with the `Auto` value, you will get the same output as with `VerticalStackLayout`. For example, the following two layouts will have the same output:

```
<Grid RowDefinitions="Auto,Auto,Auto">
    <Button Text="Button1"/>
    <Button Text="Button2" Grid.Row="1"/>
    <Button Text="Button3" Grid.Row="2"/>
</Grid>

<VerticalStackLayout>
    <Button Text="Button1"/>
    <Button Text="Button2"/>
    <Button Text="Button3"/>
</VerticalStackLayout>
```

Of course, if you have only `Auto` rows, it's better to choose `VerticalStackLayout` for performance and code simplicity reasons.

> **Key point**
>
> Multiple `Auto` rows in Grid work the same way as `VerticalStackLayout`. Multiple `Auto` columns work like `HorizontalStackLayout`.

- Rows whose definition is set to `*` proportionally divide all the space left after other rows. If you need to change the proportion between `*` rows, you can use numeric multipliers. For example, in the following code snippet, we add three rows – the first row will have a height of X, the second will have a height of 2X, and the third will have a height of 3X:

```
<Grid RowDefinitions="*,2*,3*">
    <Button Text="Button1"/>
    <Button Text="Button2" Grid.Row="1"/>
    <Button Text="Button3" Grid.Row="2"/>
</Grid>
```

There's more...

Choosing the right row/column type may be challenging, due to performance and device scaling issues. Let me demonstrate to you a few common issues in grid-based layouts:

- **Cropped elements because of fixed sizes**: In cross-platform applications, screen dimensions, resolution, DPI, and font scale may vary, depending on the device and user settings. This may pose a challenge because elements that appear correctly on a developer machine may get cropped on a user device. For example, let's define grid columns and rows in the following manner:

```
<Grid ColumnDefinitions="80,*" RowDefinitions="30">
    <Label Text="First Name"
        BackgroundColor="LightGreen"/>
    <Editor Grid.Column="1"/>
</Grid>
```

With that, you may get the following output:

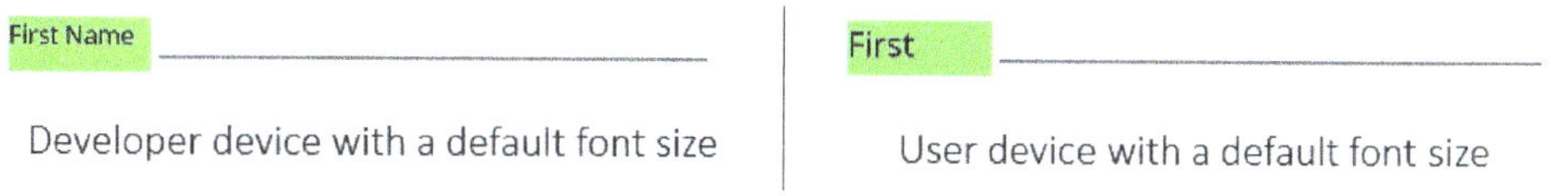

First Name _____	First _____
Developer device with a default font size	User device with a default font size

Figure 1.4 – The issue with a fixed size and different device font settings

To fix this, you can use `Auto` for the first column. However, before using it, pay attention to the next point in this list.

- **Performance issues because of too many Auto rows/columns**: Auto rows/columns may lead to performance issues, as a grid may require multiple layout calculation cycles when several child elements are arranged based on their preferred size. Of course, you are unlikely to notice significant delays even on mobile devices if your root or a few nested grids contain Auto rows, but if you have a collection whose ItemTemplate includes many Auto values, you may consider other techniques:

  - Use fixed double values, applied based on the device type/settings:

    ```
    <Grid>
        <Grid.RowDefinitions>
            <RowDefinition
                    Height="{OnIdiom Desktop=200, Phone=*}"/>
        </Grid.RowDefinitions>
    </Grid>
    ```

    We will delve into the details of this technique in the next recipe (*Implementing device-specific layouts*).

  - Create your own panel with custom measure/arrange logic. This technique will be covered in the *Implementing a custom arranging algorithm* recipe of this chapter. Typically, you will need this technique only when you have a complex layout and many elements on the screen.

- **Lists added to Auto rows**: In the *How it works…* section, we learned that to measure child elements, a grid's Auto rows use a basic rule similar to the one used in Vertical/HorizontalStackLayout – it provides the children as much space as they want. Lists, such as CollectionView, usually request the space required to display all their items. As a result, you may face the same issue with the collection infinite height as described in the *Creating horizontal/Vertical layouts* recipe:

    ```
    <Grid RowDefinitions="Auto, 50">
        <CollectionView>
            <CollectionView.ItemsSource>
                <x:Array Type="{x:Type x:String}">
                    <x:String>Item1</x:String>
                    <x:String>Item2</x:String>
                    <x:String>Item3</x:String>
                    <!--more items here-->
                    <x:String>Item100</x:String>
                </x:Array>
            </CollectionView.ItemsSource>
        </CollectionView>
        <Button Grid.Row="1" Text="Some Button"/>
    </Grid>
    ```

Refer to the right-hand side of *Figure 1.2* to see the layout produced by this code snippet.

The fix depends on your layout requirements, but typically, you would need to replace `Auto` with a `*` value:

```
<Grid RowDefinitions="*, 50">
    <!--...-->
</Grid>
```

Alternatively, you would replace `Auto` with a fixed size:

```
<Grid RowDefinitions="300, 50">
    <!--...-->
</Grid>
```

The second option is applicable when you need to create a collection with a fixed size instead of stretching it.

Creating scrollable layouts

One of the obvious techniques to add more elements to a screen such that they fit within it is to create a scrollable layout, using the `ScrollView` element. As always, even basic elements can cause issues when misused. To help you avoid pitfalls, we will create vertical and horizontal scrollable layouts and discuss their specifics in the *How it works…* and *There's more…* sections.

Getting ready

To follow the steps described in this recipe, we just need to create a blank .NET MAUI application. The default template includes sample code in the `MainPage.xaml` and `MainPage.xaml.cs` files, but you can remove it and leave only a blank `ContentPage` in XAML and a constructor with the `InitializeComponent` method in CS.

The code for this recipe is available at `https://github.com/PacktPublishing/.NET-MAUI-Cookbook/tree/main/Chapter01/c1-ScrollableLayout`.

How to do it...

To learn how to use scrollable layouts most efficiently and avoid issues, let's create simple vertical and horizontal layouts and discuss them in further sections:

1. To create a vertical scrollable layout, it's sufficient to wrap the part you would like to scroll in the `ScrollView` element:

MainPage.xaml

```
<ScrollView>
    <VerticalStackLayout>
        <Button Text="Tall Button 1"
            HeightRequest="500"/>
        <Button Text="Tall Button 2"
            HeightRequest="500"/>
    </VerticalStackLayout>
</ScrollView>
```

Run the project to see the result.

2. To enable horizontal scrolling, set `ScrollView.Orientation` to `"Horizontal"`. Replace `VerticalStackLayout` with `HorizontalStackLayout` to arrange elements horizontally:

```
<ScrollView Orientation="Horizontal">
    <HorizontalStackLayout>
        <Button Text="Tall Button 1"
            WidthRequest="500"/>
        <Button Text="Tall Button 2"
        WidthRequest="500"/>
    </HorizontalStackLayout>
</ScrollView>
```

Run the project to see the result.

How it works...

Similar to `VerticalStackLayout` and `HorizontalStackLayout`, the `ScrollView` element lets its child element occupy as much space as it requests. As such, it measures it by infinite height or width (depending on the orientation). When the desired size of a child element is greater than the space available in `ScrollView`, scrolling functionality is activated.

Setting `ScrollView.Orientation` to `Horizontal` or `Vertical` determines the direction of scrolling. You can also set `Orientation` to `Both`, to scroll in both directions.

There's more...

This is probably the most useful section in this recipe, since adding scrolling is straightforward, but ScrollView has its specifics, which should be taken into account to avoid issues. Let's take a look at a few patterns that *you should avoid* when working with ScrollView:

- Adding ScrollView with an undefined height to VerticalStackLayout:

```xml
<VerticalStackLayout>
    <ScrollView>
        <VerticalStackLayout>
            <Button Text="Tall Button 1"
                    HeightRequest="500"/>
            <Button Text="Tall Button 2"
                    HeightRequest="500"/>
            <Button Text="Tall Button 3"
                    HeightRequest="500"/>
            <Button Text="Tall Button 4"
                    HeightRequest="500"/>
        </VerticalStackLayout>
    </ScrollView>
</VerticalStackLayout>
```

You won't be able to scroll your view with this layout because, as we know from the *Creating horizontal/vertical layouts* recipe, VerticalStackLayout provides its children with infinite height. As a result, ScrollView thinks that it has infinite height, and ScrollView doesn't need to activate scrolling because its children can fit the parent panel.

- Adding CollectionView with an undefined height to ScrollView:

```xml
<ScrollView>
    <CollectionView>
        <!--...-->
    </CollectionView>
</ScrollView>
```

Here, you will encounter the same infinite height issue as with CollectionView in VerticalStackLayout or Grid, whose row is set to Auto. In all these scenarios, parent containers measure CollectionView by an infinite height. As a result, CollectionView is virtually increased to fit all its items.

Implementing device-specific layouts

Desktop and mobile devices have fundamental differences in the user experience. Here are just a few examples:

- A small versus a large screen

- A mouse versus a touchscreen

- A physical versus a virtual keyboard

- A single window versus multiple windows

There are even more differences, and all of them affect the UI – you can rarely craft a screen that will be convenient for both mobile and desktop devices without explicit adaptive logic.

While .NET MAUI gives you the power to use a single code base for multiple device types, it won't automatically adapt your layout to a specific device. However, the `OnIdiom` and `OnPlatform` markup extensions will help you implement local customization, or even replace the entire view, based on the device type or operating system. We will use both the `OnIdiom` and `OnPlatform` extensions in this recipe to see how they differ from each other.

Getting ready

To follow the steps described in this recipe, we just need to create a blank .NET MAUI application. The default template includes sample code in the `MainPage.xaml` and `MainPage.xaml.cs` files, but you can remove it and leave only a blank `ContentPage` in XAML and a constructor with the `InitializeComponent` method in CS. When copying code snippets with namespaces, don't forget to replace them with the namespaces in your project.

The code for this recipe is available at `https://github.com/PacktPublishing/.NET-MAUI-Cookbook/tree/main/Chapter01/c1-DeviceSpecificLayout`.

How to do it...

Let's use `OnIdiom` to specify a single property, specify multiple properties, and replace the entire view. Each of these techniques may be the most suitable, based on your scenario. After that, we will use `OnPlatform` to show a button on Android and hide it on iOS:

1. Use the `OnIdiom` markup extension to set a local property value based on the device type (desktop, phone, tablet, TV, or watch). To adjust the layout using `OnIdiom`, define a grid with two rows and set the first row's height using `OnIdiom`, as follows:

MainPage.xaml

```
<Grid>
    <Grid.RowDefinitions>
        <RowDefinition
            Height="{OnIdiom Desktop=200, Phone=*}"/>
        <RowDefinition Height="*"/>
    </Grid.RowDefinitions>
    <Border BackgroundColor="Coral"/>
    <Border Grid.Row="1" BackgroundColor="DarkRed"/>
</Grid>
```

As you may have noticed, we used an expanded RowDefinition syntax here to adjust each RowDefinition height separately (instead of RowDefinitions="200, *"). Run the project on a desktop and phone to see the result.

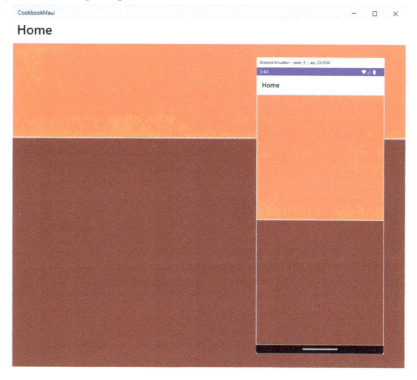

Figure 1.5 – Idiom-specific settings

2. To adjust a bunch of properties using one OnIdiom condition, define a style for each device type:

```
<ContentPage.Resources>
    <Style TargetType="Grid" x:Key="winUiBorderStyle">
        <Setter Property="Padding" Value="20"/>
        <Setter Property="Margin" Value="20"/>
    </Style>
    <Style TargetType="Grid"
            x:Key="androidBorderStyle">
        <Setter Property="Padding"
                Value="10,0,10,10"/>
        <Setter Property="Margin" Value="10"/>
    </Style>
</ContentPage.Resources>
<Border Style="{OnIdiom Desktop={StaticResource
        winUiBorderStyle}, Phone={StaticResource
        androidBorderStyle}}" BackgroundColor="Coral">
    <Border BackgroundColor="DarkRed"/>
</Border>
```

Run the project to see the result.

3. To switch the entire view based on the device type, define separate views for each device and set the ContentPage.Content property using an expanded OnIdiom tag. If you haven't created ContentView before, right-click on the project, and then select **Add** | **New Item** | **ContentView**. Name one view PhoneView and the other DesktopView:

PhoneView.xaml (for Android/iOS)

```
<ContentView
xmlns="http://schemas.microsoft.com/dotnet/2021/maui"
    xmlns:x="http://schemas.microsoft.com/winfx/2009/xaml"
    x:Class="c1_DeviceSpecificLayout.PhoneView">
    <Border>
        <Label Text="Phone View"/>
    </Border>
</ContentView>
```

DesktopView (for Windows/macOS/Linux)

```
<ContentView xmlns="http://schemas.microsoft.com/dotnet/2021/
maui"
    xmlns:x="http://schemas.microsoft.com/winfx/2009/xaml"
    x:Class="c1_DeviceSpecificLayout.DesktopView">
    <Border>
```

```xml
            <Label Text="Desktop View"/>
        </Border>
    </ContentView>
```

MainPage.xaml

```xml
<ContentPage xmlns="http://schemas.microsoft.com/dotnet/2021/
maui"
    xmlns:x="http://schemas.microsoft.com/winfx/2009/xaml"
    xmlns:local="clr-namespace: c1_DeviceSpecificLayout"
    x:Class="c1_DeviceSpecificLayout.MainPage">
    <ContentPage.Content>
        <OnIdiom x:TypeArguments="View">
            <OnIdiom.Phone>
                <local:PhoneView />
            </OnIdiom.Phone>
            <OnIdiom.Desktop>
                <local:DesktopView />
            </OnIdiom.Desktop>
        </OnIdiom>
    </ContentPage.Content>
</ContentPage>
```

Note that the TypeArguments attribute of OnIdiom should be set to View. Don't forget to add a namespace definition to MainPage to be able to reference PhoneView and DesktopView.

This technique is useful when there are significant differences between the mobile and desktop views and customizing separate controls is problematic.

4. Use the OnPlatform markup extension to specify properties that depend on an operating system:

```xml
<Button IsVisible="{OnPlatform Android=True,
        iOS=False}"/>
```

This code sets Button.IsVisible to True on Android and to False on iOS devices, showing or hiding the button, respectively, based on the operating system. You can also specify different values for other platforms supported in MAUI – MacCatalyst, Tizen, and WinUI.

How it works...

Under the hood, OnIdiom checks the current device information using the DeviceInfo class and returns a value you specified in XAML:

Here is a simplified code snippet illustrating the idea:

```csharp
public class OnIdiomExtension : IMarkupExtension {
    public object Default { get; set; }
```

```
public object Phone { get; set; }
public object Desktop { get; set; }
//...
public object ProvideValue(IServiceProvider serviceProvider) {
    //...
    if (DeviceInfo.Idiom == DeviceIdiom.Phone)
        return Phone ?? Default;
    if (DeviceInfo.Idiom == DeviceIdiom.Desktop)
        return Desktop ?? Default;
    //...
    return Default;
}
```

The OnPlatform extension works in the same way, but it uses the DeviceInfo.Platform property to get the currently running platform and return the value you specified in XAML.

There's more...

If you need to implement more complex logic, you can specify device-specific settings in C#. For example, the following code sets a grid's height based on the idiom value:

```
public MainPage() {
    InitializeComponent();
    if (DeviceInfo.Current.Idiom == DeviceIdiom.Desktop) {
        grid1.Height = CalculateDesktopHeight();
    }
    else if (DeviceInfo.Current.Idiom == DeviceIdiom.Phone)
    {
        grid1.Height = CalculateMobileHeight();
    }
}
```

The CalculateDesktopHeight and CalculateMobileHeight methods are supposed to contain custom calculation logic that cannot be easily implemented in XAML.

You can implement similar customization logic based on the DeviceInfo.Current.Platform property for each operating system. Alternatively, you can use conditional compilation and platform-specific code, as we will demonstrate in *Chapter 7, Understanding Platform-Specific APIs and Custom Handlers*.

Implementing layouts with dynamic orientation

Users can rotate mobile devices, and it's important to adapt your UI according to the current orientation. The .NET MAUI platform doesn't have a built-in class to set orientation-specific settings in XAML; however, it provides a visual state mechanism. Alternatively, you can set orientation-based properties in C#. In this recipe, we'll implement both techniques.

Getting ready

To follow the steps described in this recipe, we just need to create a blank .NET MAUI application. The default template includes sample code in the `MainPage.xaml` and `MainPage.xaml.cs` files, but you can remove it and leave only a blank `ContentPage` in XAML and a constructor with the `InitializeComponent` method in CS. When copying code snippets with namespaces, don't forget to replace them with the namespaces in your project.

The code for this recipe is available at `https://github.com/PacktPublishing/.NET-MAUI-Cookbook/tree/main/Chapter01/c1-OrientationSpecificSettings`.

How to do it...

Let's use two different techniques to specify layout settings based on the orientation – set settings in XAML using visual states and set settings in C# by subscribing to the `MainDisplayInfoChanged` event, which is raised when the orientation is changed:

1. To specify orientation-based settings in XAML, define `VisualStateGroup` with `Portrait` and `Landscape` visual states. In visual state setters, reference the elements you would like to customize by their names. Note that it's necessary to explicitly specify the parent property class in each setter:

MainPage.xaml

```xml
<VisualStateManager.VisualStateGroups>
    <VisualStateGroupList>
        <VisualStateGroup>
            <VisualState x:Name="Portrait">
                <VisualState.StateTriggers>
                    <OrientationStateTrigger
                            Orientation="Portrait" />
                </VisualState.StateTriggers>
                <VisualState.Setters>
                    <Setter TargetName="rootGrid"
                        Property="Grid.RowDefinitions"
```

```
                                Value="*,*" />
                    <Setter TargetName="border2"
                            Property="Grid.Row"
                            Value="1"/>
                </VisualState.Setters>
            </VisualState>
            <VisualState x:Name="Landscape">
                <VisualState.StateTriggers>
                    <OrientationStateTrigger
                        Orientation="Landscape" />
                </VisualState.StateTriggers>
                <VisualState.Setters>
                    <Setter TargetName="rootGrid"
                        Property="Grid.RowDefinitions"
                            Value="*,*" />
                    <Setter TargetName="border2"
                            Property="Grid.Row"
                            Value="1"/>
                </VisualState.Setters>
            </VisualState>
        </VisualStateGroup>
    </VisualStateGroupList>
</VisualStateManager.VisualStateGroups>
<Grid x:Name="rootGrid">
    <Border x:Name="border1" BackgroundColor="Coral"/>
    <Border x:Name="border2" Background="DarkRed"/>
</Grid>
```

In the preceding code snippet, we set `Grid.RowDefinitions` and `Grid.Row` for the grid and border elements, referenced using the `TargetName` property. The `VisualStateManager.VisualStateGroups` property is defined at the page/view level, which allows you to set all orientation-based settings in one place instead of creating visual states in each element. You will see the following result if you run the project and try to rotate a device:

Figure 1.6 – Landscape layout customization

2. To specify orientation-based settings in C#, subscribe to the DeviceDisplay. MainDisplayInfoChanged event and modify all required settings in the event handler:

MainPage.xaml.cs

```
protected override void OnNavigatedTo(NavigatedToEventArgs args)
{
    base.OnNavigatedTo(args);
    SetOrientationSpecificSettings();
    DeviceDisplay.MainDisplayInfoChanged +=
      OnMainDisplayInfoChanged;
}
protected override void OnNavigatedFrom(NavigatedFromEventArgs
args) {
    base.OnNavigatedFrom(args);
    DeviceDisplay.MainDisplayInfoChanged -=
      OnMainDisplayInfoChanged;
}
```

```
private void OnMainDisplayInfoChanged(object? sender,
  DisplayInfoChangedEventArgs e) {
    SetOrientationSpecificSettings();
}
void SetOrientationSpecificSettings() {
    if (DeviceDisplay.MainDisplayInfo.Orientation ==
      DisplayOrientation.Landscape)
        border1.BackgroundColor = Colors.Red;
    else
        border1.BackgroundColor = Colors.Green;
}
```

Don't forget to unsubscribe from the `MainDisplayInfoChanged` event; otherwise, `DeviceDisplay` will always hold a reference of the view, and it will never be released, causing a memory leak.

How it works...

As you may know, .NET MAUI includes the visual state mechanism. Elements can have different predefined visual statues, which are not limited by `Portrait` and `Landscape`. For example, there are states such as `Normal`, `Disabled`, and `Focused`.

In C#, you can change the state using the `VisualStateManager.GoToState` method:

```
VisualStateManager.GoToState(someVisualElement, "<stateName>");
```

You can use any name for your custom state.

In XAML, you can go to a state using a state trigger. The platform provides a built-in `OrientationStateTrigger` trigger, so when the orientation is changed, this trigger is invoked, and a corresponding state is activated.

When a state is activated, it executes the setters:

```
<VisualState x:Name="Portrait">
    <VisualState.StateTriggers>
        <OrientationStateTrigger Orientation="Portrait" />
    </VisualState.StateTriggers>
    <VisualState.Setters>
        <Setter TargetName="rootGrid" Property="Grid.RowDefinitions"
          Value="*,*" />
        <Setter TargetName="border2" Property="Grid.Row" Value="1"/>
    </VisualState.Setters>
</VisualState>
```

Each setter can be applied to a specific element on a page using the `TargetName` property. Since we define visual states at the `ContentPage` level, it's necessary to explicitly set the name of the parent class in the property setter (`"Grid.RowDefinitions"`).

As for the `DeviceDisplay` class, it includes basic information about your display, such as orientation, height, width, and density. So, if you need to fine-tune your layout based on these settings, you can use the `DeviceDisplay.Current.MainDisplayInfo` property:

```
double screenWidth = DeviceDisplay.Current.MainDisplayInfo.Width;
double screenHeight = DeviceDisplay.Current.MainDisplayInfo.Height;
double screenDensity = DeviceDisplay.Current.MainDisplayInfo.Density
```

There's more...

While the bare .NET MAUI platform doesn't include XAML extensions (similar to `OnIdiom`/ `OnPlatform`) to set orientation-specific settings, you can use third-party suites, such as DevExpress, which include additional extensions that enable you to perform this task:

```
<dx:DXButton Content="Click" Padding="{dx:OnOrientation
    Portrait='8,4', Landscape='12,8'}"/>
```

You can learn more about this functionality in DevExpress's documentation: `https://docs.devexpress.com/MAUI/404287/common-concepts/specify-device-specific-settings#xaml-use-the-onorientation-extension`.

Building a layout dynamically based on a collection

A bindable layout is a technique that allows you to generate similar UI elements without repeating XAML code blocks. Let's imagine you need to display a list of actions, and this list is dynamically retrieved from a web API service. A possible solution for this task is to add buttons to your view in C#, but .NET MAUI provides a more convenient way with the `BindableLayout.ItemsSource` property. Let's see how to utilize it.

Getting ready

To follow the steps described in this recipe, we just need to create a blank .NET MAUI application. The default template includes sample code in the `MainPage.xaml` and `MainPage.xaml.cs` files, but you can remove it and leave only a blank `ContentPage` in XAML and a constructor with the `InitializeComponent` method in CS. When copying code snippets with namespaces, don't forget to replace them with the namespaces in your project.

The code for this recipe is available at `https://github.com/PacktPublishing/.NET-MAUI-Cookbook/tree/main/Chapter01/c1-BindableLayout`.

How to do it...

Let's generate buttons with a predefined template, using `VerticalStackLayout` and the `BindableLayout` class. We will generate buttons from a collection of custom non-visual objects. Let's name the class containing information about these objects `ActionInfo`:

1. Create a `MyViewModel` class and define a collection of items that will store information about your buttons:

MyViewModel.cs

```
public class MyViewModel {
    public ObservableCollection<ActionInfo> DynamicActions {
      get; set; }
    public MyViewModel() {
        DynamicActions = new ObservableCollection<ActionInfo> {
            new ActionInfo() { Caption = "Action1" },
            new ActionInfo() { Caption = "Action2" },
            new ActionInfo() { Caption = "Action3" }
        };
    }
}
public class ActionInfo {
    public string Caption { get; set; }
}
```

2. Assign the view model to the page's `BindableContext`:

```
<ContentPage.BindingContext>
    <local:MyViewModel/>
</ContentPage.BindingContext>
```

3. Set the `BindableLayout.ItemsSource` and `BindableLayout.ItemTemplate` properties at the `VerticalStackLayout` level:

```
<VerticalStackLayout BindableLayout.ItemsSource="{Binding
DynamicActions}" Spacing="5">
    <BindableLayout.ItemTemplate>
        <DataTemplate x:DataType="{x:Type local:ActionInfo}">
            <Button Text="{Binding Caption}"/>
        </DataTemplate>
    </BindableLayout.ItemTemplate>
</VerticalStackLayout>
```

Once you run the code, you should see the following output:

Figure 1.7 – A bindable layout

How it works...

BindableLayout generates elements from a collection and adds them to the panel to which it's attached. It can work with all elements that implement the IBindableLayout interface. This interface is implemented in the layout abstract class, which is a base class for all layouts – StackLayout, HorizontalStackLayout, Grid, FlexLayout, and AbsoluteLayout.

BindableLayout takes each item in the ItemsSource collection and generates the UI for it, which is defined in ItemTemplate. To allow you to easily bind to properties in your model, BindableLayout assigns your model to BindingContext of ItemTemplate. That's why you can bind the button's Text property to Caption, defined in the ActionInfo class.

Here is a code snippet that demonstrates how BindableLayout generates items:

```
View CreateItemView(object item, DataTemplate dataTemplate)
{
    if (dataTemplate != null)
    {
        var view = (View)dataTemplate.CreateContent();
        view.BindingContext = item;
        return view;
    }
    else
    {
        return new Label
        {
```

```
            Text = item?.ToString(),
            HorizontalTextAlignment = TextAlignment.Center
        };
    }
}
```

As you can see, if `DataTemplate` is not defined, it simply creates a label with a string representation of your object.

There's more...

Here are a couple of additional tips you may find useful when using `BindableLayout`:

- Define the `BindableLayout.EmptyViewTemplate` template to show a message to a user when the source collection is empty:

    ```
    <BindableLayout.EmptyViewTemplate>
        <DataTemplate>
            <Label Text="There are no actions"/>
        </DataTemplate>
    </BindableLayout.EmptyViewTemplate>
    ```

- When generated elements exceed the space available on the screen, these elements will be cut. As such, if you need to enable scrolling, you need to wrap a panel that is used with `BindableLayout` within `ScrollView`. Typically, an even better solution is to use `CollectionView`. When you need to customize the way items are arranged in it, you can use the `ItemsLayout` property. For example, to generate items and show them in two columns, use `GridItemsLayout` as follows:

    ```
    <CollectionView ItemsSource="{Binding Tiles}">
        <CollectionView.ItemsLayout>
            <GridItemsLayout Orientation="Vertical"
                             Span="2" />
        </CollectionView.ItemsLayout>
    </CollectionView>
    ```

    `CollectionView` uses a virtualization mechanism, which means that it reuses visual elements as you scroll. This prevents performance issues when dealing with a long list of items.

Implementing a custom arranging algorithm

Built-in layout panels help you solve the most common tasks in your app. However, sometimes, you may need to achieve a unique layout, which would be difficult to implement with the default .NET MAUI panels (`Grid`, `VerticalStackLayout`, etc.). Fortunately, you can easily implement your custom layout logic, where children are measured and arranged according to your rules.

Getting ready

To follow the steps described in this recipe, we just need to create a blank .NET MAUI application. The default template includes sample code in the `MainPage.xaml` and `MainPage.xaml.cs` files, but you can remove it and leave only a blank `ContentPage` in XAML and a constructor with the `InitializeComponent` method in CS. When copying code snippets with namespaces, don't forget to replace them with the namespaces in your project.

The code for this recipe is available at `https://github.com/PacktPublishing/.NET-MAUI-Cookbook/tree/main/Chapter01/c1-CustomLayout`.

How to do it...

Let's create a panel that arranges its children in a circle with a specified radius, as demonstrated in the following figure:

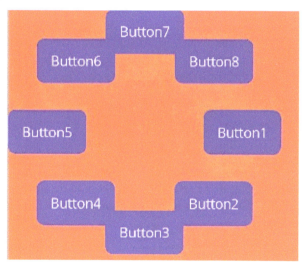

Figure 1.8 – A custom circular layout

1. Create a class inherited from `Layout` and override `CreateLayoutManager`. In `CreateLayoutManager`, return an instance of a class that will measure and arrange children in your panel:

MainWindow.xaml.cs

```
public class CircularLayout : Layout {
    protected override ILayoutManager CreateLayoutManager() {
        return new CircularLayoutManager(this);
    }
}
```

```
public double Radius {
    get { return (double)GetValue(RadiusProperty); }
    set { SetValue(RadiusProperty, value); }
}
public static readonly BindableProperty RadiusProperty =
    BindableProperty.Create("Radius", typeof(double),
        typeof(CircularLayout));
}
```

The Radius dependency property will help us arrange elements according to a specified radius.

2. Create a class that implements ILayoutManager:

```
public class CircularLayoutManager : ILayoutManager {
    readonly CircularLayout parentLayout;
    public CircularLayoutManager(CircularLayout layout) {
        this.parentLayout = layout;
    }
    public Size Measure(double widthConstraint, double
      heightConstraint) {
      throw new NotImplementedException();
    }
    public Size ArrangeChildren(Rect bounds) {
        throw new NotImplementedException();
    }
}
```

3. Implement the ILayoutManager.Measure method. In the method, iterate through all children of the panel and call Measure for each of them (this is required to update the desired size of the child items):

```
public class CircularLayoutManager : ILayoutManager {
    //…
    public Size Measure(double widthConstraint, double
      heightConstraint) {
        double radius = parentLayout.Radius;
        for (int n = 0; n < parentLayout.Count; n++) {
            var child = parentLayout[n];
            if (child.Visibility == Visibility.Collapsed) {
                continue;
            }
            child.Measure(double.PositiveInfinity, double.
              PositiveInfinity);
        }
        return new Size(parentLayout.WidthRequest, parentLayout.
```

```
            HeightRequest);
        }
    }
```

The returned value determines what desired size the panel will have.

4. Implement the `ILayoutManager.ArrangeChildren` method. For each child in the parent layout panel (`CircularLayout`), call `Arrange`. Pass a rectangle to this method, indicating what exact position and bounds a child should have:

```
public class CircularLayoutManager : ILayoutManager {
//...
    public Size ArrangeChildren(Rect bounds) {
        double radius = parentLayout.Radius;
        double angleStep = Math.PI * 2 / parentLayout.Count;
        for (int i = 0; i < parentLayout.Count; i++) {
            var child = parentLayout[i];
            if (child.Visibility == Visibility.Collapsed) {
                continue;
            }
            child.Arrange(new Rect(
                radius * Math.Cos(angleStep * i) + radius,
                radius * Math.Sin(angleStep * i) + radius,
                child.DesiredSize.Width,
                child.DesiredSize.Height));
        }
        return new Size(parentLayout.WidthRequest, parentLayout.
          HeightRequest);
    }
}
```

We use the `sin` and `cos` functions to calculate the points of the top-left point of each child. We have intentionally avoided taking into account properties such as `Padding` and `VerticalOptions`/`HorizontalOptions` to simplify the logic.

5. That's it! Now, you can use `CircularLayout` in XAML:

```
<ContentPage xmlns="http://schemas.microsoft.com/dotnet/2021/
                maui"
        xmlns:x="http://schemas.microsoft.com/winfx/2009/
                xaml"
        x:Class="c1_CustomLayout.MainPage"
        xmlns:local="clr-namespace:c1_CustomLayout"
        Title="CustomLayoutPage">
    <local:CircularLayout WidthRequest="300"
                    HeightRequest="300"
```

```
                                    BackgroundColor="There are no actions"
                                    Radius="100"
                                    VerticalOptions=Start
                                    HorizontalOptions="Start">
            <Button Text="Button1"/>
            <Button Text="Button2"/>
            <Button Text="Button3"/>
            <Button Text="Button4"/>
            <Button Text="Button5"/>
            <Button Text="Button6"/>
            <Button Text="Button7"/>
            <Button Text="Button8"/>
        </local:CircularLayout>
    </ContentPage>
```

`CircularLayout` is intentionally colored so that you can see its bounds and how child elements are distributed in the panel. The panel's children don't occupy all available space. Instead, they are arranged according to the specified radius.

Now, you can run the project to see the result.

How it works...

The platform automatically calls the layout manager's `Measure` method when it needs to update the layout. The layout manager, in turn, calls `Measure` for each of its child elements (in the preceding example, `CircularLayoutManager` calls `Measure` for each button added to `CircularLayout`). Once a child's `Measure` is called, the child calculates what size it wants to have to properly fit all its content – this size is called `DesiredSize`. The layout manager can use the `DesiredSize` property of its children to calculate its own `DesiredSize` and return this value in its `ILayoutManager`. `Measure` method. In the preceding example, we return the size based on the specified radius, without taking into account the panel's children.

In the `ArrangeChildren` method, we again iterate through all the child elements and call the `Arrange` method. This method accepts the rectangle in which a child element should be located. So, here, we specify the position and size of each element.

In .NET MAUI, layouts are created in a two-step process – measuring and arranging. Here is a simplified diagram illustrating the algorithm:

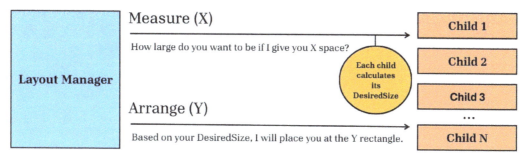

Figure 1.9 – A .NET MAUI layout algorithm

There's more...

In *step 3* of the *How to do it...* section, we measured all the child elements of our custom panel and returned a value that doesn't depend on the panel's children:

```
public class CircularLayoutManager : ILayoutManager {
    //...
    public Size Measure(double widthConstraint, double
      heightConstraint) {
        //...
        for (int n = 0; n < parentLayout.Count; n++) {
            //...
            child.Measure(double.PositiveInfinity,
              double.PositiveInfinity);
        }
        return new Size(parentLayout.WidthRequest,
          parentLayout.HeightRequest);
    }
}
```

You may ask, why measure children if we don't take their desired size into account? The answer is that if you don't call `Measure` for a child element, this element won't calculate its desired size and, as a result, won't be rendered.

> **Key point**
> Always call the `Measure` element for all panel children, even if you don't take into account their desired size during the measuring cycle.

2

Mastering the
MVVM Design Pattern

The primary purpose of **Model-View-ViewModel** (**MVVM**) is to separate the UI code (**view**) from the data and business logic (**model**). This separation is achieved through the **view model** class, which acts as an intermediary between the view and the model.

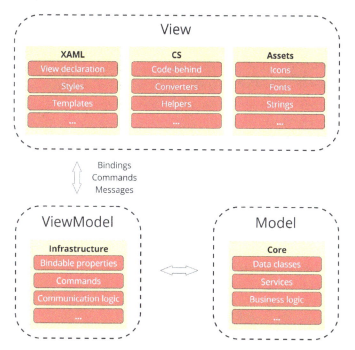

Figure 2.1 – MVVM architecture

The MVVM pattern offers several key benefits:

- **Reusability**: The business logic can be reused across different modules or applications since it is independent of the current view.

- **Testability**: In an MVVM application, you can easily isolate and test the view, model, or view model without their dependencies.

- **Clean code base and structure**: The project becomes easier to understand when UI code is confined to views, business logic and data structures are in models, and view models act as connectors between them.

- **Adaptation**: The view model allows you to adapt your model to the UI without altering the data structure and business logic.

- **Scalability**: The aforementioned advantages contribute to better scalability. As your project grows, MVVM helps maintain organized and manageable code.

Although MVVM has been used across multiple platforms for many years, its concepts are sometimes misunderstood, leading to complex and hard-to-maintain code. This chapter includes recipes for following MVVM best practices, helping you achieve a clean architecture with minimal effort.

In this chapter, we'll be covering the following recipes:

- Decoupling the UI from the view model

- Implementing auto-generated view models

- Implementing asynchronous commands

- Initializing bound collections without freezing the UI

- Interacting with the UI from the view model without breaking MVVM

- Sending messages between view models via different channels

- Injecting an application service into a view model using dependency injection

- Troubleshooting binding errors

Technical requirements

There are no specific requirements for the recipes in this chapter. All of them start with a basic .NET MAUI application created by the default Visual Studio template.

You can download all the projects created in this chapter from GitHub: `https://github.com/PacktPublishing/.NET-MAUI-Cookbook/tree/main/Chapter02`

Decoupling the UI from the view model

The .NET MAUI platform includes core features to separate the view and view model:

- **Bindings** transfer data between the view and view model
- The `BindingContext` property allows you to specify to what view model your view should be bound
- **Commands** help you pass actions (such as button clicks) from the view to the view model

Let's transform the default .NET MAUI project created by Visual Studio into an MVVM project.

Getting ready

To prepare for the first step of this recipe, create a basic .NET MAUI application from the default project template available in Visual Studio. If you are using another IDE (VS Code, Rider) and with non-default project templates, you can download a starting application from this GitHub repository: `https://github.com/PacktPublishing/.NET-MAUI-Cookbook/tree/main/Chapter02/c2-DecoupleViewAndViewModel`. This repository also contains code with the complete steps of this recipe.

How to do it...

Let's create a simple view model with a property and command. After that, we'll bind the view to the view model:

1. Create a `MyViewModel` class to store the current `Label` text and modify it. Add a command to handle the user clicking on a button in the view. Note that the `MyViewModel` class should implement the `INotifyPropertyChanged` interface to notify bindings when a property is changed:

MyViewModel.cs

```
public class MainViewModel : INotifyPropertyChanged {
    int count = 0;
    string textValue = "Click Me!";
    public string TextValue {
        get {
            return textValue;
        }
        set {
            textValue = value;
            OnPropertyChanged();
```

```
        }
    }
    public ICommand UpdateTextCommand {
        get;
        set;
    }
    public MainViewModel() {
        UpdateTextCommand = new Command(UpdateText);
    }
    public void UpdateText() {
        count++;
        if (count == 1)
            TextValue = $"Clicked {count} time";
        else
            TextValue = $"Clicked {count} times";
    }
    protected void
      OnPropertyChanged([CallerMemberName] string
      propertyName = null) {
        PropertyChanged?.Invoke(this, new
          PropertyChangedEventArgs(propertyName));
    }
    public event PropertyChangedEventHandler?
      PropertyChanged;
}
```

2. Navigate to your view and set BindingContext to the instance of your view model:

```
<ContentPage
    xmlns="http://schemas.microsoft.com/dotnet/2021/maui"
    xmlns:x="http://schemas.microsoft.com/winfx/2009/xaml"
    xmlns:viewModel="clr-namespace:
                        c2_DecoupleViewAndViewModel"
    x:Class="c2_DecoupleViewAndViewModel.MainPage">
    <ContentPage.BindingContext>
        <viewModel:MainViewModel/>
    </ContentPage.BindingContext>
```

Note that to use MainViewModel in XAML, you need to add a namespace that includes this class.

3. Remove the Button.Click event setter and bind Button.Text and Button.Command to corresponding properties in MyViewModel:

```
<Button
    x:Name="CounterBtn"
    Text="{Binding TextValue}"
```

```
        SemanticProperties.Hint="Counts the number of times you
    click"
        Command="{Binding UpdateTextCommand}"
        HorizontalOptions="Fill" />
```

4. Remove code-behind from the `MainPage` class, leaving only the constructor:

```
public partial class MainPage : ContentPage {
    public MainPage() {
        InitializeComponent();
    }
}
```

Run the project and click the button to make sure that everything still works (but now using the MVVM pattern).

How it works...

There are two main mechanisms available in .NET MAUI that allow you to decouple your view from the view model:

- **Bindings and BindingContext**: Visual elements have the `BindingContext` property, which serves as the source for your binding. The `BindingContext` value is inherited by child elements (if it's not overridden). That's why, although we specify `BindingContext` at the `MainPage` level, we can bind child UI elements such as `Label` and `Button` to `MyViewModel` properties.

- **Commands**: Typically, UI components that execute some actions (such as buttons), have a `Command` property, which accepts an instance of a class implementing `ICommand`. When a button is clicked, it gets an instance of a command passed to its `Button.Command` property and invokes its `ICommand.Execute` method. Here is a code snippet from the .NET MAUI source code GitHub repository:

```
public static void ElementClicked(
    VisualElement visualElement,
    IButtonElement ButtonElementManager)
{
    if (visualElement.IsEnabled == true)
    {
        ButtonElementManager.Command?.Execute(
            ButtonElementManager.CommandParameter
        );
        ButtonElementManager.PropagateUpClicked();
    }
}
```

Here, the button invokes the command and passes a parameter to it. The parameter is taken from the `Button.CommandParameter` property.

There's more...

Here are a few tips that may save you time when connecting your view model to the view:

- Specify the `x:DataType` attribute if you know the bound object type at design time:

```
<ContentPage
    xmlns="http://schemas.microsoft.com/dotnet/2021/maui"
    xmlns:x="http://schemas.microsoft.com/winfx/2009/xaml"
    xmlns:viewModel="clr-namespace:CookbookMVVM"
    x:Class="c2_DecoupleViewAndViewModel.MainPage"
    x:DataType="{x:Type viewModel:MainViewModel}">
    <ContentPage.BindingContext>
        <viewModel:MainViewModel/>
    </ContentPage.BindingContext>
```

When `DataType` is set, .NET MAUI compiles bindings in advance and doesn't have to use reflection to access properties, which improves performance. Additionally, this helps you avoid binding errors caused by an incorrect binding path because the compiler will warn you if you specify a property that doesn't exist in the type specified in `DataType`.

Note that even if you specify `x:DataType`, you still need to set `BindingContext`.

- Use the following list of common bindings you might need for your app:

  - **Binding to a property**:

    ```
    Text="{Binding SomeViewModelProperty}"
    ```

  - **Binding to a nested property**:

    ```
    Text="{Binding SomeViewModelProperty.ChildProperty}"
    ```

  - **Formatting the bound value**:

    ```
    Text="{Binding SomeViewModelProperty, StringFormat='{0} some
    additional text'}"
    ```

  - **Returning another value when the bound value is null**:

    ```
    Text="{Binding SomeViewModelProperty, TargetNullValue='Value is
    empty'}".
    ```

  - **Binding to the first element in a collection property**:

    ```
    Text="{Binding ViewModelCollectionProperty[0]}"
    ```

- Binding to a dictionary value with the "Cat" key:

```
Text="{Binding ViewModelDictionaryProperty[Cat]}"
```

- Binding to another label's text:

```
Text="{Binding Source={x:Reference anotherLabel}, Path=Text}"
```

- Binding to the current object's property:

```
Text="{Binding Source={RelativeSource Mode=Self},
Path=HorizontalOptions}"
```

- Binding to a static property:

```
Text="{Binding Source={x:Static local:MyClass.Instance},
Path=SomeText}"
```

It's supposed that the `Instance` property is static, and it contains an object with the `SomeText` property.

- Remember to implement `INotifyPropertyChanged` in your view model and raise the `PropertyChanged` event in bound property setters. Otherwise, your bindings won't be updated.

- Avoid passing UI control instances to your `ViewModel` class. While it might be tempting to pass a UI element instance to the view model and call its methods directly to trigger actions, this approach tightly couples your view model to the view, breaking the MVVM pattern. Using this technique sacrifices key MVVM benefits such as testability and a decoupled logical architecture. In the *Interacting with the UI from the view model without breaking MVVM* recipe, I'll explain a better way to handle this scenario.

Implementing auto-generated view models

Following the MVVM pattern often involves writing a lot of boilerplate code for properties with `INotifyPropertyChanged` support and commands. This task can be tedious and prone to errors caused by copy-pasting. Fortunately, there's a solution to avoid writing this code manually: use the code generator available in **CommunityToolkit.Mvvm**.

Getting ready

Start with the project you got after executing the previous recipe (*Decoupling the UI from the view model*). This project is available at `https://github.com/PacktPublishing/.NET-MAUI-Cookbook/tree/main/Chapter02/c2-DecoupleViewAndViewModel`.

The code for this recipe is available at `https://github.com/PacktPublishing/.NET-MAUI-Cookbook/tree/main/Chapter02/c2-GeneratedViewModels`.

How to do it...

Let's transform the view model from the previous recipe using the code generators from CommunityToolkit.Mvvm and see how much code we will save:

1. Add the CommunityToolkit.Mvvm NuGet package to your project.

2. Define a partial ViewModel class and inherit it from ObservableObject, which implements InotifyPropertyChanged and can be used as a base class for objects that need to support property change notifications:

    ```
    public partial class MainViewModel : ObservableObject {


    }
    ```

    We'll see why the partial keyword is essential in the *How it works...* section.

3. Add a textValue field and assign the ObservableProperty attribute to turn the field into a property. The ObservableProperty attribute lets the Community Toolkit know that it should generate a property with notification support:

    ```
    public partial class MainViewModel : ObservableObject {
        [ObservableProperty]
        string textValue = "Click Me!";
    }
    ```

4. Add an UpdateText method and use the RelayCommand attribute for the method to turn it into a command:

    ```
    public partial class MainViewModel : ObservableObject {
        [RelayCommand]
        public void UpdateText() {
            //...
        }
        //...
    }
    ```

5. Here is the final view model you should get:

    ```
    public partial class MainViewModel : ObservableObject {
        int count;
        [ObservableProperty]
        string textValue = "Click Me!";
        [RelayCommand]
        public void UpdateText() {
            count++;
            if (count == 1)
                TextValue = $"Clicked {count} time";
    ```

```
        else
            TextValue = $"Clicked {count} times";
    }
}
```

You will notice that it's much more concise than the view model from the *Decoupling the UI from the view model* recipe.

> **Key point**
>
> You can use the `TextValue` property, even though you defined only the `textValue` field.

Now you can run the project to make sure that everything works.

How it works...

The MVVM Community Toolkit uses the compile-time code generation mechanism. Its code generators are built on Roslyn code analyzers, which comprehend the semantics and generate additional code even before the project is built.

You can find generated code in the Visual Studio **Solution Explorer** under the **Analyzers** node:

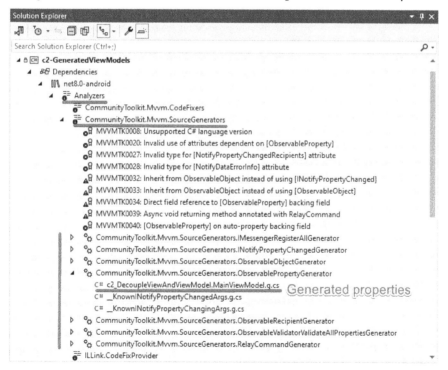

Figure 2.2 – Auto-generated classes

In the `Analyzers/SourceGenerators/ObservablePropertyGenerator/ c2_DecoupleViewAndViewModel.MainViewModel.g.cs` file, the `TextValue` property is automatically generated as follows:

```
partial class MainViewModel
{
        public string TextValue
    {
        get => textValue;
        set
        {
            if (!EqualityComparer<string>.Default
              .Equals(textValue, value))
            {
                OnTextValueChanging(value);
                OnTextValueChanging(default, value);
                OnPropertyChanging(...);
                textValue = value;
                OnTextValueChanged(value);
                OnTextValueChanged(default, value);
                OnPropertyChanged(...);
            }
        }
    }

    //...
}
```

> **Key point**
> All this code is generated in the same `MainViewModel` class. That's why we need the `partial` keyword: part of the `MainViewModel` code is written by us and part of it is generated by the Community Toolkit.

There's more...

The following tips will help you utilize more capabilities of automatically generated view models:

- Use the `INotifyPropertyChanged` attribute instead of inheriting `ObservableObject` if your view model is already inherited from another class:

```
[INotifyPropertyChanged]
public partial class MainViewModel : SomeOtherBaseClass {
```

```
//...
}
```

Since C# doesn't support multiple inheritance, if your view model is a descendant of another class, you cannot use `ObservableObject`. However, you can replace it with the `INotifyPropertyChanged` attribute and continue using the power of auto-generated properties/commands.

- As you can see from the generated code I provided in the *How it works...* section of this recipe, the property setter calls the `OnTextValueChanging` and `OnTextValueChanged` methods. This allows you to execute your custom logic before or after a property is changed:

```
public partial class MainViewModel : ObservableObject {
    //...
    [ObservableProperty]
    string textValue = "Click Me!";
    partial void OnTextValueChanging(string? oldValue, string
      newValue) {
      //called before TextValue is changed
    }
    partial void OnTextValueChanged(string? oldValue, string
      newValue) {
      //called after TextValue is changed
    }
}
```

Note that you still need to use the `partial` keyword for the methods. You can define the methods with one parameter to receive only the new value or with two parameters to receive the old and new values.

- When one property depends on another, use the `NotifyPropertyChangedFor` attribute. For example, if we have a `FullName` property that depends on `FirstName` and `LastName`, we can use `NotifyPropertyChangedFor` in the following manner:

```
public partial class MainViewModel : ObservableObject {
    [ObservableProperty]
    [NotifyPropertyChangedFor(nameof(FullName))]
    string? firstName;

    [ObservableProperty]
    [NotifyPropertyChangedFor(nameof(FullName))]
    string? lastName;

    public string? FullName => $"{FirstName} {LastName}";
}
```

With `NotifyPropertyChangedFor`, when you change `FirstName`/`LastName`, UI elements bound to `FullName` will also be updated, because the `FirstName` and `LastName` property setters will raise a `PropertyChanged` event not only for themselves but additionally for `FullName`.

- If your command's `CanExecute` state depends on a property, assign the `NotifyCan ExecuteChangedFor` attribute to the property and automatically notify this command when this property is changed:

```
public partial class MainViewModel : ObservableObject {
    [ObservableProperty]
    [NotifyCanExecuteChangedFor(nameof(UpdateTextCommand))]
    int count;

    [ObservableProperty]
    string textValue = "Click Me!";

    [RelayCommand(CanExecute = nameof(CanUpdateText))]
    public void UpdateText() {
        Count++;
        if (Count == 1)
            TextValue = $"Clicked {Count} time";
        else
            TextValue = $"Clicked {Count} times";
    }
    public bool CanUpdateText() {
        return Count < 3;
    }
}
```

Here, the `UpdateText` command can be executed only if `Count` is less than 3. Once `Count` becomes 3 or greater, the command bound to `UpdateText` will automatically be disabled. Note that in the `RelayCommand` attribute, you need to specify the name of the `CanExecute` method.

Implementing asynchronous commands

As you may know, .NET MAUI runs all UI-related operations in a single UI thread. However, your application may require executing long-running commands, such as loading data from a remote server, reading a large file, generating a report, etc. By default, commands are executed in the UI thread, meaning that when a command is running, the UI will be frozen. A good practice for user experience is not to block the UI when such a command is executed.

You can create tasks or even separate threads manually, but the Community Toolkit allows you to easily achieve the goal with asynchronous commands. It allows you to automatically track the command execution state or cancel the command.

Getting ready

Start with the project you got after executing the second recipe of this chapter: *Implementing auto-generated view model properties.* This project is available at `https://github.com/PacktPublishing/. NET-MAUI-Cookbook/tree/main/Chapter02/c2-GeneratedViewModels`.

The code for this recipe is available at `https://github.com/PacktPublishing/.NET-MAUI-Cookbook/tree/main/Chapter02/c2-AsyncCommands`.

How to do it...

Let's use `CommunityToolkit.Mvvm` to generate an asynchronous command with a long-running operation and an additional command to cancel the long-running operation:

1. Add a long-running method to your view model in the following manner:

MyViewModel.cs

```
public partial class MyViewModel : ObservableObject {
    [RelayCommand(IncludeCancelCommand = true)]
    public async Task UpdateTextAsync(CancellationToken token) {
        try {
            await Task.Delay(5000, token);
        }
        catch (OperationCanceledException) {
            return;
        }
        //other logic
    }
}
```

Here are the key elements of the preceding code snippet:

*   `RelayCommand` indicates that the Community Toolkit should generate a command from your method.

*   `IncludeCancelCommand` automatically generates the second command, which cancels the current command.

*   `async` makes the method asynchronous.

- `Task` allows the Community Toolkit to work with the task returned by the asynchronous `UpdateTextAsync` method.

- `token` allows you to stop its execution when cancellation is requested.

- `try/catch` allows you to handle the cancel operation and prevent the application from crashing.

- `Task.Delay` is used just to imitate a long-running operation. In your real app, it may be a remote service request or a heavy downloading/uploading operation.

2. Bind two buttons in the view to the long-running command and the cancel command. This will allow you to start the command with the first button and cancel it with the second button:

```
<VerticalStackLayout Spacing="10">
    <Button Text="Go!" Command="{Binding
UpdateTextCommand}"/>
    <Button Text="Cancel" Command="{Binding
UpdateTextCancelCommand}"/>
</VerticalStackLayout>
```

Note that the Community Toolkit generated not only `UpdateTextCommand` but also `UpdateTextCancelCommand` because we specified the `IncludeCancelCommand` parameter in the `RelayCommand` attribute.

Run the project to see the result. You may notice that when you click **Go**, the **Cancel** button is automatically enabled, allowing you to stop the method execution.

How it works...

The Community Toolkit includes the `IAsyncRelayCommand` interface designed for asynchronous commands:

```
public interface IAsyncRelayCommand : IRelayCommand,
INotifyPropertyChanged
{
    Task? ExecutionTask { get; }
    bool CanBeCanceled { get; }
    bool IsCancellationRequested { get; }
    bool IsRunning { get; }
    Task ExecuteAsync(object? parameter);
    void Cancel();
}
```

It allows you to check whether the command is still running (the `IsRunning` property) and cancel the command execution (the `Cancel` method). When you assign the `RelayCommand` attribute with the `IncludeCancelCommand` parameter to your method, the following code is generated:

```
partial class MyViewModel
{
    public IAsyncRelayCommand UpdateTextCommand =>
        updateTextCommand ??= new AsyncRelayCommand(
            new Func<CancellationToken, Task>(UpdateTextAsync)
        );
    public ICommand UpdateTextCancelCommand =>
        updateTextCancelCommand ??= IAsyncRelayCommandExtensions
        .CreateCancelCommand(UpdateTextCommand);
}
```

As you can see, the Community Toolkit creates two commands to which you can bind from your UI.

There's more...

Here are a few additional tips related to async commands:

- You can bind to the `IAsyncRelayCommand.IsRunning` property to show a wait indicator when an operation is running. It's a good way to let an end user know that the long-running operation is in progress by displaying an activity indicator:

    ```
    <ActivityIndicator IsRunning="{Binding UpdateTextCommand.
    IsRunning}"/>
    ```

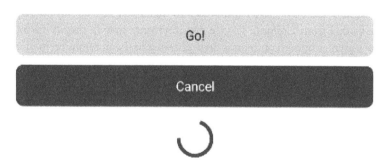

Figure 2.3 – ActivityIndicator bound to an asynchronous command

- You can call `IAsyncRelayCommand.Cancel` directly to cancel the command execution:

    ```
    public void Cancel() {
        UpdateTextCommand.Cancel();
    }
    ```

Note that you can cancel the inner method execution only if it supports cancellation. For this purpose, we passed it to the `Task.Delay` method in the *How to do it...* section:

```
public async Task UpdateTextAsync(CancellationToken token) {
    //...
        await Task.Delay(5000, token);
    //...
}
```

Initializing bound collections without freezing the UI

.NET MAUI allows you to represent collections using the `CollectionView` element. Typically, applications contain many collections, and often data for these collections is loaded on demand when a view is opened. It's essential to know how to initialize and update bound collections and avoid performance issues.

Getting ready

Start with the project you got after executing the second recipe of this chapter: *Implementing auto-generated view model properties*. This project is available at `https://github.com/PacktPublishing/.NET-MAUI-Cookbook/tree/main/Chapter02/c2-GeneratedViewModels`.

The code for this recipe is available at `https://github.com/PacktPublishing/.NET-MAUI-Cookbook/tree/main/Chapter02/c2-CollectionInitialization`.

How to do it...

Let's create a collection in the view model and bind it to `CollectionView`. Because data for the collection may be loaded from a remote service, we don't want to lock the UI during the loading operation, so we use asynchronous commands demonstrated in the previous recipe:

1. We will use automatically generated properties from the Community Toolkit to avoid boilerplate code. Define the collection property that will be displayed in the UI:

MyViewModel.cs

```
public partial class MyViewModel : ObservableObject {
    [ObservableProperty]
    ObservableCollection<Customer> customers;
}
```

> **Key point**
>
> The property should be `ObservableCollection<T>`, not `List<T>`, because `ObservableCollection` supports the `INotifyCollectionChanged` interface, which is required to notify bound UI controls about adding/removing collection items.

`Customer` is a simple POCO class with two properties:

```
public class Customer {
    public int ID {
        get;
        set;
    }
    public string Name {
        get;
        set;
    }
}
```

2. Since our loading operation may take considerable time, let's define an async method to initialize the view model and mark it with the `RelayCommand` attribute. To allow running the `Initialize` command only once, introduce the `IsInitialized` property:

```
public partial class MyViewModel : ObservableObject {
    //...
    [ObservableProperty]
    [NotifyCanExecuteChangedFor(nameof(InitializeCommand))]
    bool isInitialized;

    [RelayCommand(CanExecute = nameof(CanInitialize))]
    async Task InitializeAsync() {
        Customers = new ObservableCollection<Customer>(
    await DummyService.GetCustomersAsync());
        IsInitialized = true;
    }
    bool CanInitialize() => !IsInitialized;
}
```

`DummyService` is a simple class imitating a service that waits for 5 seconds and returns a list with two items:

```
public static class DummyService {
    public static async Task<IEnumerable<Customer>>
        GetCustomersAsync() {
        await Task.Delay(5000);
        return new List<Customer>() {
```

```
            new Customer(){ ID = 1, Name = "Jim" },
            new Customer(){ ID = 2, Name = "Bob" }
        };
    }
}
```

3. Add the CommunityToolkit.Maui NuGet and call UseMauiCommunityToolkit in the MauiProgram.CreateMauiApp method to initialize the toolkit:

```
public static class MauiProgram {
    public static MauiApp CreateMauiApp() {
        var builder = MauiApp.CreateBuilder();
        builder
            .UseMauiApp<App>()
            .UseMauiCommunityToolkit()
            //…
}
```

UseMauiCommunityToolkit is located in the CommunityToolkit.Maui namespace.

Note that CommunityToolkit.Maui and CommunityToolkit.Mvvm are separate NuGet packages.

4. In the view, add EventToCommandBehavior to the ContentPage.Behaviors collection. Set EventToCommandBehavior.EventName to Loaded and bind EventToCommandBehavior.Command to InitializeCommand. This will call InitializeCommand when the page is loaded:

```
<ContentPage xmlns=http://schemas.microsoft.com/dotnet/2021/maui
xmlns:x="http://schemas.microsoft.com/winfx/2009/xaml"
xmlns:viewModel="clr-namespace:c2_DecoupleViewAndViewModel"
xmlns:toolkit="http://schemas.microsoft.com/dotnet/2022/maui/
toolkit"
x:Class="c2_DecoupleViewAndViewModel.MainPage"
x:DataType="{x:Type viewModel:MyViewModel}">
    <ContentPage.Behaviors>
        <toolkit:EventToCommandBehavior
            EventName="Loaded"
            Command="{Binding InitializeCommand}"/>
    </ContentPage.Behaviors>
```

Note that you need to add the toolkit namespace to work with classes available in CommunityToolkit.Maui.

5. Define `CollectionView` and bind it to the `Customers` collection. Let's add `ActivityIndicator` to let a user know that data is being loaded:

```
<Grid>
    <CollectionView ItemsSource="{Binding Customers}">
        <CollectionView.ItemTemplate>
            <DataTemplate
                x:DataType="{x:Type viewModel:Customer}">
                <HorizontalStackLayout>
                    <Label Text="{Binding ID}"/>
                    <Label Text="{Binding Name}"/>
                </HorizontalStackLayout>
            </DataTemplate>
        </CollectionView.ItemTemplate>
    </CollectionView>
    <ActivityIndicator
        IsRunning="{Binding InitializeCommand.IsRunning}"/>
</Grid>
```

Run the project to see the result.

How it works...

The main trick used in this recipe is that collection initialization is performed asynchronously when the page is loaded. The `Loaded` event is transferred to a command in the view model using `EventToCommandBehavior`, available in `CommunityToolkit.Maui`. The asynchronous initialization command is automatically created from the `Initialize` method by the code generator.

There's more...

Here are some tips that will help you avoid common issues related to collection binding and initialization:

*   The bound collection property should implement the `INotifyCollectionChanged` interface. This allows the bound control (`CollectionView`) to track changes in the collection and update the visual state. Typically, `ObservableCollection<T>` is used for such usage scenarios. You can also use `BindingList<T>`; however, since it doesn't implement `INotifyCollectionChanged`, not all controls support it.

> **Key point**
> It's insufficient to support the `PropertyChanged` notification at the property-collection level because it will be triggered only when you set the property to a new value. However, `PropertyChanged` won't be raised if you modify the existing collection (add/remove items).

- When initializing a collection, assign a populated collection to the bound property instead of adding elements one by one. This will help avoid performance issues because when you add many elements to a bound collection, `CollectionView` processes each modification separately. It's much more efficient to populate a collection in advance and then assign it to the property bound to `CollectionView`.

- To avoid deadlocks, don't wait for a task result in the UI thread when loading collection data asynchronously. For example, the following code will produce a deadlock:

```
public partial class MyViewModel : ObservableObject {
    //…
    public MyViewModel() {
        Customers = DummyService.GetCustomersAsync().Result;
    }
}
public static class DummyService {
    public static async Task<ObservableCollection<Customer>>
      GetCustomersAsync() {
        await Task.Delay(5000);
        return new ObservableCollection<Customer>() {
        new Customer(){ ID = 1, Name = "Jim" },
        new Customer(){ ID = 2, Name = "Bob" }
    };
    }
}
```

Here is the sequence that results in a deadlock:

- Calling `DummyService.GetCustomersAsync().Result` suspends the UI thread until `GetCustomersAsync` finishes.

- Execution control is passed to the `GetCustomersAsync` method where `Task.Delay` is executed in a separate thread.

- When `Task.Delay` completes, control is returned to the UI thread. However, this thread is already locked because of the first step, which is waiting for the `GetCustomersAsync` method to complete.

This situation results in a deadlock: the functions in the first and third steps are waiting for each other.

Interacting with the UI from the view model without breaking MVVM

Commands help you invoke a method in a view model when some action is executed in the UI. However, sometimes you may need to perform the opposite task: call a method in a UI control when some logic is executed in your view model. For example, let's assume, you need to scroll `CollectionView` down each time a user adds a new item to the bound collection in the view model. Let's see how to accomplish this task using **WeakReferenceMessenger**, available in `CommunityToolkit.Mvvm`.

> **Definition**
> `WeakReferenceMessenger` enables communication between different parts of an application without creating strong references between objects. Weak references allow you to avoid memory leaks even if you don't unregister a message handler.

Getting ready

Start with the project you got after executing the fourth recipe of this chapter: *Initializing bound collections without freezing the UI*. This project is available at `https://github.com/PacktPublishing/`. `NET-MAUI-Cookbook/tree/main/Chapter02/c2-CollectionInitialization`.

The code for this recipe is available at `https://github.com/PacktPublishing/.NET-MAUI-Cookbook/tree/main/Chapter02/c2-UiAndViewModelInteraction`.

How to do it...

Let's create a method in the view model that adds a new item to a collection and notifies the bound `CollectionView` that it should scroll to the added item:

1. Add a button to `MainPage.xaml` and bind it to `AddCustomerCommand`, which will be added in the next step:

MainPage.xaml

```xml
<Grid RowDefinitions="50,*">
    <Button Text="Add Customer"
            Command="{Binding AddCustomerCommand}"/>
    <CollectionView x:Name="customersCollectionView"
                    ItemsSource="{Binding Customers}"
                    Grid.Row="1">
        <!--...-->
    </CollectionView>
</Grid>
```

2. Create a command in your `MyViewModel` class that adds a new customer to the `Customers` collection. In this command, call the `WeakReferenceMessenger.Send` method after updating the collection:

MyViewModel.cs

```
public partial class MyViewModel : ObservableObject {
    [ObservableProperty]
    [NotifyCanExecuteChangedFor(nameof(AddCustomerCommand))]
    ObservableCollection<Customer>? customers;

    [RelayCommand(CanExecute = nameof(CanAddCustomer))]
    void AddCustomer() {
        if (Customers != null) {
            Customers.Add(new Customer() {
                ID = Customers.Count,
                Name = "New Customer" });
            WeakReferenceMessenger.Default.Send(
                Customers.Last());
        }
    }
    bool CanAddCustomer() {
        return Customers != null;
    }
}
```

The `Send` method accepts any object, and you will be able to access this object when handling the message.

You may notice that we added the `RelayCommand.CanExecute` parameter and the `NotifyCanExecuteChangedFor` attribute to disable the bound button when the `Customers` property is null and automatically enable it once the property is initialized. This technique is described in the *Implementing auto-generated view models* recipe. They are not obligatory for sending messages, but we can add them to consolidate the technique.

3. In the `MainPage` constructor, register a handler for the message we're sending in the view model:

MainPage.xaml.cs

```
public MainPage() {
    InitializeComponent();
    WeakReferenceMessenger.Default.Register<Customer>(
    this, (r, customer) =>
    {
        customersCollectionView.ScrollTo(customer);
```

```
    });
}
```

You may notice that the `Customer` object we sent in the view model is now available in the `customer` variable. Since this code is executed at the view level, we can easily access our `CollectionView` and call its `ScrollTo` method.

How it works...

The `WeakReferenceMessenger` class offers you a centralized way to manage messages across the application. There are two main methods in the class: `Send` and `Register`.

As the name suggests, the `Send` method sends a message:

```
WeakReferenceMessenger.Default.Send(newCustomer);
```

The `Register` method accepts a handler that will be invoked when a message with the specified type is sent. In our case, this type is `Customer`:

```
WeakReferenceMessenger.Default.Register<Customer>(this, (recipient,
customer) =>
{
    //...
});
```

In the message handler, the `recipient` parameter will contain the current class, because we pass `this` as the first parameter. The `customer` parameter will contain an instance of the `Customer` class passed to the `Send` method.

The key advantage of `WeakReferenceMessenger` is that modules can communicate without holding a strong reference to each other. This helps you to create a loosely coupled architecture.

There's more...

Another technique to implement interaction between the view and view model without holding strong references is to use view services using interfaces. Let's solve the same task with `CollectionView` scrolling using a service. For this, declare an `ICollectionScrollService` interface in the view and implement it to call the `CollectionView.ScrollTo` method:

```
public interface ICollectionScrollService {
    public void ScrollToItem(object item);
}
public class CollectionScrollService : ICollectionScrollService {
    CollectionView collection;
    public CollectionScrollService(CollectionView collection) =>
```

```
    this.collection = collection;
  public void ScrollToItem(object item) {
      collection.ScrollTo(item);
  }
}
```

After that, pass an instance of this service to your view model in the `view` constructor:

```
public partial class MainPage : ContentPage {
    public MainPage() {
        InitializeComponent();
        BindingContext = new MyViewModel(customersCollectionView);
    }
}
```

Now you can invoke the `ScrollTo` method of `CollectionView` from your view model without breaking MVVM because you have an abstraction level represented by a service interface:

```
public class MyViewModel {
    //...
    ICollectionScrollService collectionScrollService;
    public MyViewModel (ICollectionScrollService
    collectionScrollService) =>
    this.collectionScrollService = collectionScrollService;
    void AddCustomer() {
        //...
        Customers.Add(new Customer());
        collectionScrollService.ScrollToItem(Customers.Last());
    }
]
```

The advantage of UI services is that you can easily reuse the same implementation in different views without registering any messages. Additionally, a single service may incorporate multiple methods related to the attached UI component. This will help you to keep all interaction functionality related to this component in a single class.

However, services require more complex view model initialization. Additionally, if you decide to write unit tests for your view model, you will have to mock the UI service with a dummy implementation.

Sending messages between view models via different channels

`WeakReferenceMessenger` allows you to organize communication not only between the view and view model but also between different view models. This helps you create communication between parent/child view models or even between view models in different modules. Additionally, `WeakReferenceMessenger` allows you to create different messaging channels to handle the same message type differently based on the channel.

Getting ready

Start with a new project and add the `CommunityToolkit.MVVM` NuGet package.

The code for this recipe is available at `https://github.com/PacktPublishing/.NET-MAUI-Cookbook/tree/main/Chapter02/c2-ViewModelCommunication`.

How to do it...

Let's create a simple app with three view models: `AlertGeneratorViewModel`, `SecurityMonitorViewModel`, and `PerformanceMonitorViewModel`. `AlertGeneratorViewModel` will generate alerts of two types: security and performance. `SecurityMonitorViewModel` and `PerformanceMonitorViewModel` will handle these messages based on the alert type – we will implement this part using separate channels:

1. Define a class to store alert messages. `CommunityToolkit.Mvvm` offers a base `ValueChangedMessage` class for custom message types:

   ```
   public class AlertMessage(string? value) :
   ValueChangedMessage<string?>(value) { }
   ```

2. Define a static `AlertTypes` class to store alert token types. You can use simple strings as tokens, but the class will help you avoid spelling issues when using the tokens:

   ```
   public static class AlertTypes {
       public static string Security = "SecurityAlert";
       public static string Performance = "Performance";
   }
   ```

3. Create an `AlertGeneratorViewModel` class that will send alerts. Let's send different types for even and odd alerts:

   ```
   public partial class AlertGeneratorViewModel : ObservableObject
   {
       [ObservableProperty]
       string? alertText;
   ```

```
        int alertCount = 0;
        [RelayCommand]
        public void GenerateAlert() {
            string channelType = ++alertCount % 2 == 0 ?
                AlertTypes.Security : AlertTypes.Performance;
            WeakReferenceMessenger.Default.Send(
              new AlertMessage(AlertText),
              channelType);
        }
    }
```

4. Create view models for the Security and Performance views. Register message handlers based on the required token/alert type:

PerformanceMonitorViewModel.cs

```
    public partial class PerformanceMonitorViewModel :
    ObservableObject {
        [ObservableProperty]
        ObservableCollection<string> performanceAlerts;
        public PerformanceMonitorViewModel() {
            performanceAlerts = new ObservableCollection<string>();
            WeakReferenceMessenger.Default.Register<AlertMessage,
        string>(this, AlertTypes.Performance, (r, alert) =>
            {
                PerformanceAlerts.Add(alert.Value);
            });
        }
    }
```

SecurityMonitorViewModel.cs

```
    //…
    public SecurityMonitorViewModel() {
        securityAlerts = new ObservableCollection<string>();
        WeakReferenceMessenger.Default.Register<AlertMessage,
        string>(this, AlertTypes.Security, (r, alert) =>
        {
            SecurityAlerts.Add(alert.Value);
        });
    }
```

I trimmed the code in `SecurityMonitorViewModel` because it has the same structure as `PerformanceMonitorViewModel`. The key point is that the message handlers should be registered for different alert types.

5. Now you can create views and bind them to view models:

AlertGeneratorView.xaml

```xml
<ContentView.BindingContext>
    <vm:AlertGeneratorViewModel/>
</ContentView.BindingContext>
<Grid ColumnDefinitions="*, 150">
    <Entry Text="{Binding AlertText, Mode=TwoWay}"/>
    <Button Text="Send Alert" Grid.Column="1"
            Command="{Binding GenerateAlertCommand}"/>
</Grid>
```

PerformanceMonitorView.xaml

```xml
<ContentView.BindingContext>
    <vm:PerformanceMonitorViewModel/>
</ContentView.BindingContext>
<VerticalStackLayout>
    <Label Text="Performance" FontSize="30"/>
    <CollectionView ItemsSource="{Binding PerformanceAlerts}"/>
</VerticalStackLayout>
```

SecurityMonitorView.xaml CollectionView's

```xml
<ContentView.BindingContext>
    <vm:SecurityMonitorViewModel/>
</ContentView.BindingContext>
<VerticalStackLayout>
    <Label Text="Security" FontSize="30"/>
    <CollectionView ItemsSource="{Binding SecurityAlerts}"/>
</VerticalStackLayout>
```

MainPage.xaml

```xml
<Grid RowDefinitions="40, *" ColumnDefinitions="*,*">
    <views:AlertGeneratorView Grid.ColumnSpan="2"/>
    <views:PerformanceMonitorView Grid.Row="1"/>
    <views:SecurityMonitorView Grid.Row="1"
```

```
rid.Column="1"/>
</Grid>
```

In all the preceding code snippets, vm corresponds to `clr-namespace:c2_View ModelCommunication.ViewsModels` and `views` corresponds to `clr-names pace:c2_ViewModelCommunication.Views`.

How it works...

The `WeakReferenceMessenger` class allows you to process messages from different channels separately. This allows you not to create a separate class for each message type. Instead, you can use the same class and distinguish channels by tokens. In this example, we used string tokens, but you can use integer values or custom types implementing the `IEquatable<Token>` interface.

The `Register` method accepts a token value. As a result, `WeakReferenceMessenger` invokes the registered handler only when a message with this token value is sent.

The following diagram illustrates how you can implement communication between view models by sending messages to different channels using tokens:

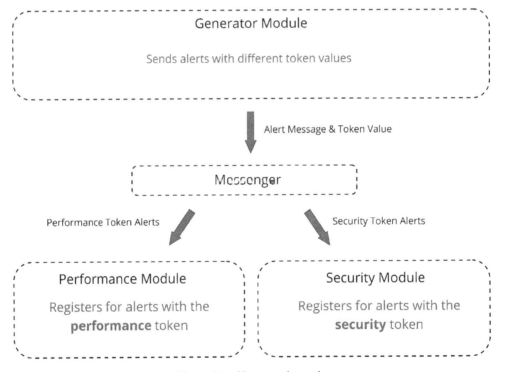

Figure 2.4 – Message channels

There's more...

The messaging system available in CommunityToolkit.MVVM offers even more useful capabilities. Let me outline some of them:

- The WeakReferenceMessenger.Default class doesn't use strong references to store message handlers. This means that even if you don't unsubscribe from a message, you won't get a memory leak. However, according to best practices, it's recommended to unregister from messages when you don't need them anymore because otherwise the registered message handler will be invoked until it's destroyed. Use the Unregister method for this purpose.

  You can use built-in classes to define your own message types. In the *How to do it...* section, we sent an instance of Customer as a message for simplicity. However, you can create a specialized message class by inheriting it from the ValueChangedMessage<T> class.

- You can implement the IRecipient<T> interface instead, specifying the message type in the Register method. This way, you can easily determine that a class handles specific messages:

```
public class MyViewModel : IRecipient<AlertMessage> {
    public MyViewModel () {
        WeakReferenceMessenger.Default.Register(this);
    }
    public void Receive(AlertMessage message) {
        // …
    }
}
```

- WeakReferenceMessenger allows you to not only send messages but also request information from message handlers. For this, inherit your message class from the RequestMessage<T> class and call Reply in the message handler:

```
public class AlertRequest : RequestMessage<string> { }
//…
WeakReferenceMessenger.Default.Register<MyViewModel,
  AlertRequest >(this, (r, request) => {
    request.Reply("some test");
});
//…
string requestedAlert = WeakReferenceMessenger.Default
    .Send<AlertRequest>();
```

- You can even request replies asynchronously using AsyncRequestMessage:

```
public class AlertRequest : AsyncRequestMessage<string>{ }
//…
WeakReferenceMessenger.Default.Register<MyViewModel,
```

```
   AlertRequest>(this, (r, request) => {
      request.Reply(r.GetAlertAsync());
   });
   // …
   string requestedAlert = await WeakReferenceMessenger.Default
      .Send<AlertRequest>();
```

It's supposed that `GetAlertAsync` returns `Task<string>`.

Injecting an application service into a view model using dependency injection

Dependency injection (**DI**) is a form of the **inversion of control** (**IoC**) pattern. The core idea of DI is that classes don't create the objects they rely on. Instead, a DI framework resolves the objects centrally and injects them into dependent classes. This technique allows you to easily manage dependencies and achieve loosely coupled architecture, share more code, and create unit tests for separate modules.

In this recipe, we will use DI to inject a data service into a view model:

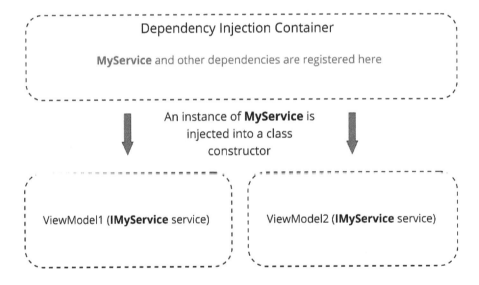

Figure 2.5 – DI service injection

Getting ready

Start with the project you got after executing the fourth recipe of this chapter: *Initializing and updating bound collections*. This project is available at `https://github.com/PacktPublishing/.NET-MAUI-Cookbook/tree/main/Chapter02/c2-CollectionInitialization`.

The code for this recipe is available at `https://github.com/PacktPublishing/.NET-MAUI-Cookbook/tree/main/Chapter02/c2-MvvmDependencyInjection`.

How to do it...

In the *Initializing bound collections without freezing the UI* recipe, we initialized a collection as a static `DummyService` class:

```
public partial class MyViewModel : ObservableObject {
    //...
    async Task InitializeAsync() {
       Customers = new ObservableCollection<Customer>(
    await DummyService.GetCustomersAsync());
       //...
    }
}
```

This creates a strong coupling between `MyViewModel` and `DummyService`. Let's use DI to enhance our architecture:

1. Create an interface for `DummyService` and make this class non-static:

    ```
    public interface IDummyService {
        Task<IEnumerable<Customer>> GetCustomersAsync();
    }
    public class DummyService : IDummyService {
        public async Task<IEnumerable<Customer>> GetCustomersAsync()
        {
            await Task.Delay(5000);
            return new List<Customer>() {
            new Customer(){ ID = 1, Name = "Jim" },
            new Customer(){ ID = 2, Name = "Bob" }};
        }
    }
    ```

2. Create a `MyViewModel` constructor accepting `IDummyService` and modify the `InitializeAsync` method so that it uses the service instance passed to the constructor:

    ```
    public partial class MyViewModel {
        //....
        IDummyService DataService;
        public MyViewModel(IDummyService dataService) {
            DataService = dataService;
        }
        async Task InitializeAsync() {
    ```

```
        Customers = new ObservableCollection<Customer>(
    await DataService.GetCustomersAsync());
        IsInitialized = true;
    }
}
```

3. Register `IdummyService`, `MyViewModel`, and `MainPage` in the DI container:

```
public static class MauiProgram {
    public static MauiApp CreateMauiApp() {
        var builder = MauiApp.CreateBuilder();
        builder
            .UseMauiApp<App>()
            .UseMauiCommunityToolkit()
            .RegisterViewModels()
            .RegisterViews()
            .RegisterAppServices();
        return builder.Build();
    }
    public static MauiAppBuilder RegisterViewModels(
      this MauiAppBuilder mauiAppBuilder) {
        mauiAppBuilder.Services.AddTransient<MyViewModel>();
        return mauiAppBuilder;
    }
    public static MauiAppBuilder RegisterViews(
      this MauiAppBuilder mauiAppBuilder) {
        mauiAppBuilder.Services.AddTransient<MainPage>();
        return mauiAppBuilder;
    }
    public static MauiAppBuilder RegisterAppServices(
      this MauiAppBuilder mauiAppBuilder) {
        mauiAppBuilder.Services.AddSingleton<IDummyService,
            DummyService>();
        return mauiAppBuilder;
    }
}
```

Here, we register our classes using the `AddSingleton` and `AddTransient` methods. We'll explain the difference between these methods in the *There's more…* section. We also added the `RegisterViewModels`, `RegisterViews`, and `RegisterAppServices` methods to logically group registrations.

4. Create a `DISource` markup extension. We will use it to resolve an instance of `MyViewModel` and assign it to `MainPage` in XAML:

```
public class DISource : IMarkupExtension {
    public Type Type { get; set; }
    public object ProvideValue(IServiceProvider serviceProvider)
    {
        return Application.Current.MainPage.Handler
            .MauiContext.Services.GetService(Type);
    }
}
```

Note that we use `GetService` to resolve the registered view model by its type.

5. Use `DISource` to set `MainPage.BindingContext` in XAML:

```
<ContentPage
    ...
    xmlns:local="clr-namespace:c2_DecoupleViewAndViewModel"
    x:Class="c2_DecoupleViewAndViewModel.MainPage"
    BindingContext="{local:DISource Type={x:Type
        viewModel:MyViewModel}}">
```

You may notice that we need to specify only the view model's type, and `DISource` will create a view model instance from the DI container.

Now you can run the project to make sure that everything works.

How it works...

There are two main concepts in DI:

- **Registration**: This is the process of informing the DI container about which interfaces and classes should be instantiated and how. We registered our view, view model, and service in the `MauiProgram.CreateMauiApp` method using `MauiAppBuilder`, available on the .NET MAUI platform by default. We used the `AddTransient` method to register our classes.

- **Resolution**: This is the process of retrieving the required dependencies from the DI container. When you ask the DI container to create a class instance, it checks what constructors this class has and what parameters it accepts. If the DI container finds a type registered before that matches a constructor parameter, it automatically injects an instance of this type into the constructor. In our case, when the DI container created `MyViewModel`, it knew about the `IDummyService` (because we registered it) and automatically injected an instance of `DummyService` into the constructor.

Classes are resolved using the `GetService` method:

```
IDummyService service = Application.Current.MainPage.Handler.
MauiContext.Services.GetService<IDummyService>();
```

In the *How to do it...* section, we created the `DISource` markup extension to resolve view models without writing code-behind. Another solution would be to create a `MainPage` constructor accepting `MyViewModel` and assign `BindingContext` there:

```
public MainPage(MyViewModel viewModel) {
    InitializeComponent();
    BindingContext = viewModel;
}
```

In .NET MAUI, the root object that handles navigation between pages is called Shell. The Shell automatically resolves pages from the DI container. That's why even though you don't explicitly call `GetService` to create `MainPage`, `MyViewModel` is passed to the constructor.

There's more...

The built-in .NET MAUI DI container contains three registration types:

- **Transient**: When you request a class instance from a DI container, a new instance will be created for each request. We used this registration type for the main page and view model:

    ```
    mauiAppBuilder.Services.AddTransient<MainPage>();
    mauiAppBuilder.Services.AddTransient<MyViewModel>();
    ```

    If you register a page using `AddTransient`, a new page instance will be created each time you navigate to it using the `GoToAsync` method. Note that pages added directly to Shell won't be recreated even if you use `AddTransient`. For this reason, a new `MainPage` instance won't be created if you navigate to another page and then go back. However, if you create a child page and navigate to it from `MainPage` using `GoToAsync`, a page instance will be requested from the DI container during navigation, and if it's registered as transient, a new instance will be created.

> **Key point**
> *Transient* is good for rarely used pages, lightweight services, and thread-unsafe objects.

- **Singleton**: A single shared instance will be returned by the DI container each time a registered class is resolved. We used this technique for `DummyService`:

    ```
    mauiAppBuilder.Services.AddSingleton<IDummyService,
    DummyService>();
    ```

If a page is registered as singleton, it will be created only once. If you navigate to this page once again, the same instance will be used. This may help you reduce the subsequent page opening time.

> **Key point**
>
> *Singleton* is good for frequently used pages and services that share data/state across the application.

- **Scoped**: A single object instance will be created within the scope. You need to explicitly create a new scope and access its `ServiceProvider` to create scoped instances. If we register `DummyService` as scoped, in the following code snippet, `ds1` will be equal to `ds2`; however, `d2` won't be equal to `ds3`, because `ds3` is created in a separate scope:

```
IServiceProvider serviceProvider = Application.Current.MainPage.
Handler.MauiContext.Services;
IDummyService ds1, ds2, ds3;
using (var scope1 = serviceProvider.CreateScope()) {
    ds1 = scope1.ServiceProvider.GetService<IDummyService>();
    ds2 = scope1.ServiceProvider.GetService<IDummyService>();
}
using (var scope2 = serviceProvider.CreateScope()) {
    ds3 = scope2.ServiceProvider.GetService<IDummyService>();
}
```

> **Key point**
>
> *Scoped* may be useful for sharing the same service instance across multiple views on the same page.

Troubleshooting binding errors

As you may have noticed from previous recipes in this chapter, binding is one of the core mechanisms used in the MVVM pattern. Views in real apps include dozens of bindings and it's important to know how to troubleshoot a binding when something doesn't work.

One of the techniques that helps you avoid binding errors is assigning the `x:DataType` attribute, which resolves bindings at compile time. This will not only let you know that you made a typo in a binding but will also improve the performance. However, `x:DataType` only works when you know exactly what object will be used in `BindingContext`. Sometimes, your binding source may contain properties with the `object` type, and in such cases `x:DataType` can't be used. Moreover, you may need to create complex bindings with `RelativeSource` and `x:Reference` mechanisms, as described in the *There's more…* section of the *Decoupling the UI from the view model* recipe in this chapter. However, there is a simple trick that will help you always diagnose and fix issues in almost any binding type: you can create a binding converter and gradually complicate your binding to see when it fails.

Getting ready

Start with a new project and add the `CommunityToolkit.MVVM` NuGet package.

The code of this recipe is available at `https://github.com/PacktPublishing/.NET-MAUI-Cookbook/tree/main/Chapter02/c2-TroubleshootBindings`.

How to do it...

The general idea is to create a dummy binding converter and use it in the binding you want to debug. It's better to start with a simple binding and gradually complicate it, checking what objects come to the converter. Let's create a list of items in `CollectionView` and bind a command in each item to the `delete` command declared in the view model:

1. Create a `MyViewModel` class with a collection property and a `delete` command:

    ```
    public partial class MyViewModel : ObservableObject {
        [ObservableProperty]
        ObservableCollection<Customer> customers;
        public MyViewModel() {
            Customers = new ObservableCollection<Customer>();
            for (int i = 1; i < 30; i++) {
                Customers.Add(new Customer() { ID = i, Name = "Name"
                    + i });
            }
        }
        [RelayCommand]
        public void DeleteCustomer(Customer customer) {
            Customers.Remove(customer);
        }
    }

    public class Customer {
        public int ID {
            get;
            set;
        }
        public string? Name {
            get;
            set;
        }
    }
    ```

2. Now let's define `CollectionView` with `ItemTemplate`. Add a label to the template to display the customer name and a button to delete the current customer:

```
<ContentPage.BindingContext>
    <local:MyViewModel/>
</ContentPage.BindingContext>
<CollectionView ItemsSource="{Binding Customers}">
    <CollectionView.ItemTemplate>
        <DataTemplate>
            <Grid ColumnDefinitions="*, 100">
                <Label Text="{Binding Name}"/>
                <Button Command="{Binding
DeleteCustomerCommand}"
                        CommandParameter="{Binding}"
                        Text="Delete"
                        Grid.Column="1"/>
            </Grid>
        </DataTemplate>
    </CollectionView.ItemTemplate>
</CollectionView>
```

If you run the project, you will see the following result; however, the **Delete** buttons won't work:

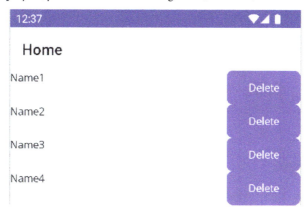

Figure 2.6 – CollectionView with buttons

The `Delete` action won't work, because `Binding` in the `Button.Command` property couldn't find `DeleteCustomerCommand`.

3.   Let's create a dummy converter to understand what comes to the binding and why the button doesn't invoke the `DeleteCustomer` command. For this, create a DummyConverter class, implementing the `IValueConverter` interface:

```
public class DummyConverter : IValueConverter {
    public object? Convert(object? value, Type targetType,
      object? parameter, CultureInfo culture) {
       return null;
    }
    public object? ConvertBack(object? value, Type targetType,
      object? parameter, CultureInfo culture) {

       return null;
    }
}
```

4.   Then, define DummyConverter in the page sources and assign it to the `Binding.Converter` property. Replace the previous binding path (`DeleteCustomerCommand`) with a dot `.`:

```
<ContentPage.Resources>
    <local:DummyConverter x:Key="dummyConverter"/>
</ContentPage.Resources>
...
<Button Command="{Binding ., Converter={StaticResource
dummyConverter}}" ... />
```

A dot means that you are binding to the entire object that comes to the binding source.

5.   Now you can add a breakpoint to the `DummyConverter.Convert` method, run the project, and check what object comes to the `value` parameter:

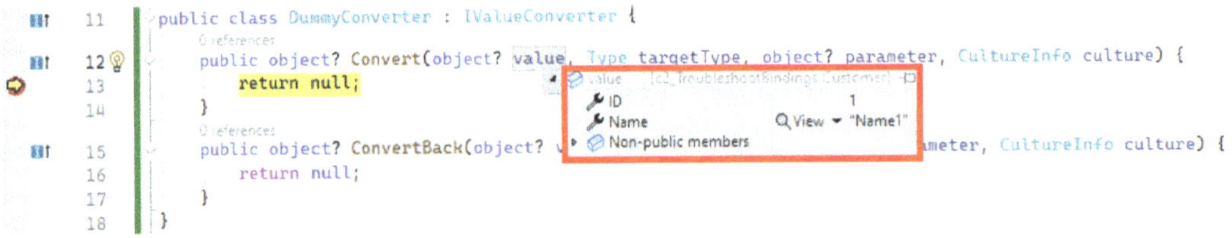

Figure 2.7 – Converter debugging

You may notice that we receive the `Customer` class, not `MyViewModel`, so it's expected that the `Binding` can't find the `DeleteCustomerCommand` property.

6. Now we understand that we need to bind to MyViewModel to access DeleteCustomerCommand. However, how can we do it from the ItemTemplate of CollectionView? One of the possible solutions is to use a RelativeSource binding, which will help us access MyViewModel through the BindingContext of CollectionView:

```
<Button Command="{Binding BindingContext,
        Source={RelativeSource
                AncestorType={x:Type CollectionView}},
        Converter={StaticResource dummyConverter}}"
        CommandParameter="{Binding}"
```

If you run the project and check what value comes to DummyConverter, you should see an instance of MyViewModel.

7. Now we can bind to MyViewModel.DeleteCustomerCommand and remove Dummy Converter:

```
<Button Command="{Binding
        Source={RelativeSource
                AncestorType={x:Type CollectionView}},
        Path=BindingContext.DeleteCustomerCommand}"
        CommandParameter="{Binding}"
        Text="Delete"
        Grid.Column="1"/>
```

This time, our binding should work as expected, and clicking the Delete button will remove the current item from CollectionView.

How it works...

The idea behind this technique is pretty straightforward: you create a test converter and check what value comes from the binding. If the converter is not invoked, this means that the binding fails and you need to simplify the binding path to determine what comes at a higher level. Sometimes, however, bindings may work once and they don't update their value when the bound object is modified. The most common reason is that the bound object doesn't implement the INotifyPropertyChanged interface or it doesn't raise INotifyPropertyChanged.PropertyChanged even when the property is changed.

There's more...

Visual Studio provides log information about the binding errors to the **Output** window. You can open it using the **Views | Output** menu. While sometimes it's not as helpful as debugging a binding using a converter, it may help you detect binding errors on a large page. The original binding error from the *How to do it…* section will look as follows:

```
Microsoft.Maui.Controls.Xaml.Diagnostics.BindingDiagnostics:
Warning: 'DeleteCustomerCommand' property not found on 'c2_
TroubleshootBindings.Customer', target property: 'Microsoft.Maui.
Controls.Button.Command'
```

For simple usage scenarios, this error provides sufficient information to detect a binding error and understand its cause.

3

Advanced XAML and UI Techniques

Would you like to learn all the pro tips to make your app's UI shine with minimal effort? If yes, then this chapter is for you. .NET MAUI offers a wide range of XAML features, many inherited from Windows Presentation Foundation (WPF), such as **styles**, **triggers**, and **DataTemplates**. These basic mechanisms are perfect for most simple usage scenarios. However, in this chapter, we will explore advanced techniques that will help you achieve the desired user experience and organize your view code efficiently. You will also master best practices on features such as attached properties and behaviors, elements, and graphical animations. We will create a custom, reusable view and a bar chart drawn with `Microsoft.Maui.Graphics`.

In this chapter, we'll be covering the following recipes:

- Extending a UI element without subclassing using attached properties
- Implementing attached behavior to reuse UI logic
- Implementing `ContentView` with dependency properties to reuse UI elements
- Assigning custom animations to elements in XAML
- Creating motion graphics with Lottie animations
- Implementing dark/light theme switching
- Implementing theme support for images and the status bar
- Drawing custom elements on a canvas

Technical requirements

There are no specific requirements for the recipes in this chapter. All of them start with a basic .NET MAUI application created by the default Visual Studio template.

You can download all the projects created in this chapter from GitHub: `https://github.com/PacktPublishing/.NET-MAUI-Cookbook/tree/main/Chapter03`

Extending a UI element without subclassing using attached properties

Have you ever used extension methods in C#?

```
public class ClassA {
    //...
}
public static class ClassAExtensions {
    public static void MethodX(this ClassA a) {
        //...
    }
}
//...
ClassA classA = new ClassA();
classA.MethodX();
```

This is a great concept that helps you extend the functionality of a certain class without creating a descendant. In .NET MAUI, you can create not only methods but also *extensions* or **attached properties** for UI elements without subclassing them. Even if you haven't created custom attached properties yet, I'm sure you've already used them in the Grid panel:

```
<Grid ColumnDefinitions="*,*" RowDefinitions="*,*">
    <Label Grid.Row="1" Grid.Column="1"/>
</Grid>
```

Here, `Grid.Row` and `Grid.Column` are attached properties: they are not defined in the `Label` class, but you can attach them to labels and other UI elements. In this recipe, we will create a custom attached property to extend the functionality of the `Entry` element.

Getting ready

To follow the steps described in this recipe, we just need to create a blank .NET MAUI application.

The code for this recipe is available at `https://github.com/PacktPublishing/.NET-MAUI-Cookbook/tree/main/Chapter03/c3-AttachedProperties`.

How to do it...

Let's create a custom attached property for the Entry element. The property will incorporate custom logic to select all text in the Entry when it's focused. This will be achieved by subscribing to the Entry's Focused event in the changed callback of the attached property. When the attached property is created, we will be able to set it in XAML and the focusing logic will be activated for a specific Entry element.

1. Create a static EntrySelection class with a static field and assign it to an object returned by the BindableProperty.CreateAttached method. CreateAttached registers a property with specified parameters and returns a BindableProperty instance. A property should be registered only once, so it's important to use the static keyword:

```
public static class EntrySelection {
    public static readonly BindableProperty
        SelectAllOnFocusProperty =
        BindableProperty.CreateAttached("SelectAllOnFocus",
            typeof(bool),
            typeof(EntrySelection),
            false,
            propertyChanged: OnSelectAllOnFocusChanged);
public static bool GetSelectAllOnFocus(
        BindableObject view) =>
        (bool)view.GetValue(SelectAllOnFocusProperty);

public static void SetSelectAllOnFocus(
        BindableObject view, bool value) =>
        view.SetValue(SelectAllOnFocusProperty, value);

public static void OnSelectAllOnFocusChanged(
        BindableObject obj, object oldValue, object newValue){

    }

}
```

> **Key point**
>
> The property name (SelectAllOnFocus) passed to the CreateAttached method as a parameter should match the field name (SelectAllOnFocusProperty) and accessor methods (GetSelectAllOnFocus and SetSelectAllOnFocus).

2. In the `OnSelectAllOnFocusChanged` method, subscribe to the `Entry.Focused` event and set the `CursorPosition` and `SelectionLength` properties to select all text in the entry:

```
public static void OnSelectAllOnFocusChanged(BindableObject obj,
  object oldValue, object newValue) {
    if (obj is Entry entry) {
        if ((bool)newValue)
            entry.Focused += EntryFocused;
        else
            entry.Focused -= EntryFocused;
    }
}
private static void EntryFocused(object? sender, FocusEventArgs
  e) {
    if (sender is Entry entry) {
        entry.Dispatcher.Dispatch(() =>
        {
            entry.CursorPosition = 0;
            entry.SelectionLength = entry.Text == null ? 0 :
              entry.Text.Length;
        });
    }
}
```

In the preceding code snippet, we used the `Dispatcher.Dispatch` method to postpone selection modification. This is required because the `Entry` element executes its internal logic when it receives the focus, and this can remove our selection if we set it as soon as the `Focused` event is raised. We additionally unsubscribe from the `Focused` event when the `newValue` parameter is `false`. This disables the selection behavior when the attached property is set to `false`.

3. Now we can use the attached property in the view. Create a simple layout with two `Entry` elements and bind the `EntrySelection.SelectAllOnFocus` attached property to the `CheckBox` that will enable or disable the property:

```
xmlns:local="clr-namespace:c3_AttachedProperties"
<VerticalStackLayout>
    <CheckBox x:Name="selectOnFocusCheckBox" IsChecked="True"/>
    <Entry Text="SelectAll editor"
        local:EntrySelection.SelectAllOnFocus="{Binding
Source={x:Reference selectOnFocusCheckBox}, Path=IsChecked}"/>
    <Entry Text="Normal editor"/>
</VerticalStackLayout>
```

Now you can run the project and see how it works. You will notice that when you focus the first `Entry`, all the text is selected. However, if you disable the `CheckBox` and focus the `Entry` once again, the text won't be selected.

How it works...

.NET MAUI offers the following two main UI property types:

- **Bindable (or dependency) property**: These are the properties you use in most UI elements – for example, `Entry.Text`, `Entry.IsEnabled`, and so on. All these properties are defined in the `Entry` class and can be set only on the `Entry` element.

- **Attached property**: As demonstrated in the *How to do it...* section, these properties are defined in an external class and can be set on other UI elements.

`BindableProperty.CreateAttached` is the core method used to create an attached property. However, you need to also add accessor methods (`GetSelectAllOnFocus` and `SetSelectAllOnFocus` in our example). As mentioned in the *How to do it...* section, it's essential to follow the naming convention where the accessor methods include the property name.

There's more...

Here are a few tips you may find helpful when working with attached properties:

- Use the `GetPropertyName` and `SetPropertyName` accessor methods to get or set attached properties in C#. For example, you can use the following code to set the `SelectAllOnFocus` property on the `Entry` element:

  ```
  EntrySelection.SetSelectAllOnFocus(selectAllEntry, true);
  ```

- Just like regular bindable properties, you can set attached properties in a `Style`:

  ```
  <Style TargetType="Entry">
      <Setter Property="local:EntrySelection.SelectAllOnFocus"
      Value="True"/>
  </Style>
  ```

- You cannot bind to attached properties from other elements. For instance, the following code won't work:

  ```
  <Entry x:Name="selectAllEntry"
          local:EntrySelection.SelectAllOnFocus="True"/>
  <CheckBox IsChecked="{Binding Source={x:Reference
  selectAllEntry},
              Path=(local:EntrySelection. SelectAllOnFocus)}"/>
  ```

  In .NET MAUI, attached properties can only be used as a binding *target*, not as a binding *source*.

Implementing attached behavior to reuse UI logic

Attached properties are useful for encapsulating simple reusable logic or assigning information to a UI element. However, because attached properties are implemented in static classes, they do not retain state, which may be necessary for advanced usage scenarios. One powerful technique to address this is by using **attached behavior**.

Here are a few examples where you could create a custom attached behavior and reuse it for multiple elements:

- Creating custom editor validation rules
- Implementing drag-and-drop logic
- Implementing image zooming
- Handling any UI-related events when you wish to keep code-behind clean

Getting ready

To follow the steps described in this recipe, we just need to create a blank .NET MAUI application.

The code for this recipe is available at `https://github.com/PacktPublishing/.NET-MAUI-Cookbook/tree/main/Chapter03/c3-AttachedBehavior`.

How to do it...

Let's create attached behavior that zooms into an image when it's double-tapped:

1. Create a `DoubleTapToZoomBehavior` class and inherit it from `Behavior`. Use `Image` as a generic parameter:

```
public class DoubleTapToZoomBehavior : Behavior<Image> {
}
```

2. Add `BindableProperty` to specify the scale factor that will be applied when an image is double-tapped:

```
public double ScaleFactor {
    get { return (double)GetValue(ScaleFactorProperty); }
    set { SetValue(ScaleFactorProperty, value); }
}
public static readonly BindableProperty ScaleFactorProperty =
    BindableProperty.Create("ScaleFactor", typeof(double),
        typeof(DoubleTapToZoomBehavior) , 2d);
```

Making the property bindable will allow you not only to set it when using `DoubleTapToZoomBehavior`, but also to bind it to a view model or another control. We also specify 2d as the default value `ScaleFactor` if it's not specified explicitly.

3. Override the `OnAttachedTo` method to add a `TapGestureRecognizer` to the collection of `GestureRecognizers`:

```
Image image;
TapGestureRecognizer tapGestureRecognizer;
protected override void OnAttachedTo(Image bindable) {
    base.OnAttachedTo(bindable);
    tapGestureRecognizer = new TapGestureRecognizer() {
        NumberOfTapsRequired = 2
    };
    image = bindable;
    tapGestureRecognizer.Tapped += OnImageDoubleTap;
    image.GestureRecognizers.Add(tapGestureRecognizer);
}
```

`TapGestureRecognizer` allows you to handle taps in elements inherited from the `View` class. We added the `image` field to save the image to which the behavior is attached. We set the `NumberOfTapsRequired` property to 2 to handle only double taps.

4. Implement the `OnImageDoubleTap` method and add the `isZoomed` field to store the current state:

```
bool isZoomed;
private void OnImageDoubleTap(object sender, TappedEventArgs e)
{
    Point? tappedPoint = e.GetPosition(image);
    if (isZoomed) {
        image.ScaleTo(1);
        image.TranslateTo(0, 0);
    }
    else {
        double translateFactor = ScaleFactor - 1;
        double traslateX = (image.Width / 2 - tappedPoint.
          Value.X) * translateFactor;
        double traslateY = (image.Height / 2 - tappedPoint.
          Value.Y) * translateFactor;
        image.TranslateTo(traslateX, traslateY);
        image.ScaleTo(ScaleFactor);
    }
    isZoomed = !isZoomed;
}
```

The `TranslateTo` and `ScaleTo` methods scale and move the image with an animation so that the tapped point is always located under the finger. We also use the `ScaleFactor` property that we defined in the second step to calculate proper image scaling and shifting.

5. Override the `OnDetachingFrom` method to remove `TapGestureRecognizer` when `DoubleTapToZoomBehavior` is detached from the parent image:

```
protected override void OnDetachingFrom(Image bindable) {
    base.OnDetachingFrom(bindable);
    image.GestureRecognizers.Remove(tapGestureRecognizer);
    tapGestureRecognizer.Tapped -= OnImageDoubleTap;
    image = null;
}
```

Note that if we don't remove `TapGestureRecognizer`, it will continue handling the `Tapped` event even after detaching the behavior from the image. We also set the `image` field to null in order to not hold a reference to the parent `Image` object.

6. Finally, you can attach `DoubleTapToZoomBehavior` to an image in your view:

```
<Image Source="dotnet_bot.png">
    <Image.Behaviors>
        <local:DoubleTapToZoomBehavior
                                ScaleFactor="3.5"/>
    </Image.Behaviors>
</Image>
```

Now you can run the project and double-tap the image to see how zooming works.

How it works...

When a behavior is attached to a visual element, it calls the `OnAttachedTo` virtual method. The `bindable` parameter contains the UI element to which the behavior is attached. Since we attached `DoubleTapToZoomBehavior` to an image, we received this image in `OnAttachedTo`. Typically, this method is used to subscribe the parent object's events or perform other setup configurations.

The `OnDetachingFrom` method is called when a behavior is removed from the `Behaviors` collection. In `OnDetachingFrom`, it's important to unsubscribe from all events to prevent the event handler from being called after detaching a behavior. Additionally, it's recommended to remove object references to external objects to avoid memory leaks. That's why we set the `image` field to `null` in `OnDetachingFrom`. I'll describe how object references may cause memory leaks in the *Getting rid of memory leaks* recipe in *Chapter 8, Optimizing Performance*.

The behavior class is a `BindableObject` descendant. This allowed us to create a `BindableProperty` in `DoubleTapToZoomBehavior` to configure the behavior. Creating properties in behaviors adds more flexibility because you can use the same behavior class, but with different settings based on the requirements of a specific view.

There's more...

Here are a few tips you may find useful when working with behaviors:

- You can attach or detach behaviors in C# using the `Behaviors` collection:

```
image.Behaviors.Add(new DoubleTapToZoomBehavior() { ScaleFactor
= 3 });
image.Behaviors.RemoveAt(0);
```

- To add a behavior in `Style`, create an attached property in the `DoubleTapToZoomBehavior` class and modify the `Behaviors` collection in the `PropertyChanged` callback:

```
public static readonly BindableProperty AttachBehaviorProperty =
    BindableProperty.CreateAttached("AttachBehavior",
        typeof(bool), typeof(DoubleTapToZoomBehavior),
        false, propertyChanged: OnAttachBehaviorChanged );

public static bool GetAttachBehavior(BindableObject view) {
    return (bool)view.GetValue(AttachBehaviorProperty);
}

public static void SetAttachBehavior(BindableObject view, bool
value) {
    view.SetValue(AttachBehaviorProperty, value);
}

static void OnAttachBehaviorChanged(BindableObject view, object
oldValue, object newValue) {
    Image img = view as Image;
    if (img == null) {
        return;
    }
    bool attachBehavior = (bool)newValue;
    if (attachBehavior) {
        img.Behaviors.Add(new DoubleTapToZoomBehavior());
    }
    else {
```

```
            Behavior toRemove = img.Behaviors.FirstOrDefault(b => b
                is DoubleTapToZoomBehavior);
            if (toRemove != null) {
                img.Behaviors.Remove(toRemove);
            }
        }
    }
}
```

After that, you can attach the behavior in XAML using the following code:

```
<Style TargetType="Image">
    <Setter Property="local:DoubleTapToZoomBehavior.IsActive"
Value="True"/>
</Style>
```

Implementing ContentView with dependency properties to reuse UI elements

How much code is redundant in your application? Developers have been creating various techniques to avoid repeated code and yet according to different research, the percentage of repeated code may vary from 10% to 20% in an average project (`https://plg.uwaterloo.ca/~migod/846/papers/bellon-tse07.pdf`). In this recipe, we will see how to create reusable UI elements with `ContentView` and decrease the amount of repeated code.

Getting ready

To follow the steps described in this recipe, we just need to create a blank .NET MAUI application.

The code for this recipe is available at `https://github.com/PacktPublishing/.NET-MAUI-Cookbook/tree/main/Chapter03/c3-ReusableContentView`.

How to do it...

Let's create a reusable card element with a toggle button that starts editing or saves changes. We will use `ContentView` with a dependency property to set card text.

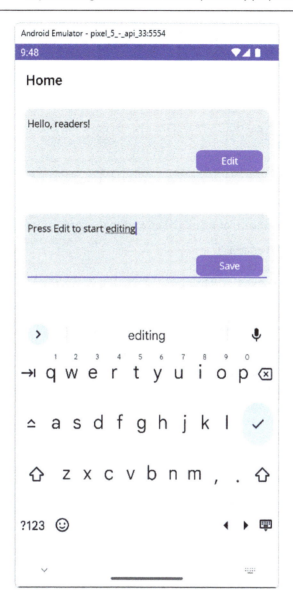

Figure 3.1 – ContentView cards

1. Right-click on the project in **Solution Explorer** and select **Add | New Item | .NET MAUI ContentView (XAML)**. Name the view EditableCard.

2. Add the `Text` bindable property to the `EditableCard` class:

```
public string Text {
    get { return (string)GetValue(TextProperty); }
    set { SetValue(TextProperty, value); }
}
public static readonly BindableProperty TextProperty =
BindableProperty.Create("Text", typeof(string),
    typeof(EditableCard));
```

We will use this property to pass data from external elements to `EditableCard` and bind it to the `Entry` element.

3. Assign `BindingContext` of `EditableCard` to the current class instance:

```
public EditableCard() {
    InitializeComponent();
    BindingContext = this;
}
```

This will allow us to bind to the `EditableCard.Text` property in XAML.

4. Add UI elements to present a card with editable text:

```
<Border StrokeShape="RoundRectangle 10,10,10,10"
StrokeThickness="0">
    <Border.Shadow>
        <Shadow Brush="LightGray"
        Offset="20,20"
        Radius="20"
        Opacity="0.8" />
    </Border.Shadow>
    <Grid BackgroundColor="LightGray">
        <Entry x:Name="editor"
                Text="{Binding Text}"
                IsReadOnly="True"/>
        <Button x:Name="editButton"
                Text="Edit"
                Clicked="OnEditButtonClicked"
                HorizontalOptions="End"
                VerticalOptions="End"
                WidthRequest="100"
                HeightRequest="30"
                Padding="0"
                Margin="10"/>
    </Grid>
</Border>
```

In the preceding code snippet, we use the following controls:

- `Border` to create a rounded shape
- `Grid` to arrange elements
- `Entry` to edit text
- `Button` to start or stop editing

We also added an `OnEditButtonClicked` event handler. We will implement it in the next step.

5. Navigate to `EditableCard.xaml.cs` and add the `OnEditButtonClicked` method:

```
bool isEditing;
private void OnEditButtonClicked(object sender, EventArgs e) {
    isEditing = !isEditing;
    if (isEditing) {
        editor.IsReadOnly = false;
        editor.Focus();
        editor.CursorPosition = editor.Text == null ? 0 :
          editor.Text.Length;
        editButton.Text = "Save";
    }
    else {
        editor.IsReadOnly = true;
        editButton.Focus();
        editButton.Text = "Edit";
    }
}
```

6. Finally, you can use the `EditableCard` class in `MainPage.xaml`. Let's add two cards with different text:

```
<VerticalStackLayout Spacing="52" Padding="14">
    <local:EditableCard HorizontalOptions="Fill"
                        HeightRequest="100"
                        Text="Hello, readers!"/>
    <local:EditableCard HorizontalOptions="Fill"
                        HeightRequest="100"
                        Text="Press Edit to start
editing"/>
</VerticalStackLayout>
```

If you run the project, you should see the result shown in *Figure 3.1*.

How it works...

If you have experience with WPF or WinForms, you can think of ContentView as being similar to UserControl. ContentView lets you encapsulate XAML and C# code into reusable blocks. By adding BindableProperty, you can configure your custom ContentView or pass data to it, as we did with the Text property.

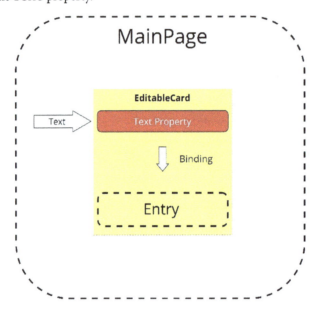

Figure 3.2 – Structure of ContentView with a custom bindable property

There's more...

ContentView is not the only way to reuse UI elements in .NET MAUI. The platform provides DataTemplates that allow you to define XAML code and then reuse it in different parts of your application:

```xml
<DataTemplate x:Key="customerTemplate">
    <Border>
        <Label Text="{Binding CustomerName}"/>
    </Border>
</DataTemplate>
...
<CollectionView x:Name="collection1"
          ItemTemplate="{StaticResource customerTemplate}"
              />
<CollectionView x:Name="collection2"
```

```
        ItemTemplate="{StaticResource customerTemplate}"
            />
```

However, if you wish to display one separate item, you will need to use `CollectionView` or `BindableLayout` with a single element, which is not the best solution.

There are third-party libraries that allow you to solve this task in a more elegant manner. For example, the DevExpress .NET MAUI suite offers the `DXContentPresenter` element, which can visualize any type of content using a specified `DataTemplate`:

```
<dxc:DXContentPresenter Content="{Binding Customer}"
        ContentTemplate="{StaticResource customerTemplate }"/>
```

The `BindingContext` of `DataTemplate` will be set to the object specified as `Content`. This allows you to bind to the object from the template. You can learn more about `DXContentPresenter` at `https://docs.devexpress.com/MAUI/DevExpress.Maui.Core.DXContentPresenter`.

Assigning custom animations to elements in XAML

How many animations will you notice if you open any app on your phone and navigate through a few screens? Even though animations are not usually part of the core functionality, they play an important role in the user experience by bringing the interface to life and highlighting important elements.

While .NET MAUI offers methods for animating elements in C#, it doesn't have a built-in API to define animations declaratively in XAML. Fortunately, `CommunityToolkit.Maui` provides the `AnimationBehavior` and `BaseAnimation` classes for this task. `AnimationBehavior` is attached to a UI element and serves as a container for an animation. `BaseAnimation` is a base class for built-in animations that implement animating logic. In this recipe, we will use these capabilities to create a blinking animation when a button appears on the screen.

Getting ready

To follow the steps described in this recipe, we just need to create a blank .NET MAUI application.

The code for this recipe is available at `https://github.com/PacktPublishing/.NET-MAUI-Cookbook/tree/main/Chapter03/c3-CustomAnimations`.

How to do it...

Let's create a blinking button using `AnimationBehavior`. The animation will start when the button is shown on the page. Below is an image demonstrating the stages of the button fade animation:

Figure 3.3 – Button fade animation

1. Add the `CommunityToolkit.Maui` NuGet package to your project.

2. Create `AttentionAnimation`, inherited from `BaseAnimation`, and override the `Animate` method to implement the fade-in and fade-out animations:

```
class AttentionAnimation : BaseAnimation {
    public override async Task Animate(VisualElement view,
      CancellationToken token = default) {
        for (int i= 0; i < 6; i++){
            await view.FadeTo(0.5, Length, Easing);
            await view.FadeTo(1, Length, Easing);
        }
    }
}
```

We're calling `FadeTo` in a cycle to animate `Opacity` six times from 0.5 to 1.

3. Add a button to the main page and attach `AttentionAnimation` to it using `AnimationBehavior`:

```
xmlns:toolkit="http://schemas.microsoft.com/dotnet/2022/maui/
toolkit"


<Button Text="!"
        Padding="5"
        CornerRadius="25">
    <Button.Behaviors>
        <toolkit:AnimationBehavior EventName="Loaded">
            <toolkit:AnimationBehavior.AnimationType>
                <local:AttentionAnimation Length="100"
                    Easing= "{x:Static Easing.SinIn}"/>
            </toolkit:AnimationBehavior.AnimationType>
        </toolkit:AnimationBehavior>
    </Button.Behaviors>
</Button>
```

To start the animation when the button is shown, set `AnimationBehavior.EventName` to `Loaded`. You can additionally specify the `Length` and `Easing` properties to change the animation duration and easing function.

Now you can run the project to see how the button repeatedly changes its opacity according to the animation we implemented.

How it works...

The .NET MAUI Community Toolkit includes the `AnimationBehavior` class that helps you assign animations in XAML and trigger them based on a specific condition. You can consider `AnimationBehavior` as a container and infrastructure of your animation (it's not an animation itself). The animation applied to the parent element is assigned to the `AnimationBehavior.AnimationType` property.

`AnimationType` accepts an instance inherited from the `BaseAnimation` abstract class. `BaseAnimation` has only one method that needs to be overridden–`Animate`. `AnimationBehavior` passes the attached parent element to the `view` parameter. In the `Animate` method, you can use standard .NET MAUI animations, such as the following:

- `FadeTo` to change the opacity
- `BackgroundColorTo` to change the background color
- `ScaleTo` to enlarge or shrink an element
- `RotateTo` to rotate an element to a specified angle
- `TranslateTo` to move an element

It's important to note that animations can be started simultaneously and subsequently. For example, in the following code snippet, the fade and background animations will be started one after another because of the `await` keyword:

```
public override async Task Animate(VisualElement view,
CancellationToken token = default) {
        await view.FadeTo(1, Length, Easing);
        await view.BackgroundColorTo(Colors.Red);
}
```

To start them simultaneously, it's sufficient to remove `await` to let the execution flow continue after calling the first method (`FadeTo`).

There's more...

By default, if you don't specify `EventName`, `AnimationBehavior` starts an animation when you tap an element. If you set `EventName`, `AnimationBehavior` subscribes to the specified event and uses it as an animation trigger. `AnimationBehavior` offers an additional way to start an animation: `AnimateCommand`. Let's see how you can use it:

- You can bind `AnimateCommand` to another UI element that executes commands, for example, `Button`:

```
xmlns:tr="clr-namespace:System.Threading;assembly=mscorlib"
<!--...-->
<toolkit:AnimationBehavior x:Name="animationBehavior" >
<!--...-->
</toolkit:AnimationBehavior>
<!--...-->
<Button Text="Trigger"
        Command="{Binding Source={x:Reference
animationBehavior}, Path=AnimateCommand}"
        CommandParameter="{x:Static tr:CancellationToken.
None}"/>
```

When the **Trigger** button is tapped, it will call the bound `AnimateCommand`, and `AnimationBehavior` will start an animation. Note that it's necessary to pass a cancellation token as a command parameter (at least the None value).

- You can bind `AnimateCommand` to a property in your view model and trigger the animation from the view model. For this, define a command property in your view model without initializing it:

```
public partial class MyViewModel : ObservableObject {
    public ICommand CompleteAnimationCommand { get; set; }

    public void Complete() {
        //...
        CompleteAnimationCommand.Execute(CancellationToken.None);
    }
}
```

After that, bind `AnimationBehavior.AnimateCommand` to this property:

```
<toolkit:AnimationBehavior
  AnimateCommand="{Binding CompleteAnimationCommand}">
    <!--...-->
</toolkit:AnimationBehavior>
```

`AnimationBehavior` automatically initializes `AnimateCommand` and passes a command instance to your ViewModel using `OneWayToSource` binding.

Creating motion graphics with Lottie animations

.NET MAUI animations let you perform visual manipulations with UI elements, such as moving, rotating, and scaling. However, if you or your designer want to impress users with an animated graphic illustration, it can be challenging to achieve with the built-in animations. One of the easiest solutions is to use **Lottie** animations. Lottie is a vector-based, JSON-encoded animation format. You can find many ready-to-use animations at `https://lottiefiles.com`. Let's see how to use these animations to enhance your .NET MAUI app.

Getting ready

To follow the steps described in this recipe, we just need to create a blank .NET MAUI application.

The code for this recipe is available at `https://github.com/PacktPublishing/.NET-MAUI-Cookbook/tree/main/Chapter03/c3-LottieAnimations`.

How to do it...

Let's use a Lottie animation instead of a standard `ActivityIndicator` to indicate a running process. We will add a button that starts an async five-second thread delay and plays an animation during this period:

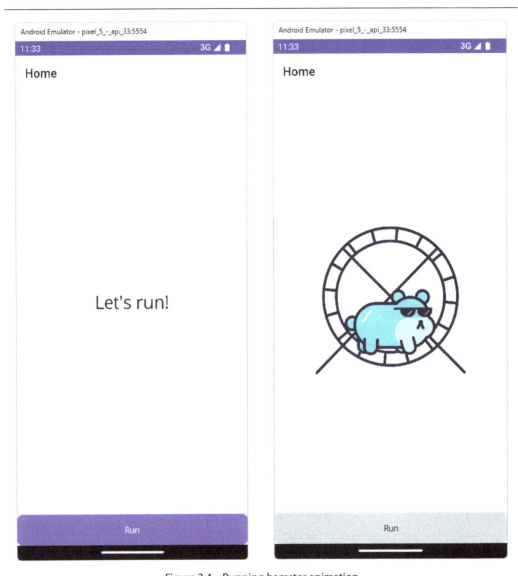

Figure 3.4 – Running hamster animation

1. We will need to install three NuGet packages in this recipe:

    - `SkiaSharp.Extended.UI.Maui` to use the `SKLottieView` element playing an animation

    - `CommunityToolkit.Maui` to use `InvertedBoolConverter`, which will help us show or hide a status label based on a Boolean property in a view model

    - `CommunityToolkit.Mvvm` to use auto-generated properties and commands

So, navigate to the NuGet Package Manager and install these packages.

2. In the `MauiProgram.CreateMauiApp` method, call `UseSkiaSharp` and `UseMauiCommunityToolkit` to initialize handlers from `SkiaSharp.Extended.UI.Maui` and `CommunityToolkit.Maui`:

```
builder
    .UseMauiApp<App>()
    .UseSkiaSharp()
    .UseMauiCommunityToolkit();
    //…
```

3. You can visit `https://lottiefiles.com` and find the animation you believe is good for your project and download the JSON file for this Lottie animation. You may need to create an account. Download the animation as a JSON file.

Add the downloaded JSON file to the `Resource/raw` folder in your project. Make sure that the `Build Action` property is set to `MauiAsset`:

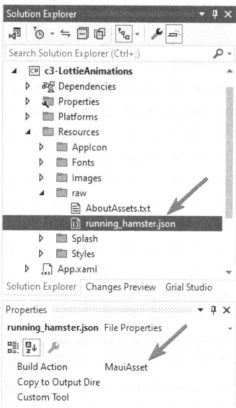

Figure 3.5 – Animation file location

4. Now you can use the animation in the view. Add the `SKLottieView` element to the main page and set `Source` to the name of the Lottie file name:

```
xmlns:skia="clr-namespace:SkiaSharp.Extended.
UI.Controls;assembly=SkiaSharp.Extended.UI"
<skia: RepeatCount="-1"
                    Source="running_hamster.json"/>
```

When `RepeatCount` is set to -1, the animation will be repeated until you explicitly stop it by setting `IsAnimationEnabled` to `False`. You can run the project and see what the animation looks like.

5. Let's add a command that triggers that animation from the view model during a long-running operation. For this, create a `MyViewModel` class with an auto-generated property and command:

```
public partial class MyViewModel : ObservableObject {
    [ObservableProperty]
    string statusMessage = "Let's run!";

    [RelayCommand]
    async Task HamsterRunAsync() {
        await Task.Delay(5000);
        StatusMessage = "Complete! Let's run again?";
    }
}
```

The text in `StatusMessage` will be used as a placeholder when the animation is hidden.

6. On the main page, specify the `BindingContext`, bind `Button` to `HamsterRunCommand`, and `Label` to `StatusMessage`. To conditionally hide the `SKLottieView` and `Label` elements, use the `HamsterRunCommand.IsRunning` property:

```
xmlns:toolkit="http://schemas.microsoft.com/dotnet/2022/maui/
toolkit"
<ContentPage.BindingContext>
    <local:MyViewModel/>
</ContentPage.BindingContext>
<ContentPage.Resources>
    <toolkit:InvertedBoolConverter
      x:Key="invertedBoolConverter"/>
</ContentPage.Resources>
<Grid RowDefinitions="*,50">
    <Label Text="{Binding StatusMessage}"
           IsVisible="{Binding HamsterRunCommand.IsRunning,
Converter={StaticResource invertedBoolConverter}}"/>
    <skia:SKLottieView RepeatCount="-1"
           IsVisible="{Binding RunCommand.IsRunning}"
```

```
                        Source="running_hamster.json"/>
        <Button Text="Run"
                Command="{Binding HamsterRunCommand}"
                Grid.Row="1"/>
    </Grid>
```

As you may remember from *Chapter 2*, *Mastering the MVVM Design Pattern*, asynchronous commands provide the `IsRunning` property, which allows us to conditionally show or hide `Label` and `SKLottieView`. `InvertedBoolConverter`, which is available in the Community Toolkit, inverts the `IsRunning` value bound to `Label`.

That's it; now you can run the project to see the final result.

How it works...

The core element of the recipe is `SKLottieView`. It parses the JSON animation file and draws it using the **SkiaSharp** engine. As you may know, **Skia** is a cross-platform graphics library used in Chromium, Android, Flutter, and other platforms and products.

In this recipe, we used asynchronous commands to display the `SKLottieView` element only during long-running operations. These async commands expose the `IsRunning` property, allowing us to easily toggle the visibility of the element based on the command's execution state:

```
<skia:SKLottieView Source="running_hamster.json"
        IsVisible="{Binding HamsterRunCommand.IsRunning}"/>
```

The command was automatically created by `CommunityToolkit` because we assigned the `RelayCommand` attribute to the async `HamsterRunAsync` method returning a task.

There's more...

Lottie animations offer several key advantages:

- **Vector-based**: This means that a Lottie animation can be scaled to any size without losing quality
- **JSON-encoded**: The lightweight JSON format takes up much less space than the GIF or MP4 format
- **Cross-platform compatible**: Lottie animations are supported by most UI platforms, which means that you can easily use them in different UI clients
- **Ready-to-use animations**: Lottie has rapidly gained popularity among designers and developers, leading to the creation of a wealth of animations that are available for free or at a low cost

Implementing dark/light theme switching

According to various studies, between 30% and 50% of end users prefer dark themes. Among us software developers, this percentage tends to be even higher. Whether you prefer dark or light themes, it's widely accepted that giving users the option to choose their preferred mode is best practice.

.NET MAUI offers a mechanism to set properties based on the current application theme; however, it doesn't include a built-in component to switch a theme in the UI, so let's create it!

Getting ready

To follow the steps described in this recipe, we just need to create a blank .NET MAUI application.

The code for this recipe is available at `https://github.com/PacktPublishing/.NET-MAUI-Cookbook/tree/main/Chapter03/c3-DarkAndLightThemes`.

How to do it...

Let's create a theme selector using the `Picker` element. We will bind it to a class with static properties so that you can use the theme selector in any application view. To switch the theme at the application level, we will use the standard `Application.Current.UserAppTheme` property:

1. Create a `ThemeInfo` class to store the application theme object and its caption that will be displayed in the `Picker` element:

    ```
    public class ThemeInfo {
        public AppTheme AppTheme { get; }
        public string Caption { get; }

        public ThemeInfo(AppTheme theme, string caption) {
            AppTheme = theme;
            Caption = caption;
        }
    }
    ```

2. Add the `CommunityToolkit.Mvvm` NuGet package so that we can use `ObservableObject` and auto-generated properties. After that, create a `ThemeSettings` class to store the list of available themes and information about the currently selected theme:

    ```
    public partial class ThemeSettings : ObservableObject {
        public static List<ThemeInfo> AvailableThemes { get; } = new
          List<ThemeInfo>() {
                new ThemeInfo(AppTheme.Unspecified, "System"),
                new ThemeInfo(AppTheme.Light, "Light"),
                new ThemeInfo(AppTheme.Dark, "Dark")
    ```

```
        };
    public static ThemeSettings Current { get; } = new
        ThemeSettings() {
            SelectedTheme = AvailableThemes.First()
        };


    [ObservableProperty]
    public ThemeInfo selectedTheme;


    partial void OnSelectedThemeChanged(ThemeInfo oldValue,
        ThemeInfo newValue) {
            Application.Current.UserAppTheme = newValue.AppTheme;
    }
}
```

We introduced the Current property to use the **Singleton** pattern.

Singleton

Singleton is a design pattern that restricts the instantiation of a class to a single instance. This is useful when only one object is needed to coordinate actions in an application. The Singleton pattern helps to provide a global point to access an object.

When SelectedTheme is changed, we set the UserAppTheme property, which is responsible for changing the theme in a .NET MAUI application. UserAppTheme accepts one of the following values: Unspecified, Light, or Dark. When the Unspecified value is used, the application will inherit the system theme mode (dark or light, not the color).

3. Add the Picker element to the main page and use x:Static to bind its ItemsSource and SelectedItem to the static properties we created in ThemeSettings. Specify ItemDisplayBinding to display the ThemeInfo.Caption property value:

```
xmlns:local="clr-namespace:c3_DarkAndLightThemes"
<Picker ItemsSource="{Binding Source={x:Static
local:ThemeSettings.ThemesList}}"
        SelectedItem="{Binding Source={x:Static
local:ThemeSettings.Current}, Path=SelectedTheme}"
        ItemDisplayBinding="{Binding Caption}"/>
```

Note that since we inherited ThemeSettings from ObservableObject, its SelectedTheme property supports INotifyPropertyChanged, which means that once we modify SelectedTheme in another part of our program, the Binding in Picker. SelectedItem will be updated, and a user will see the actual value.

Now you can run the project and switch a theme using the `Picker` component.

How it works...

The default blank .NET MAUI project template in Visual Studio includes styles for most standard components, such as `Label`, `CheckBox`, and so on. You can find these styles in the `Resources/Styles` folder:

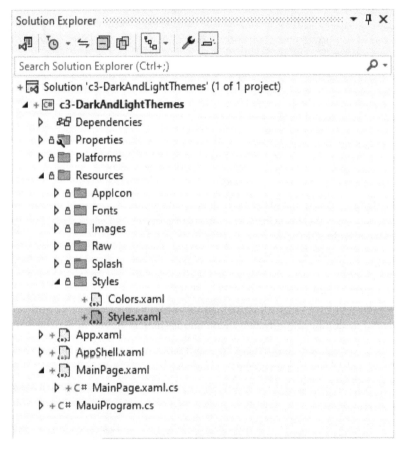

Figure 3.6 – Default styles

Each style sets theme-dependent properties using the AppThemeBinding markup extension:

```
<Style TargetType="Label">
    <Setter Property="TextColor"
        Value="{AppThemeBinding
                Light={StaticResource Black},
                Dark={StaticResource White}}" />
    <!--...-->
</Style>
```

AppThemeBinding tracks the current application theme stored in Application.UserAppTheme and returns corresponding values specified in the Light and Dark properties.

Now, let me summarize how choosing a theme using Picker works. When implementing the ThemeSettings class to switch themes using Picker, we added the OnSelectedThemeChanged method where we set UserAppTheme. Since Picker.SelectedItem is bound to SelectedTheme, once a user selects an item in the Picker, the OnSelectedThemeChanged is changed, and the application theme is switched thanks to setting UserAppTheme.

There's more...

Since ThemeSettings is inherited from ObservableObject, it supports INotifyPropertyChanged, and changing the SelectedTheme property in C# will properly update the Picker element in the UI:

```
ThemeSettings.Current.SelectedTheme = ThemeSettings.ThemesList.
FirstOrDefault(t => t.Caption == "Dark");
```

To find a theme in the list, we had to use the FirstOrDefault function. To make our theme-changing API more convenient, we can add three static fields to store the instances of the System, Light, and Dark themes:

```
public partial class ThemeInfo : ObservableObject {
    public static ThemeInfo System = new(AppTheme.Unspecified,
        "System");
    public static ThemeInfo Light = new(AppTheme.Light, "Light");
    public static ThemeInfo Dark = new(AppTheme.Dark, "Dark");
    //...
    }
}
```

This will allow us to use these fields when populating the `ThemeSettings.ThemesList` collection and when switching a theme in code:

```
public partial class ThemeSettings : ObservableObject {
    public static List<ThemeInfo> ThemesList { get; } = new
      List<ThemeInfo>() {
        ThemeInfo.System,
        ThemeInfo.Light,
        ThemeInfo.Dark
    };
}
//...
ThemeSettings.Current.SelectedTheme = ThemeInfo.Dark;
```

Implementing theme support for images and the status bar

When dark themes first started gaining popularity, it was common for some parts of applications to remain unthemed. Needless to say, this would look odd in modern applications.

Elements such as images and **status bars** are an integral part of any mobile user interface. If you are not familiar with mobile-specific terminology, the status bar is the topmost stripe that shows the time, battery level, and other information.

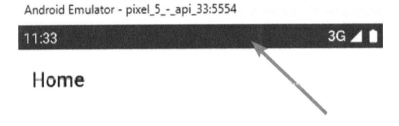

Figure 3.7 – Android status bar

In this recipe, we will learn how to dynamically change the color of images and the status bar according to the current theme.

Getting ready

Start with the project you got after finishing the previous recipe (*Implementing dark/light theme switching*). This project is available at `https://github.com/PacktPublishing/.NET-MAUI-Cookbook/tree/main/Chapter03/c3-DarkAndLightThemes`.

The code for this recipe is available at `https://github.com/PacktPublishing/.NET-MAUI-Cookbook/tree/main/Chapter03/c3-ThemedImagesAndStatusBar`.

How to do it...

Let's use the standard `AppThemeBinding` markup extension combined with `IconTintColorBehavior` and `StatusBarBehavior` from `CommunityToolkit.Maui` to theme an image and status bar, respectively:

1. Add any test SVG image to the `Resources/Images` folder. For example, you can use the checkmark image available in this GitHub repository: `https://github.com/PacktPublishing/.NET-MAUI-Cookbook/blob/main/Chapter03/c3-CustomDrawing/c3-CustomDrawing/Resources/Images/check_mark.svg`. Make sure that the image's build action is set to `MauiImage`:

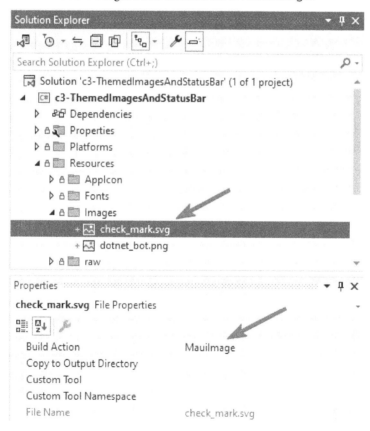

Figure 3.8 – Image build action

2. Add the `Image` element to the page and set its **Source** property to the name of the SVG image:

    ```
    <Image Source="check_mark.png"/>
    ```

> **Key point**
>
> Although we added an SVG image, we should reference it as PNG because .NET MAUI converts SVG to PNG when building your project for a specific platform.

3. Add the `CommunityToolkit.Maui` NuGet package to your project. Assign `IconTintColorBehavior` and `StatusBarBehavior` to the `Image` and `ContentPage` elements:

    ```
    <ContentPage.Behaviors>
        <toolkit:StatusBarBehavior
            StatusBarColor="{AppThemeBinding Dark=Orange,
    Light=Gray}"
    </ContentPage.Behaviors>
    <VerticalStackLayout>
        <Image Source="check_mark.png">
            <Image.Behaviors>
                <toolkit:IconTintColorBehavior
                    TintColor="{AppThemeBinding Dark= Orange,
    Light=Gray}"/>
            </Image.Behaviors>
        </Image>
        <!--...-->
    </VerticalStackLayout>
    ```

We use AppThemeBinding to specify the `StatusBarColor` and `TintColor` properties based on the current theme.

You can run the project and see how colors are applied to the image and status bar. However, if you try switching a theme using the `Picker` we implemented in the previous recipe, you will notice that the image and status bar don't react to changes (at least, this issue existed in `CommunityToolkit.Maui` in v 9.0.1). Let's fix this.

4. Add the `Label` element to the page and bind `StatusBarColor` and `TintColor` to `Label.TextColor` using `x:Reference`:

    ```
    <ContentPage.Behaviors>
        <toolkit:StatusBarBehavior
            StatusBarColor="{Binding Source={x:Reference
    themedLabel}, Path=TextColor}"/>
    </ContentPage.Behaviors>
    <VerticalStackLayout>
        <Image Source="check_mark.png">
    ```

```
            <Image.Behaviors>
                <toolkit:IconTintColorBehavior
                    TintColor="{Binding Source={x:Reference
        themedLabel}, Path=TextColor}"/>
            </Image.Behaviors>
        </Image>
        <Label x:Name="themedLabel"
            Text="Hello, readers!"
            TextColor="{AppThemeBinding Dark=Orange,
        Light=Gray}"/>
        <!--...-->
    </VerticalStackLayout>
```

Now, if you run the project and switch a theme using the `Picker` element, the image and status bar should properly react to the theme change.

How it works...

In this recipe, we used `StatusBarBehavior` and `IconTintColorBehavior` (available in `CommunityToolkit.Maui`). Both behaviors use platform-specific code to change the color of elements they are attached to.

Since `StatusBarBehavior` and `IconTintColorBehavior` require access to platform-specific APIs, they are not the `Behavior<T>` descendants that we used in the second recipe of this chapter (*Implementing attached behavior to reuse UI logic*). Instead, they are inherited from the `BasePlatformBehavior` class, which allows you to implement internal logic based on the platform for which the application is compiled.

In *step 4* of the *How to do it...* section, we used a "hacky" solution and bound `StatusBarColor` and `TintColor` to `Label.TextColor` to fix the issue with dynamic theme switching. Alternatively, we could create `StatusBarBehavior` and `IconTintColorBehavior` descendants to address this challenge, but this would require writing platform-specific code, which is covered in *Chapter 7, Understanding Platform-Specific APIs and Custom Handlers*.

There's more...

`StatusBarBehavior` has another useful feature: it allows you to change not only the status bar background but also its foreground. This is helpful when you set a custom background color and need to maintain text contrast. Use the `StatusBarStyle` property for this purpose:

```
<toolkit:StatusBarBehavior
    StatusBarStyle="LightContent"
    StatusBarColor="Black"/>
```

Note that it accepts only one of two values: `LightContent` and `DarkContent`. You cannot specify a custom color.

`IconTintColorBehavior` allows us to change the SVG tint color; however, what if we need to replace the entire image in dark/light mode? You can use `AppThemeBinding` and specify different image sources for dark and light modes:

```
<Image Source="{AppThemeBinding Dark=moon.png, Light=sun.png}"/>
```

An alternative solution is to use `AppThemeObject` (available in the Community Toolkit). It allows you to define any theme-dependent resource and use it in your application. To reference `AppThemeObject`, use the `AppThemeResource` markup extension:

```
<ContentPage.Resources>
    <toolkit:AppThemeObject Light="check_mark.png" Dark="dotnet_bot.
      png" x:Key="themedImage" />
</ContentPage.Resources>
<!--...-->
<Image Source="{toolkit:AppThemeResource themedImage}"/>
```

Drawing custom elements on a canvas

Whether you need to implement a custom chart, gauge, or even a simple 2D game, you can use .NET MAUI drawing capabilities. The platform includes XAML elements, such as line, ellipse, rectangle, and so on. For instance, here is how you can draw a green ellipse with a red border:

```
<Ellipse Fill="Green"
         Stroke="Red"
         StrokeThickness="2"
         WidthRequest="100"
         HeightRequest="50"/>
```

Built-in drawing elements work well for simple scenarios, but they might not be optimal if you need to draw a custom control.

In this recipe, we will use `Microsoft.Maui.Graphics`, which allows you to implement more flexible and performant logic in C#.

Getting ready

To follow the steps described in this recipe, we just need to create a blank .NET MAUI application.

The code for this recipe is available at `https://github.com/PacktPublishing/.NET-MAUI-Cookbook/tree/main/Chapter03/c3-CustomDrawing`.

How to do it...

Let's create a simple horizontal bar chart consisting of colored rectangles. We will use `GraphicsView`, which is basically a .NET MAUI wrapper over a platform canvas:

Figure 3.9 – Segmented bar chart

1. When using `GraphicsView`, all drawing logic should be implemented in a custom class implementing the `IDrawable` interface. Let's start with creating a basic interface implementation and drawing a green rectangle:

```
public class BarChartDrawable : IDrawable {
    public void Draw(ICanvas canvas, RectF dirtyRect) {
    canvas.FillColor = Colors.Green;
    canvas.FillRectangle(0, 0, 20, 20);
}
```

The `FullColor` property specifies the rectangle color and the `FillRectangle` method draws the rectangle with a specified position and size.

2. To draw `BarChartDrawable`, it's sufficient to add `GraphicsView` to the page and assign an instance of `BarChartDrawable` to the `GraphicsView.Drawable` property:

```
<GraphicsView HeightRequest="20">
    <GraphicsView.Drawable>
        <local:BarChartDrawable/>
    </GraphicsView.Drawable>
</GraphicsView>
```

If you run the project, you should see a green rectangle on the page.

3. Define fields to customize the rectangle size, distance between sibling rectangle segments, corner radius, and the current chart bar value, which will affect the number of drawn segments. Additionally, create an array to store the chart palette:

```
public class BarChartDrawable : IDrawable {
    Color[] Palette = [Colors.LightGreen, Colors.Gold, Colors.
Coral];
```

```
float spacing = 5;
float cornerRadius = 4;
public float Value { get; set; } = 1;
public void Draw(ICanvas canvas, RectF dirtyRect)
{
    //…
}
```
}

4.   Implement an algorithm to draw bar chart segments based on the `Value` property. We will use the `FillRoundedRectangle` method to draw rounded rectangles representing the segments:

```
public void Draw(ICanvas canvas, RectF dirtyRect) {
    canvas.SaveState();
    float rectSize = dirtyRect.Height;
    int maxStep = (int)(dirtyRect.Width / (rectSize + spacing));
    int valueBasedSteps = (int)(maxStep * Value);

    for (int step = 0; step < valueBasedSteps; step++) {
        canvas.FillColor = Palette[Palette.Length * step /
maxStep];
        canvas.FillRoundedRectangle(
            x: (rectSize + spacing) * step,
            y: 0,
            width: rectSize,
            height: rectSize,
            cornerRadius: cornerRadius);
    }
    canvas.RestoreState();
}
```

Note that we call the `SaveState` and `RestoreState` methods to keep the original canvas state. The state includes information such as fill color, font, and scale. Although, in our case, we don't necessarily need to save the state, in most cases it's recommended to restore the original state so that each call of the `Draw` method doesn't depend on the previous call.

5.   Modify XAML and add two different bar charts with different values:

```
<VerticalStackLayout Spacing="10">
    <GraphicsView HeightRequest="20">
        <GraphicsView.Drawable>
            <local:BarChartDrawable Value="0.3" />
        </GraphicsView.Drawable>
    </GraphicsView>
    <GraphicsView HeightRequest="20">
```

```
            <GraphicsView.Drawable>
                <local:BarChartDrawable Value="0.8" />
            </GraphicsView.Drawable>
        </GraphicsView>
    </VerticalStackLayout>
```

Now you can run and test the project. You should see the output demonstrated in *Figure 3.9*.

How it works...

GraphicsView serves as a canvas for custom 2D graphics based on the Microsoft.Maui.Graphics rendering engine. GraphicsView defines a Drawable property of the IDrawable type. This property specifies the content that will be drawn on the canvas. To create drawable content, you need to define an object that derives from IDrawable and implement its Draw method. This method takes ICanvas (the drawing canvas) and RectF (which contains size and location information) as arguments.

There's more...

The BarChartDrawable component we implemented earlier is good when you need to display a static value, but you will face the following issues if you wish to change the value dynamically:

- The BarChartDrawable.Value property is not bindable. This means that you can set it directly in XAML or C#, but you cannot use Binding with it.

- GraphicsView automatically draws its content when it's shown. However, if we change the BarChartDrawable.Value property value, GraphicsView won't know about it, because it won't know about the property change. To redraw graphics in this usage scenario, you need to call the GraphicsView.Invalidate method.

We can resolve both issues by creating a ContentView with BindableProperty and calling Invalidate in the property changed callback. Let's add a new ContentView and name it SegmentedBarChartView. In the XAML code of SegmentedBarChartView, add GraphicsView with BarChartDrawable:

```
<ContentView xmlns="http://schemas.microsoft.com/dotnet/2021/maui"
            xmlns:x="http://schemas.microsoft.com/winfx/2009/xaml"
            xmlns:local="clr-namespace:c3_DarkAndLightThemes"
            x:Class="c3_DarkAndLightThemes.SegmentedBarChartView">
    <GraphicsView HeightRequest="20" x:Name="graphicsView">
        <GraphicsView.Drawable>
            <local:BarChartDrawable/>
        </GraphicsView.Drawable>
```

```
    </GraphicsView>
  </ContentView>
```

In the code-behind of ContentView, add a bindable property named Value. In the property changed callback, update the BarChartDrawable.Value property and call GraphicsView. Invalidate:

```
public partial class SegmentedBarChartView : ContentView {
    public float Value {
        get { return (float)GetValue(ValueProperty); }
        set { SetValue(ValueProperty, value); }
    }

    public static readonly BindableProperty ValueProperty =
        BindableProperty.Create("Value",
            typeof(float),
            typeof(SegmentedBarChartView),
            defaultValue: 0f,
            propertyChanged: (b, o, n) =>
    ((SegmentedBarChartView)b).OnValueChanged()

    void OnValueChanged() {
        ((BarChartDrawable)graphicsView.Drawable).Value = Value;
        graphicsView.Invalidate();
    }

    public SegmentedBarChartView() {
        InitializeComponent();
    }
}
```

Now we can use SegmentedBarChartView on the main page and bind its Value property. Let's bind it to a slider:

```
<local:SegmentedBarChartView
    Value="{Binding Source={x:Reference slider}, Path=Value}"/>
<Slider Minimum="0"
        Maximum="1"
        Value="0.2"
        x:Name="slider"/>
```

4

Connecting to a Database and Implementing CRUD Operations

How many apps on your phone don't store information in some sort of database? Probably not many. Even simple apps, such as calculators, often save a history of operations.

Back in 2022, when .NET MAUI had its first official release, I built a simple .NET MAUI application. I was surprised to encounter noticeable lags despite the UI being relatively simple. After profiling the app, I discovered that the problem lay in how I was loading data from the database. In this chapter, I will describe how to avoid the issues I encountered and implement best practices for database communication.

In each recipe covered in this chapter, we will build on the project from the previous step. By the end of this chapter, you'll have implemented a CRUD application that retrieves information from both local and remote storage. You'll learn how to create separate views to display and edit information, and how to effectively pass data and updates between these views. We'll also implement the **unit of work** and **repository** patterns with caching support, showing you how these patterns make it easy to replace one data retrieval mechanism with another.

In this chapter, we'll be covering the following topics:

- Connecting to a local SQLite database via **Entity Framework Core (EF Core)**
- Implementing create and delete operations
- Implementing detail and edit forms
- Implementing the unit of work and repository patterns
- Handling errors while saving data to a database
- Validating editors in the UI before data posting

- Implementing data caching for enhanced performance
- Connecting to a remote web API service

Technical requirements

There are no specific requirements for the recipes in this chapter. Each recipe builds on the project from the previous recipe.

You can download all the projects created in this chapter from GitHub at `https://github.com/PacktPublishing/.NET-MAUI-Cookbook/tree/main/Chapter04`.

Connecting to a local SQLite database via Entity Framework Core

When discussing data retrieval from a database, some might assume they'll have to handle complex SQL queries. While SQL queries may be necessary for intricate scenarios, most of the time you'll work with **object-relational mapping (ORM)**, which provides a high-level abstraction for database operations.

> Object-relational mapping
>
> **Object-relational mapping** is a technique offering a high-level abstraction over database objects, such as tables and rows. In simple words, tables are turned into collections, rows into objects, and cell values into properties. ORM handles all low-level operations, including SQL generation, object mapping, and database schema management.

In this chapter, we'll use **EF Core** as our object-relational mapper and **SQLite** as our database. This combination is a popular choice for storing data locally in .NET MAUI applications because SQLite is a very lightweight database suitable for mobile devices, and EF Core abstracts developers from low-level SQL operations. We will connect to a database generated on the fly, asynchronously load data, and display it in `CollectionView`.

Getting ready

To follow the steps described in this recipe, we just need to create a blank .NET MAUI application.

The code for this recipe is available at `https://github.com/PacktPublishing/.NET-MAUI-Cookbook/tree/main/Chapter04/c4-LocalDatabaseConnection`.

How to do it...

Let's create a simple application that displays CollectionView with data loaded from a database. We'll use the **code-first** approach, where the database is automatically generated (if it doesn't already exist) based on the objects we create in code. Code-first is convenient for actively developed projects when the database structure may change frequently. If you already have a complex database, you may want to use the **database-first** technique.

To ensure the UI remains responsive during data loading, we'll use the technique from the *Initializing bound collections without freezing the UI* recipe in *Chapter 2, Mastering the MVVM Design Pattern*:

1. Let's install all the NuGet packages we will need in this recipe:

    *   We need Microsoft.EntityFrameworkCore.Sqlite to use Entity Framework classes.

    *   We need CommunityToolkit.Mvvm to use auto-generated view model properties and commands.

    *   We need CommunityToolkit.Maui to use EventToCommandBehavior and transform the Loaded event into a command in a view model that will load data asynchronously. Don't forget to call UseMauiCommunityToolkit in the MauiProgram.CreateMauiApp method to use features from CommunityToolkit.Maui.

2. EF Core uses the DbContext object as an entry point to query and update data in the database. To work with entities, create a class that inherits from DbContext and add a public property of the DbSet<T> type. According to EF Core conventions, each DbSet<T> property represents a table in the database. Let's create a CrmContext class with a property named Customers, meaning that the database will have one Customers table:

CrmContext.cs

```
public class CrmContext : DbContext {
    public DbSet<Customer> Customers { get; set; }
}
```

Define the Customer class as follows:

Customer.cs

```
public class Customer {
    public int Id { get; set; }
    public string FirstName { get; set; }
    public string LastName { get; set; }
    public string Email { get; set; }
}
```

To organize files in your project, you can create a separate folder named `DataAccess` and move all files with data-related logic there.

3. EF Core works with different databases. To specify that we will use SQLite, override the `OnConfiguring` method in your `DbContext` class and call `UseSqlite`, passing the database file location as a parameter.

Here's how you can do it in the `CrmContext` class:

CrmContext.cs

```
public class CrmContext : DbContext {
    //…
    protected override void
      OnConfiguring(DbContextOptionsBuilder optionsBuilder)
      {
        string dbPath =
          Path.Combine(FileSystem.AppDataDirectory,
          "localdatabase.db");

    optionsBuilder.UseSqlite($"Filename={dbPath}");
        base.OnConfiguring(optionsBuilder);
    }
}
```

`FileSystem.AppDataDirectory` represents the name of the folder where an application can store local data. This folder's location may vary depending on the platform currently in use (such as Android, iOS, Windows, or macOS). We used the `localdatabase.db` file, we used the `.db` extension, but you can specify other extension names (e.g., `.sqlite`), and SQLite will continue working with the file.

4. To add initial data to the database, override the `DbContext.OnModelCreating` method and call the `HasData` method with initial data as a parameter:

CrmContext.cs

```
protected override void OnModelCreating(ModelBuilder builder) {
    builder.Entity<Customer>().HasData(new Customer {
        Id = 1,
        FirstName = "John",
        LastName = "Doe",
        Email = "john.doe@example.com"
    });
}
```

We added only one customer to initialize the database, but you can add more if required.

5. Initialize the database. Navigate to the App class constructor and call the `Batteries_V2.Init` and `CrmContext.EnsureCreated` methods:

App.xaml.cs

```
public App() {
    SQLitePCL.Batteries_V2.Init();
    using var context = new CrmContext();
    context.Database.EnsureCreated();

    InitializeComponent();
    MainPage = new AppShell();
}
```

The `SQLitePCL.Batteries_V2.Init` method is necessary for initializing SQLitePCLRaw on iOS devices. SQLitePCLRaw comprises a collection of low-level, cross-platform libraries designed to facilitate access to SQLite databases.

The `EnsureCreated` method within EF Core creates a database if it doesn't already exist.

6. This is all you need to start working with an SQLite database. Now, you can access and modify the `Customers` table using the `CrmContext.Customers` property. However, we'll create a basic UI to display data as a collection.

Let's create a folder named `ViewModels` and add the `MainViewModel` class there. In `MainViewModel`, define two fields: `customers` and `refreshing`:

MainViewModel.cs

```
public partial class MainViewModel : ObservableObject {
    [ObservableProperty]
    ObservableCollection<Customer> customers;

    [ObservableProperty]
    bool refreshing;
}
```

We will use the `Customers` property to bind to `CollectionView` and `Refreshing` to bind to the `RefreshView` element, which supports loading indication and pull-to-refresh functionality.

7. Load items from the database to the local collection. Add the `LoadCustomersAsync` method, which creates a `CrmContext` instance, and assigns the `Customers` property. We'll use this method as a command in `RefreshView`, so annotate the method with the `RelayCommand` attribute to create a corresponding command:

MainViewModel.cs

```
[RelayCommand]
async Task LoadCustomersAsync() {
    await Task.Run(() =>
    {
        using CrmContext context = new CrmContext();
        Customers = new ObservableCollection<Customer>(context.
            Customers);
    });
    Refreshing = false;
}
```

The `using` statement ensures that `CrmContext` and all its unmanaged resources will be automatically disposed of when they are no longer needed.

> **Key point**
>
> `CrmContext` is created within an asynchronous task, which prevents freezing the UI while interacting with the database. It's important to note that even though `DbContext` includes async methods, such as `SaveChangesAsync`, the SQLite data provider itself is synchronous internally. Therefore, running tasks asynchronously is crucial to maintain UI responsiveness.

8. Add the `Showing` command to the view model. This command will be invoked when a page is shown. In this command, we will simply set `Refreshing` to `true`, which will trigger the `RefreshView` bound to the `Refreshing` property:

MainViewModel.cs

```
[RelayCommand]
void Showing() {
    Refreshing = true;
}
```

9. Let's create a simple UI using `CollectionView` to display data. We'll wrap `CollectionView` within `RefreshView`. `RefreshView` enables pull-to-refresh functionality and executes a command bound to the `RefreshView.Command` property. This command is also triggered when `RefreshView.IsRefreshing` is set to `true`. Additionally, we'll utilize `EventToCommandBehavior` to invoke `ShowingCommand` when the `ContentPage.Appearing` event is raised:

MainPage.xaml

```
xmlns:vm="clr-namespace:c4_LocalDatabaseConnection.ViewModels"
xmlns:local="clr-namespace:c4_LocalDatabaseConnection"
xmlns:toolkit="http://schemas.microsoft.com/dotnet/2022/maui/
toolkit"
<ContentPage.BindingContext>
    <vm:MainViewModel/>
</ContentPage.BindingContext>
<ContentPage.Behaviors>
    <toolkit:EventToCommandBehavior
    EventName="Appearing"
    Command="{Binding ShowingCommand}"/>
</ContentPage.Behaviors>
<ContentPage.Resources>
    <DataTemplate x:Key="customerTemplate"
                  x:DataType="local:Customer">
        <Grid RowDefinitions="40,40"
            ColumnDefinitions="*,*"
            Padding="10">
            <Label Text="{Binding FirstName}"/>
            <Label Text="{Binding LastName}"
                Grid.Column="1"/>
            <Label Text="{Binding Email}"
                TextColor="DarkGray"
                Grid.Row="1"
                Grid.ColumnSpan="2"/>
        </Grid>
    </DataTemplate>
</ContentPage.Resources>
<Grid>
    <RefreshView IsRefreshing="{Binding Refreshing}"
        Command="{Binding LoadCustomersCommand}">
        <CollectionView ItemsSource="{Binding Customers}"
                ItemTemplate="{StaticResource
customerTemplate}"/>
```

```
            </RefreshView>
        </Grid>
```

Finally, you can run the project to see the result.

How it works...

In EF Core, DbContext serves as the primary object responsible for database interactions. It abstracts away low-level SQL operations, providing APIs for tasks such as retrieving and modifying data, change tracking, and transaction management.

Furthermore, DbContext allows you to configure database connections and can automatically create a database if it doesn't already exist. This abstraction simplifies database interaction tasks within .NET applications.

Figure 4.1 – Business logic, DbContext, and database

There's more...

In this recipe, we created a new database if it doesn't exist. However, many applications may already have a populated database. In such cases, you can add the database file to the Resources/Raw folder in your project and copy it to the directory stored in FileSystem.AppDataDirectory when the application starts. The following code snippet demonstrates how to asynchronously copy the database file to AppDataDirectory if it doesn't exist there yet:

```
public partial class App : Application {
    public App() {
        Task.Run(async () => await CopyToAppDataDirectory("crm.db"));
        InitializeComponent();
        //…
    }

    public async Task<string> CopyToAppDataDirectory(string filename)
    {
        string targetFile = Path.Combine(FileSystem.Current.
          AppDataDirectory, filename);
        if (!File.Exists(targetFile)) {
```

```
            using Stream inputStream = await FileSystem.Current.
              OpenAppPackageFileAsync(filename);
            using FileStream outputStream = File.Create(targetFile);
            await inputStream.CopyToAsync(outputStream);
        }
        return targetFile;
    }
}
```

It's important to note that since `CopyToAppDataDirectory` runs asynchronously, you must ensure it completes before accessing the database to avoid any issues with data availability.

> **Important**
>
> When debugging an application, previously stored application data isn't automatically removed. Therefore, if you make any changes related to the database structure or data schema, you may need to manually uninstall the previously deployed application from your device or emulator to ensure that the changes take effect correctly.

Implementing create and delete operations

In your application, you may often need to allow users to create and delete items in a list. From the UI perspective, these operations are typically facilitated using a **floating action button** (**FAB**) to create items and **swipe actions** to delete them.

In this recipe, we will build upon the application created in the previous recipe and implement a typical UI along with the underlying logic to enable users to create and delete items in a collection.

Getting ready

Start with the project you got after finishing the previous recipe (*Connecting to a local SQLite database via Entity Framework Core*). This project is available at `https://github.com/PacktPublishing/.NET-MAUI-Cookbook/tree/main/Chapter04/c4-LocalDatabaseConnection`.

The code for this recipe is available at `https://github.com/PacktPublishing/.NET-MAUI-Cookbook/tree/main/Chapter04/c4-CreateDelete`.

How to do it...

Let's implement swipe actions to delete items from the collection and add the FAB to create new items. Clicking the FAB will navigate to a separate form to edit the properties of the newly created item:

Figure 4.2 – UI to create and delete items

1. Implement item deletion logic in the view model. Add the `DeleteCustomer` command to the `MainViewModel` class, where you can remove an item from the `CrmContext`. `Customers` collection and call `SaveChanges` to synchronize local changes with the database:

MainViewModel.cs

```
[RelayCommand]
void DeleteCustomer(Customer customer) {
    CrmContext context = new CrmContext();
    context.Customers.Remove(customer);
    context.SaveChanges();
    Customers.Remove(customer);
}
```

Note that we also removed the customer from the view model's `Customers` collection so that the item is removed from the bound `CollectionView`.

2. Add a swipe item to `CollectionView`. Navigate to `MainPage.xaml` and enclose the content within `ItemTemplate` of `CollectionView` with a `SwipeView` element. Define an item in the `RightItems` collection and bind its `Command` to the `DeleteCustomer` command created in the previous step. Bind `CommandParameter` to the current customer to access it within the `DeleteCustomer` method:

MainPage.xaml

```
<CollectionView.ItemTemplate>
    <DataTemplate x:DataType="{x:Type vm:Customer}">
        <SwipeView>
            <SwipeView.RightItems>
                <SwipeItem Text="Delete"
                BackgroundColor="IndianRed"
                Command="{Binding Path=BindingContext
                  .DeleteCustomerCommand,
                  Source={RelativeSource Mode=FindAncestor,
                  AncestorType={x:Type CollectionView}}}"
                CommandParameter="{Binding}"/>
            </SwipeView.RightItems>
            <Grid>
                <!--...-->
            </Grid>
        </SwipeView>
    </DataTemplate>
</CollectionView.ItemTemplate>
```

> **Key point**
>
> To bind `SwipeItem.Command` to the `MainViewModel.DeleteCustomerCommand` property, we need to use a `RelativeSource` binding because the `BindingContext` of `ItemTemplate` is a `Customer` object, not `MainViewModel`. The specified `RelativeSource` binding locates `CollectionView` in the visual tree and accesses the `BindingContext` of `CollectionView`, which is `MainViewModel`.

You can run the project to test how the **Delete** swipe item functions.

3.   Add a FAB to add new items. Add the button to the page and bind it to the ShowNewFormCommand:

MainPage.xaml

```
<Grid>
    <RefreshView ...>
        <!--...-->
    </RefreshView>
    <Button Text="+"
        Command="{Binding ShowNewFormCommand}"
        WidthRequest="56"
        HeightRequest="56"
        FontSize="24"
        HorizontalOptions="End"
        VerticalOptions="End"
        Margin="16"/>
</Grid>
```

Note that we can simply add `Button` next to the `RefreshView` element. Since both `RefreshView` and `Button` are in the same `Grid`, `Button` will be located over `RefreshView` because it's added as the last element.

4.   Implement navigation to the editing page. Create the ShowNewFormAsync method in the `MainViewModel` class. Call GoToAsync within it to navigate to the page where users can input customer information when creating a new item. To inform `CustomerEditPage` about the item being edited, pass the `Item` parameter to the GoToAsync method. Additionally, pass the `ParentRefreshAction` parameter containing a function that will refresh `CollectionView` after adding a new customer:

MainViewModel.cs

```
[RelayCommand]
async Task ShowNewFormAsync() {
    await Shell.Current.GoToAsync(nameof(CustomerEditPage),
        parameters: new Dictionary<string, object>
```

```
        {
            { "ParentRefreshAction", (Func<Customer, Task>)
    RefreshAddedAsync },
            { "Item", new Customer() },
        });
    }
    Task RefreshAddedAsync(Customer addedCustomer) {
        Customers.Add(addedCustomer);
        return Task.CompletedTask;
    }
```

You might wonder why we don't add a new customer to the `Customers` collection before navigating to `CustomerEditPage`. The reason is that if a user starts adding a new customer and then decides to cancel (by pressing the back button), this empty customer will remain in the collection. Therefore, we pass `RefreshAddedAsync` as a `ParentRefreshAction` parameter. `ParentRefreshAction` will only be invoked if the user presses the **Save** button, ensuring that only valid, completed entries are added to the collection.

Note that the `CustomerEditPage` class doesn't exist yet; we will create it in *step 7*.

5. Create the editing page view model. Create the `CustomerEditViewModel` class and add it to the `ViewModels` folder. First, let's implement logic to receive and save the `ParentRefreshAction` and `Item` parameters. Implement the `IQueryAttributable` interface and extract the `Item` and `ParentRefreshAction` parameters from the query.

```
    public partial class CustomerEditViewModel : ObservableObject,
    IQueryAttributable {
        [ObservableProperty]
        Customer item;

        protected Func<Customer, Task> ParentRefreshAction { get;
          set; }
        public void ApplyQueryAttributes(IDictionary<string, object>
          query) {
            if (query.TryGetValue("Item", out object currentItem)) {
                Item = (Customer)currentItem;
            }
            if (query.TryGetValue("ParentRefreshAction", out object
              parentRefreshAction)) {
                ParentRefreshAction = (Func<Customer, Task>)
                  parentRefreshAction;
            }
            query.Clear();
        }
    }
```

It's important to call the `query.Clear` method because in certain usage scenarios with .NET MAUI's navigation mechanism, parameters may be repeatedly passed to the `ParentRefreshAction` method even if you didn't explicitly add these parameters. Clearing the query ensures that only intended parameters are processed each time the navigation occurs.

6. Save changes after editing an item. Add the `SaveAsync` command that will be called when a user clicks the **Save** button in the UI. In `SaveAsync`, save the edited object using `SaveChanges`, call `ParentRefreshAction`, and navigate back:

CustomerEditViewModel.cs

```
[RelayCommand]
async Task SaveAsync() {
    using CrmContext context = new CrmContext();
    context.Customers.Add(Item);
    context.SaveChanges();
    await ParentRefreshAction(Item);
    await Shell.Current.GoToAsync("..");
}
```

> **Key point**
>
> The `ParentRefreshAction` delegate contains the `MainViewModel.RefreshAddedAsync` method, which refreshes the `MainViewModel.Customers` collection bound to `CollectionView`. This step is crucial because `CrmContext.Customers` and `MainViewModel.Customers` are separate collections. If you update `CrmContext.Customers` without refreshing `MainViewModel.Customers`, the changes won't be reflected in the `CollectionView` bound to `MainViewModel.Customers`. Thus, invoking `MainViewModel.RefreshAddedAsync` ensures that the UI accurately reflects any updates made to the data in `CrmContext.Customers`.

7. Create an item editing view. Create a `Views` folder and add a new `ContentPage` (XAML) named `CustomerEditPage` to it. Implement a basic UI with vertically stacked `Entry` elements:

CustomerEditPage.xaml

```
xmlns:vm="clr-namespace:c4_LocalDatabaseConnection.ViewModels"

<ContentPage.BindingContext>
    <vm:CustomerEditViewModel/>
</ContentPage.BindingContext>
<Grid>
    <VerticalStackLayout VerticalOptions="Start">
        <Entry Placeholder="First Name"
```

```
            Text="{Binding Item.FirstName}"/>
            <Entry Placeholder="Last Name"
            Text="{Binding Item.LastName}"/>
            <Entry Placeholder="Email" Text="{Binding Item.Email}"
            ReturnCommand="{Binding SaveCommand}"/>
            <Button Text="Save" Command="{Binding SaveCommand}"/>
        </VerticalStackLayout>
        <ActivityIndicator VerticalOptions="Center"
                    HorizontalOptions="Center"
                    IsRunning="{Binding SaveCommand.IsRunning}"/>
    </Grid>
```

Note that each `Entry` is bound to a corresponding sub-property of the `Item` property. The `ActivityIndicator` element is used to indicate a saving operation in progress, enhancing perceived UI responsiveness.

8. Register `CustomerEditPage` in the routing mechanism so that the `Shell.GoToAsync` method knows how to navigate to the editing page:

AppShell.xaml.cs

```
public AppShell() {
    InitializeComponent();
    Routing.RegisterRoute(nameof(CustomerEditPage),
typeof(CustomerEditPage));
}
```

Now, you can run the project and utilize swipe actions to delete an item and use the floating "plus" button to add a new customer.

How it works...

We've implemented the delete and create actions. Deleting items is straightforward because all the logic is handled within the `MainViewModel` class. However, creating items is more complex because we need to pass information about the edited item to the new item form and execute the refresh action after saving data to the database. If a user clicks the back button instead of the **Save** button, we shouldn't keep the collection in its modified state. Therefore, we cannot add a new item to the bound `Customers` collection in advance; we need to add it conditionally.

One effective technique to handle this scenario is to pass a refresh function delegate from `MainViewModel` to `CustomerEditViewModel`. This delegate will be called from the `Save` method of `CustomerEditViewModel`, ensuring that the main view updates only when a user successfully saves the edited.

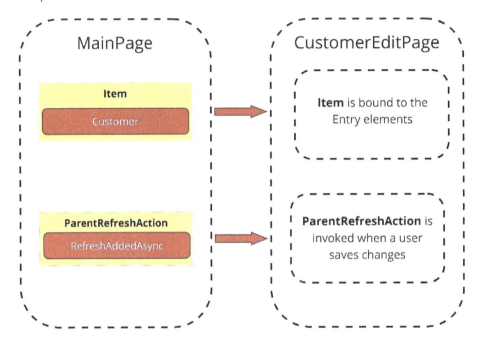

Figure 4.3 – Parameters passed to new item form

There's more...

In certain versions, Visual Studio creates a default .NET MAUI project with a white back button and white title background. This can lead to issues where the back button and title are not visible in `CustomerEditPage`.

To resolve this, navigate to the `Resources/Styles/Styles.xaml` file, locate the implicit style for the `Shell` element, and set `Shell.ForegroundColor` to `Black`:

```
<Style TargetType="Shell" ApplyToDerivedTypes="True">
    <Setter Property="Shell.ForegroundColor" Value="Black" />
    <!--...-->
</Style>
```

Implementing detail and edit forms

Typically, mobile applications organize lists, item details, and editing views on separate screens to ensure a clean design that fits well on mobile screens and optimizes performance. To implement CRUD operations effectively, you typically need at least three views:

- **List of items**: This displays a collection of items. We've already implemented this screen in the previous recipe.

- **Item detail form**: It's challenging to fit all necessary information about an item into a list item template. Therefore, it's considered best practice to display additional details about a selected item on a separate page.

- **Item edit form**: This form contains editing elements to modify item information.

While saving data changes using Entity Framework is straightforward with `DbContext.SaveChanges`, implementing the required UI can be challenging, especially for those new to the task. Key considerations include the following:

- Passing information between different views

- Refreshing the collection when an item is updated

- Handling cancellation of item editing without updating the parent collection

- Optimizing performance by refreshing specific items instead of reloading the entire collection

In this recipe, you'll learn how to efficiently implement these tasks.

Getting ready

Start with the project you completed in the previous recipe (*Implementing the create delete operations*). This project is available at `https://github.com/PacktPublishing/.NET-MAUI-Cookbook/tree/main/Chapter04/c4-CreateDelete`.

The code for this recipe is available at `https://github.com/PacktPublishing/.NET-MAUI-Cookbook/tree/main/Chapter04/c4-ItemEditing`.

How to do it...

Let's create an application with the following views: a collection view to display customers, a customer details view, and a customer editing view. When a user taps on an item, we'll navigate to the detail view. In the detail view, users can tap an **Edit** button to navigate to the editing view:

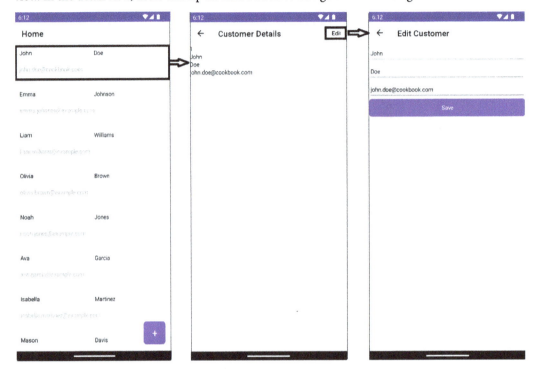

Figure 4.4 – Collection detail and edit views

1. Add the item tap recognizer to `CollectionView`. Navigate to the `MainPage.xaml` file and add `TapGestureRecognizer` to the `customerTemplate DataTemplate`. This gesture recognizer allows us to call a command to navigate to the detail view when a user taps an item in `CollectionView`. Bind `TapGestureRecognizer.Command` to `ShowDetailFormCommand` and `TapGestureRecognizer.CommandParameter` to the current item:

MainPage.xaml

```
<DataTemplate x:DataType="local:Customer" x:key="
customerTemplate">
  <!--...-->
    <Grid>
        <Grid.GestureRecognizers>
```

```
        <TapGestureRecognizer
Command="{Binding Path=BindingContext.ShowDetailFormCommand,
Source={RelativeSource Mode=FindAncestor, AncestorType={x:Type
CollectionView}}}"
        CommandParameter="{Binding}"/>
      </Grid.GestureRecognizers>
    </Grid>
        <!--...-->
</DataTemplate>
```

We used `RelativeSource` binding to bind `TapGestureRecognizer.Command` to `ShowDetailFormCommand` of `MainViewModel`, similar to how we handled `SwipeItem.Command` in the previous recipe.

2. Navigate to the detail view when an item is tapped. Create the `ShowDetailFormAsync` command in the `MainViewModel` class to navigate to the customer details form. Pass the tapped customer as the `Item` parameter and the `RefreshEditedAsync` method as a `ParentRefreshAction` parameter. In `RefreshEditedAsync`, find the edited customer's index in the bound collection by its `Id` property and replace it with the updated customer instance:

MainViewModel.cs

```
[RelayCommand]
async Task ShowDetailFormAsync(Customer customer) {
    await Shell.Current.GoToAsync(nameof(CustomerDetailPage),
            parameters: new Dictionary<string, object>
            {
                    { "ParentRefreshAction", (Func<Customer,
Task>)RefreshEditedAsync },
                    { "Item", customer }
            });
}

async Task RefreshEditedAsync(Customer updatedCustomer) {
    int editedItemIndex = -1;
    await Task.Run(() =>
    {
        editedItemIndex = Customers.Select((customer, index) =>
new { customer, index }).
                                    First(item => item.customer.
Id == updatedCustomer.Id).index;
    });
    if (editedItemIndex == -1)
        return;
```

```
                Customers[editedItemIndex] = updatedCustomer;
    }
```

We will call the `RefreshEditedAsync` method once a user saves changes in the edit form.

3. Create a view model to display tapped customer information. Create the `CustomerDetailViewModel` class and move the `item`, `ParentRefreshAction`, and `ApplyQueryAttributes` members from the `CustomerEditViewModel` class to `CustomerDetailViewModel`. Make the `ApplyQueryAttributes` method virtual because we will override it later:

CustomerDetailViewModel.cs

```
public partial class CustomerDetailViewModel : ObservableObject,
IQueryAttributable {
    [ObservableProperty]
    Customer item;

    public Func<Customer, Task> ParentRefreshAction { get; set;
}

    public virtual void ApplyQueryAttributes(IDictionary<string,
object> query) {
        if (query.TryGetValue("Item", out object currentItem)) {
            Item = (Customer)currentItem;
        }
        if (query.TryGetValue("ParentRefreshAction", out object
parentRefreshAction)) {
            ParentRefreshAction = (Func<Customer, Task>)
parentRefreshAction;
        }
        query.Clear();
    }
}
```

4. Implement logic to navigate from the detail form to the edit form. Add the `ShowEditFormAsync` command that will be invoked when a user presses the **Edit** button on the detail page. In `ShowEditFormAsync`, retrieve a new instance of a customer from `CrmContext` and pass it as an `Item` parameter.

Pass `ItemEditedAsync` as a `ParentRefreshAction` parameter. This method will be called when a user presses the **Save** button in the edit form. In `ItemEditedAsync`, set `Item` to update the displayed customer and call `ParentRefreshAction` to refresh the item in the `Customers` collection of `MainViewModel`:

```
[RelayCommand]
async Task ShowEditFormAsync() {
```

```
    CrmContext context = new CrmContext();
    Customer editedItem = context.Customers.FirstOrDefault(c =>
c.Id == Item.Id);

    await Shell.Current.GoToAsync(nameof(CustomerEditPage),
        parameters: new Dictionary<string, object>
                    {
                        { "ParentRefreshAction", (Func<Customer,
Task>)ItemEditedAsync },
                        { "Item", editedItem }
                    });
}
async Task ItemEditedAsync(Customer customer) {
    Item = customer;
    await ParentRefreshAction(customer);
}
```

> **Key point**
>
> We need to create a new customer instance, because a user may start editing a customer and then cancel the edit operation by pressing the back button. Creating a new instance will prevent updating a customer displayed in the collection until a user saves it.

5. Implement a customer detail view. Create `CustomerDetailPage` and bind `Label` elements to the sub-properties of `Item`. The `Item` property contains the `Customer` object, so we can bind to its `Id`, `FirstName`, `LastName`, and `Email`:

```xml
xmlns:vm="clr-namespace:c4_LocalDatabaseConnection.ViewModels"

<ContentPage.BindingContext>
    <vm:CustomerDetailViewModel/>
</ContentPage.BindingContext>
<ContentPage.ToolbarItems>
    <ToolbarItem Text="Edit" Command="{Binding
ShowEditFormCommand}"/>
</ContentPage.ToolbarItems>
<VerticalStackLayout>
    <Label Text="{Binding Item.Id}"/>
    <Label Text="{Binding Item.FirstName}"/>
    <Label Text="{Binding Item.LastName}"/>
    <Label Text="{Binding Item.Email}"/>
</VerticalStackLayout>
```

6. Update the customer edit view model. Inherit `CustomerEditViewModel` from `CustomerDetailViewModel`, and add the `IsNewItem` property. We will use `IsNewItem` to determine whether an edit form is used for creating a new item or for editing an existing item. Remove `Item` and `ParentRefreshAction` because they already exist in the inherited `CustomerDetailViewModel` class:

CustomerEditViewModel.cs

```
public partial class CustomerEditViewModel :
CustomerDetailViewModel {
    [ObservableProperty]
    bool isNewItem;

    //[ObservableProperty]
    //Customer item;

    //public Func<Customer, Task> ParentRefreshAction { get;
set; }
    //...
}
```

7. Obtain the `IsNewItem` parameter during navigation from the detail view to the edit view. Update the `ApplyQueryAttributes` method to extract the `IsNewItem` parameter value:

CustomerEditViewModel.cs

```
public override void ApplyQueryAttributes(IDictionary<string,
object> query) {
    if (query.TryGetValue("IsNewItem", out object isNew)) {
        IsNewItem = (bool)isNow;
    }
    base.ApplyQueryAttributes(query);
}
```

8. Update the save method to execute different saving logic for new and updated customers. Modify the `SaveAsync` method to add or modify a customer based on the `IsNewItem` property value:

CustomerEditViewModel.cs

```
[RelayCommand]
async Task SaveAsync() {
    CrmContext context = new CrmContext();
    if (IsNewItem) {
```

```
            context.Customers.Add(Item);
        }
        else {
            context.Customers.Attach(Item);
            context.Entry(Item).State = EntityState.Modified;
        }
        context.SaveChanges();
        await ParentRefreshAction(Item);
    await Shell.Current.GoToAsync("..");
}
```

The Attach method informs DbContext that an item should be tracked by this DbContext instance. Setting State to Modified informs DbContext that the entity is modified and should be saved when DbContext.SaveChanges is called.

9. Pass the IsNewItem parameter from MainViewModel to the editing form when a new item is created. Navigate to the MainViewModel class and update the ShowNewFormAsync method to pass true to the IsNewItem parameter to let CustomerEditViewModel know that it's used for new item editing when ShowNewFormAsync is called:

MainViewModel.cs

```
async Task ShowNewFormAsync()
{
    await Shell.Current.GoToAsync(
        nameof(CustomerEditPage),
        parameters: new Dictionary<string, object>
        {
            { "ParentRefreshAction",
                (Func<Customer, Task>)RefreshAddedAsync },
            { "Item", new Customer() },
            { "IsNewItem", true }
        });
}
```

10. Register a navigation route for CustomerDetailPage:

AppShell.cs

```
public AppShell() {
    InitializeComponent();
    //…
    Routing.RegisterRoute(nameof(CustomerDetailPage),
typeof(CustomerDetailPage));
}
```

Now, you can run the project, tap an item to see its details, and navigate to a separate edit screen to edit the item.

How it works...

In this recipe, we employed a technique similar to the one used in *Implementing the create and delete operations* recipe for passing data and refreshing information when navigating between views. However, two key changes were made:

- `MainPage` now passes the `IsNewItem` parameter to `CustomerEditPage`, indicating that `CustomerEditPage` will be used for editing a new item.

- `CustomerDetailPage` passes its own `RefreshParentAction` to `CustomerEditPage`. The refresh action of `CustomerDetailPage` updates the displayed item only if changes are saved by the user. Additionally, `RefreshParentAction` triggers the refresh action of `MainViewModel`, which updates the `Customers` collection bound to `CollectionView`.

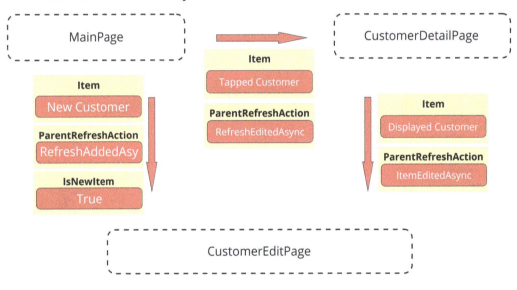

Figure 4.5 – Display and edit view parameters

There's more...

In `CustomerDetailPage`, we display the same title for both new item and edit item operations. Since `CustomerEditViewModel` includes the `IsNewItem` property, we can conditionally modify the page title using a data trigger. Set the default `ContentPage.Title` to **Edit Customer** and create a trigger bound to the `IsNewItem` property. In the trigger, set `Title` to **New Customer**:

```
<ContentPage xmlns="http://schemas.microsoft.com/dotnet/2021/maui"
    xmlns:x="http://schemas.microsoft.com/winfx/2009/xaml"
    xmlns:vm="clr-namespace:c4_LocalDatabaseConnection.ViewModels"
    x:Class="c4_LocalDatabaseConnection.Views.CustomerEditPage"
             Title="Edit Customer">
    <ContentPage.Triggers>
        <DataTrigger Binding="{Binding IsNewItem}"
TargetType="ContentPage">
            <Setter Property="Title" Value="New Customer"/>
        </DataTrigger>
    </ContentPage.Triggers>
        <!--...-->
</ContentPage>
```

Implementing the unit of work and repository patterns

The **unit of work** and **repository** patterns provide an additional abstraction layer between the database and the view model. They enable you to eliminate data storage-related logic from the view model, promoting modular reuse across different parts of your application. These patterns facilitate clear separation of concerns and mitigate concurrency issues when multiple transactions are executed simultaneously.

A repository is responsible for accessing domain objects, typically corresponding to individual tables in a database. On the other hand, a unit of work encapsulates multiple repositories and ensures that transactions involving multiple tables are either fully processed or entirely rejected. This capability is crucial for maintaining data consistency.

When integrated with EF Core, a unit of work typically manages a single instance of `DbContext`, shared among its constituent repositories. Each repository leverages this shared `DbContext` to access and manipulate data. Additionally, the unit of work provides a centralized method to commit changes made across all repositories.

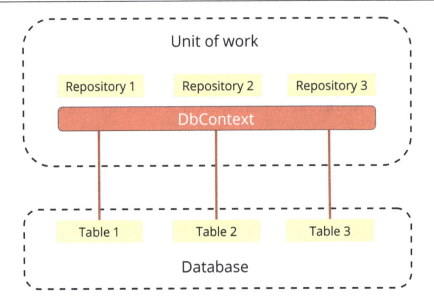

Figure 4.6 – Unit of work and repositories

Best practice dictates creating a new instance of the unit of work for each discrete operation. For instance, when starting an editing operation, it's advisable to instantiate a fresh unit of work. This approach isolates the editing process from other ongoing operations, ensuring transactional integrity.

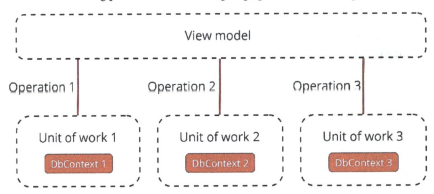

Figure 4.7 – Unit of work per operation

Since each unit of work operates with its own instance of `DbContext`, simultaneous execution of multiple transactions doesn't lead to conflicts. EF Core optimizes database communication internally, ensuring efficient performance without the overhead of separate database connections for each `DbContext` instance.

Getting ready

Begin with the project you've been working on since the completion of the previous recipe (*Implementing detail and edit forms*). You can find this project at `https://github.com/PacktPublishing/.NET-MAUI-Cookbook/tree/main/Chapter04/c4-ItemEditing`.

For the code related to this recipe, refer to `https://github.com/PacktPublishing/.NET-MAUI-Cookbook/tree/main/Chapter04/c4-UnitOfWork`.

How to do it...

Let's set up a repository for the `Customers` table and a unit of work to manage it. In our view models, we'll utilize the unit of work instead of directly interacting with `DbContext` to access and persist data:

1. Create a repository interface. Add an `IRepository` file to the `DataAccess` folder and add an interface with basic methods for CRUD operations:

IRepository.cs

```
public interface IRepository<TEntity> where TEntity : class {
    Task<TEntity> GetByIdAsync(int id);
    Task<IEnumerable<TEntity>> GetAllAsync();
    Task AddAsync(TEntity item);
    Task UpdateAsync(TEntity item);
    Task DeleteAsync(TEntity item);
}
```

2. Create a repository class. Add the `CustomerRepository` class to the `DataAccess` folder and create a constructor that accepts a `CrmContext` instance and saves it to a read-only field. We will use this `CrmContext` instance to manage data:

CustomerRepository.cs

```
public class CustomerRepository {
    readonly DbSet<Customer> DbSet;
    readonly CrmContext Context;

    public CustomerRepository(CrmContext context) {
        Context = context;
```

```
                              DbSet = context.Set<Customer>();
                  }
         }
```

The `DbContext.Set` method creates a `DbSet` instance of a specified type. We will use `DbSet` to get data from the `Customers` table.

3. Implement the `IRepository` interface in the `CustomerRepository` class:

CustomerRepository.cs

```
public class CustomerRepository : IRepository<Customer> {
    //…
    public async Task<IEnumerable<Customer>> GetAllAsync() {
        return await Task.Run(() => DbSet.ToList());
    }
    public async Task AddAsync(Customer item) {
        DbSet.Add(item);
        await Task.CompletedTask;
    }
    public async Task DeleteAsync(Customer item) {
        DbSet.Remove(item);
        await Task.CompletedTask;
    }
    public async Task<Customer> GetByIdAsync(int id) {
        return await Task.Run(() => DbSet.Find(id));
    }
    public async Task UpdateAsync(Customer item) {
        DbSet.Attach(item);
        Context.Entry(item).State = EntityState.Modified;
        await Task.CompletedTask;
    }
}
```

In our implementation, we utilize `Task.Run` exclusively within the `GetAllAsync` and `GetByIdAsync` methods. For other methods, such as those that don't directly interact with the database, we simply return `Task.CompletedTask`. Despite this, we maintain the async signature for future scenarios involving remote services.

4. Create a class for the unit of work. Create the `CrmUnitOfWork` class within the `DataAccess` folder. `CrmUnitOfWork` serves as the primary entry point for data access and change tracking. Include a public `Items` property for accessing data and a `Context` field for managing changes. To ensure proper resource management, implement `IDisposable` and invoke `DbContext.Dispose` within the `Dispose` method of `IDisposable`.

This ensures that the `DbContext` releases its unmanaged resources when `CrmUnitOfWork` is no longer needed.

CrmUnitOfWork.cs

```
public class CrmUnitOfWork : IDisposable, IUnitOfWork<Customer>
{
    readonly CrmContext Context = new CrmContext();
    IRepository<Customer> customerRepository;
    public IRepository<Customer> Items =>
        customerRepository ??= new CustomerRepository(Context);
    public async Task SaveAsync() {
        await Task.Run(() => Context.SaveChanges());
    }
    public void Dispose() {
        Context.Dispose();
    }
}
public interface IUnitOfWork<TEntity> where TEntity : class {
    IRepository<TEntity> Items { get; }
    Task SaveAsync();
}
```

The `IUnitOfWork` interface will help you use different units of work implementations without changing other classes that use a specific unit of work.

5. Modify the customer loading mechanism to use a unit of work. We'll update our view models to interact with `CrmUnitOfWork` instead of `CrmContext` directly. Navigate to `MainViewModel` and modify the `LoadCustomersAsync` method to use `CrmUnitOfWork`. We need to create a new instance of `CrmUnitOfWork` and call the `GetAllAsync` method, which will asynchronously return customers:

MainViewModel.cs

```
[RelayCommand]
async Task LoadCustomersAsync() {
    using var uniOfWork = new CrmUnitOfWork();
    Customers = new ObservableCollection<Customer>(await
uniOfWork.Items.GetAllAsync());
    Refreshing = false;
}
```

6. Update the customer deletion logic to use a unit of work. Replace DeleteCustomer with the DeleteCustomerAsync method in MainViewModel and integrate CrmUnitOfWork:

MainViewModel.cs

```
[RelayCommand]
async Task DeleteCustomerAsync(Customer customer) {
    using var uniOfWork = new CrmUnitOfWork();
    await uniOfWork.Items.DeleteAsync(customer);
    await uniOfWork.SaveAsync();
    Customers.Remove(customer);
}
```

You may notice that after calling DeleteAsync, we need to call SaveAsync to save changes to the database. If you don't save them, the item will be deleted only from the local collection.

7. Update the saving logic in the edit view model to use a unit of work. In the CustomerEditViewModel class, modify the SaveAsync method to use CrmUnitOfWork. Call AddAsync or UpdateAsync depending on the IsNewItem property value:

CustomerEditViewModel.cs

```
async Task SaveAsync() {
    using var uof = new CrmUnitOfWork();
    if (IsNewItem)
        await uof.Items.AddAsync(Item);
    else
        await uof.Items.UpdateAsync(Item);
    await uof.SaveAsync();
    await ParentRefreshAction(Item);
    await Shell.Current.GoToAsync("..");
}
```

8. Lastly, incorporate CrmUnitOfWork into the detail view model by modifying CustomerDetailViewModel.ShowEditFormAsync:

CustomerDetailViewModel.cs

```
async Task ShowEditFormAsync() {
    using var uof = new CrmUnitOfWork();
    Customer editedItem = await uof.Items.GetByIdAsync(Item.Id);
    await Shell.Current.GoToAsync(nameof(CustomerEditPage),
        parameters: new Dictionary<string, object>
                    {
                { "ParentRefreshAction", (Func<Customer, Task>)
```

```
          ItemEditedAsync },
                        { "Item", editedItem }
                            });
      }
```

How it works...

In our example, the unit of work exposes two members:

- The `Items` property accessing the `customers` repository
- The `SaveAsync` method for saving changes

The repository provides basic methods for data access and modification:

- `GetByIdAsync`: To get an item by its ID
- `GetAllAsync`: To get all items
- `AddAsync`: To add an item to the context
- `UpdateAsync`: To update an item in the context
- `DeleteAsync`: To delete an item from the context

> **Key point**
>
> While `AddAsync`, `UpdateAsync`, and `DeleteAsync` modify items in the context, they don't make any changes in the database. The database is updated only when you call the `CrmUnitOfWork.SaveAsync` method.

There's more...

In the `CustomerRepository.GetAllAsync` method, we retrieve all customers unconditionally:

```
public async Task<IEnumerable<Customer>> GetAllAsync() {
    return await Task.Run(() => DbSet.ToList());
}
```

This means that if you need to get all customers whose names start with "A," you need to load all items from the database and then filter them on the client side.

To load only required entities, you can add a filtering expression to the `GetAllAsync` method as a parameter:

```
public async Task<IEnumerable<Customer>>
GetAllAsync(Expression<Func<Customer, bool>> filter = null) {
```

```
        IQueryable<Customer> query = DbSet;
        if (filter != null) {
            query = query.Where(filter);
        }
        return await Task.Run(() => query.ToList());
    }
```

If the filter parameter is not null, call the `IQueryable.Where` method. This method appends the filter expression to the future request. Note that the expression is not executed when you call the `Where` method. It will be executed only when you call `query.ToList`.

Now, you can retrieve filtered items using `GetAllAsync` in the following manner:

```
    IEnumerable<Customer> filteredCustomers = await customerRepository.
    GetAllAsync(c => c.FirstName.StartsWith("A"));
```

You can use a similar technique to return sorted items. Modify `GetAllAsync` so that it accepts an ordering function:

```
    public async Task<IEnumerable<Customer>>
    GetAllAsync(Func<IQueryable<Customer>, IOrderedQueryable<Customer>>
    orderBy = null) {
        IQueryable<Customer> query = DbSet;
        if (orderBy != null) {
            query = orderBy(query);
        }
        return await Task.Run(() => query.ToList());
    }
```

The `IOrderedQueryable` interface represents the result returned by methods such as `OrderBy`, `OrderByDescending`, `ThenBy`, or `ThenByDescending`. To use the `GetAllAsync` method, pass an expression that calls `OrderBy`:

```
    IEnumerable<Customer> sortedCustomers = customersRepository.
    GetAllAsync(q => q.OrderBy(c => c.FirstName));
```

Handling errors while saving data to a database

How do you handle the situation when a user tries to save data that doesn't correspond to the database model? For example, what steps would you take if a user attempts to save an entity with a duplicate ID? Additionally, how would you handle a scenario where data is being requested from a remote service, but the device loses internet connection during the process?

When working with a database, we should always be prepared for potential failures during database transactions. These issues can arise from factors outside of your code's control.

It's important to ensure your application properly manages errors without disrupting the UX. Inform users promptly when an operation cannot be completed.

Getting ready

Start with the project you got after finishing the previous recipe (*Implementing the unit of work and repository patterns*). This project is available at `https://github.com/PacktPublishing/.NET-MAUI-Cookbook/tree/main/Chapter04/c4-UnitOfWork`.

The code for this recipe is available at `https://github.com/PacktPublishing/.NET-MAUI-Cookbook/tree/main/Chapter04/c4-DatabaseValidation`.

How to do it...

In this recipe, we'll establish database rules to prevent empty `FirstName` entries and duplicate `Email` addresses. If these rules are violated, users will receive an error alert like the one demonstrated in the following figure:

Figure 4.8 – Database validation error alert

1. Add database validation constraints. In the `CrmContext.OnModelCreating` method, call `HasIndex` with `IsUnique` for the unique constraint on `Email`. After that, call `Property` with the `IsRequired` method for the not null constraint on `FirstName`:

```
public class CrmContext : DbContext {
//...
    protected override void OnModelCreating(ModelBuilder
builder) {
        builder.Entity<Customer>()
            .HasIndex(c => c.Email)
            .IsUnique();
        builder.Entity<Customer>()
            .Property(c => c.FirstName)
            .IsRequired();
            //...
    }
}
```

2. Catch database exceptions. When calling `SaveAsync` in `MainViewModel.cs` and `CustomerEditViewModel.cs`, wrap the operation in try-catch blocks to catch exceptions raised by EF Core if database constraints are violated. Display an error alert with the exception message:

MainViewModel.cs

```
async Task DeleteCustomerAsync(Customer customer) {
    using var uniOfWork = new CrmUnitOfWork();
    try {
        await uniOfWork.Items.DeleteAsync(customer);
        await uniOfWork.SaveAsync();
    }
    catch (Exception ex) {
        await Shell.Current.DisplayAlert("Error", ex.Message,
"OK");
        return;
    }
    Customers.Remove(customer);
}
```

CustomerEditViewModel.cs

```
async Task SaveAsync() {
    using var uof = new CrmUnitOfWork();
    try {
        if (IsNewItem)
            await uof.Items.AddAsync(Item);
        else
            await uof.Items.UpdateAsync(Item);
        await uof.SaveAsync();
    }
    catch (Exception ex) {
        await Shell.Current.DisplayAlert("Error", ex.Message,
"OK");
        return;
    }
    await ParentRefreshAction(Item);
    await Shell.Current.GoToAsync("..");
}
```

3. To apply the updated database schema, uninstall the application to ensure EF Core creates a new database on your device or emulator. Add a new customer using the plus button, and intentionally enter an existing email or leave FirstName empty. This action should trigger the error alert shown in *Figure 4.8*.

    Note that if you clear FirstName for an existing customer, no error will occur because the Entry element sets FirstName to an empty string, not null.

How it works...

When you invoke the DbContext.SaveChanges method, the DbContext analyzes the modifications made to tracked entities and prepares SQL commands for execution in the database. Subsequently, the database evaluates these commands against the constraints defined in the affected tables. If any constraints are violated during this validation, the database throws an exception. This exception is then propagated back through DbContext and up to the view model layer, where we handle it by displaying an alert to the user.

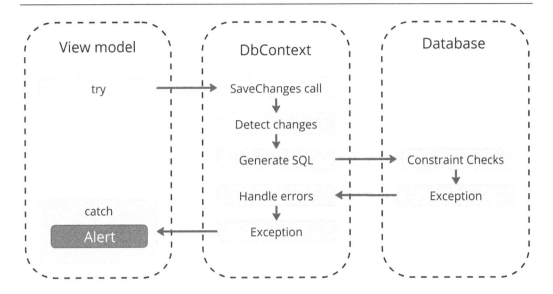

Figure 4.9 – Database exception handling

There's more...

In this recipe, we've utilized the top-level exception to display text in an alert. However, this exception typically lacks detailed information about the specific issue. Different databases raise their own distinct exception types, which offer more precise details regarding the error. For instance, SQLite raises `SqliteException`, which the EF Core wraps within `DbUpdateException`. You can handle `SqliteException` as shown in the following code:

CustomerEditViewModel.cs

```
async Task SaveAsync() {
    using var uof = new CrmUnitOfWork();
    try {
        if (IsNewItem)
            await uof.Items.AddAsync(Item);
        else
            await uof.Items.UpdateAsync(Item);
        await uof.SaveAsync();
    }
    catch (DbUpdateException ex) when (ex.InnerException is
SqliteException sqliteEx) {
        await Shell.Current.DisplayAlert("Error", sqliteEx.Message,
"OK");
        return;
```

```
    }
    catch (Exception ex) {
        await Shell.Current.DisplayAlert("Error", ex.Message, "OK");
        return;
    }
    await ParentRefreshAction(Item);
    await Shell.Current.GoToAsync("..");
}.
```

When working with asynchronous tasks, it's important to remember that `async void` methods don't propagate exceptions to the calling method. Therefore, you should avoid using them in order not to lose information about a raised exception.

> **Key point**
>
> Don't use the `async void` methods, because you won't be able to handle exceptions coming from such methods.

Validating editors in the UI before data posting

In your application, certain validation rules can be enforced at the application level before data is submitted to the database. This approach can improve UX by promptly notifying users of any invalid inputs before they attempt to save changes. The .NET MAUI Community Toolkit provides various built-in validation behaviors designed to streamline common input validation tasks. We will use these behaviors to change the appearance of editors and disable saving when a user types invalid text.

Getting ready

Begin with the project you created upon completing the previous recipe (*Handling errors while saving data to a database*). You can access this project at `https://github.com/PacktPublishing/.NET-MAUI-Cookbook/tree/main/Chapter04/c4-DatabaseValidation`.

The code specific to this recipe is available at `https://github.com/PacktPublishing/.NET-MAUI-Cookbook/tree/main/Chapter04/c4-UIValidation`.

How to do it...

Let's disable the **Save** button when the user enters an empty `FirstName` or `Email` that doesn't match the common email format. It's important to note that not all database constraints can be caught at the UI level since they require data to be saved to the database first. Therefore, validation for unique `Email` constraints will still occur at the database level:

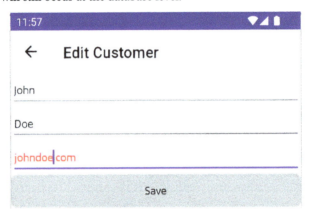

Figure 4.10 – UI validation during editing

1. Add properties to store the validation status in the view model. Navigate to the `CustomerEditViewModel` class and add the `IsEmailValid` and `IsFirstNameValid` properties. Utilize these properties in the `CanExecute` method of `SaveCommand`. In `CanSave`, return true when both `IsEmailValid` and `IsFirstNameValid` are true:

CustomerEditViewModel.cs

```
public partial class CustomerEditViewModel :
CustomerDetailViewModel {

    [NotifyCanExecuteChangedFor(nameof(SaveCommand))]
    [ObservableProperty]
    bool isEmailValid;

    [NotifyCanExecuteChangedFor(nameof(SaveCommand))]
    [ObservableProperty]
    bool isFirstNameValid;

    [RelayCommand(CanExecute = nameof(CanSave))]
    async Task SaveAsync() {
        //...
    }
```

```
    bool CanSave() =>
        IsEmailValid && IsFirstNameValid;

    //...
}
```

2. Define the appearance of an invalid editor. In `CustomerEditForm`, add a style that applies to `Entry` when it contains an invalid value. Let's set the text color to red:

CustomerEditForm.xaml

```
<ContentPage.Resources>
    <Style TargetType="Entry" x:Key="invalidEntryStyle">
        <Setter Property="TextColor" Value="Red"/>
    </Style>
</ContentPage.Resources>
```

3. Configure the validation behavior for the `First Name` editor. Attach `TextValidationBehavior` to the `Entry` responsible for editing `FirstName`. Set `InvalidStyle` to the style defined earlier. Also, bind `IsValid` to `IsFirstNameValid` to notify the view model when a value is invalid:

```
xmlns:toolkit="http://schemas.microsoft.com/dotnet/2022/maui/
    toolkit"

<Entry Placeholder="First Name"
        Text="{Binding Item.FirstName}">
    <Entry.Behaviors>
        <toolkit:TextValidationBehavior
            InvalidStyle="{StaticResource invalidEntryStyle}"
            IsValid="{Binding IsFirstNameValid}"
            Flags="ValidateOnValueChanged, ValidateOnAttaching"
            MinimumLength="1">
        </toolkit:TextValidationBehavior>
    </Entry.Behaviors>
</Entry>
```

The `MinimumLength` property ensures that a string with at least one symbol is considered valid. The `Flags` property specifies when validation occurs: in our case, on text change (`ValidateOnValueChanged`) and when `TextValidationBehavior` is attached (`ValidateOnAttaching`).

4. Configure the validation behavior for the `Email` editor. Assign `EmailValidationBehavior` to the editor responsible for `Email` editing. `EmailValidationBehavior` automatically checks if the entered email corresponds to the common email format (`abc@abc.abc`). Configure other properties similarly to `TextValidationBehavior`:

CustomerEditForm.xaml

```
xmlns:toolkit="http://schemas.microsoft.com/dotnet/2022/maui/
    toolkit"

<Entry.Behaviors>
    <toolkit:EmailValidationBehavior
        InvalidStyle="{StaticResource invalidEntryStyle}"
        IsValid="{Binding IsEmailValid}"
        Flags="ValidateOnValueChanged, ValidateOnAttaching">
    </toolkit:EmailValidationBehavior>
</Entry.Behaviors>
```

Now, you can run the project and attempt to edit an item. You'll observe that the Save button is disabled, and the editor's text turns red when you clear the `FirstName` field or enter an invalid email address.

How it works...

The `TextValidationBehavior` and `EmailValidationBehavior` classes implement basic validation logic. When the entered text doesn't meet an internal validation rule, these behaviors apply the style defined in the `InvalidStyle` property. Additionally, they set `IsValid` to false, which allows us to control the state of the `Save` command.

`TextValidationBehavior` and `EmailValidationBehavior` trigger validation based on the values specified in the `Flags` property, which accepts the following values:

- `ValidateOnAttaching`: This triggers validation when the behavior is attached to the control, which typically occurs when the control is shown.

- `ValidateOnValueChanged`: This triggers validation as soon as the validated value is changed.

- `ValidateOnFocusing`: This triggers validation when the associated control is focused.

- `ValidateOnUnfocusing`: This triggers validation when the associated control loses focus.

- `ForceMakeValidWhenFocused`: If an error exists, this removes the visual effect of an invalid value when the associated control is focused. The value is still considered invalid.

- `None`: Validation is not automatically triggered. You can use the `ForceValidate` method to trigger it manually.

There's more…

While you can implement validation logic in UI purely using default .NET MAUI capabilities, there are third-party control suites that offer advanced validation techniques and enhanced UX when an invalid value appears. For example, the DevExpress `DataFormView` allows you to validate values and display an error message by simply assigning a data annotation attribute to a property:

```
public class Customer {
    [Required(ErrorMessage = "FirstName cannot be empty")]
    public string FirstName { get; set; }
    // ...
}
```

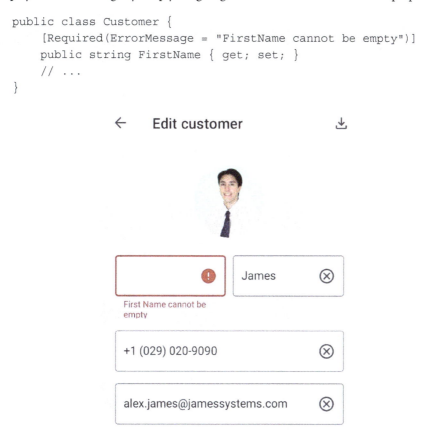

Figure 4.11 – The DevExpress data form

Additionally, the DevExpress `DataFormView` allows you to validate separate properties or the entire edited object by handling the `ValidateProperty` and `ValidateForm` events, respectively.

The `DataFormView` control automatically shows an error icon and error text to inform a user about incorrect input. You can learn more about it in the following help article: `https://docs.devexpress.com/MAUI/403640/data-form/index`.

Implementing data caching for enhanced performance

When developing a mobile application, working with a database can present certain performance challenges:

- Accessing data even from a local database can lead to noticeable delays because mobile devices typically have lower CPU capabilities
- Since typically you can't store too much data on a mobile device, you often need your application to work with remote data storage, which causes delays due to the internet connection

Implementing data caching techniques helps mitigate these challenges. You can reduce redundant database calls and enable quicker access to frequently used data. Integrating the unit of work and repository patterns, as introduced in the *Implementing the unit of work and repository patterns* recipe, allows you to seamlessly integrate caching into your data processing logic, enhancing overall application performance and UX.

In this recipe, we will enhance the repository created in the previous step by incorporating a memory cache into it. You will see that the repository abstraction does not allow us to change any code at the view and view model level.

Getting ready

Start with the project you got after finishing the previous recipe (*Validating editors in the UI before data posting*). This project is available at `https://github.com/PacktPublishing/.NET-MAUI-Cookbook/tree/main/Chapter04/c4-UIValidation`.

The code for this recipe is available at `https://github.com/PacktPublishing/.NET-MAUI-Cookbook/tree/main/Chapter04/c4-DataCaching`.

How to do it...

Let's create a caching repository by implementing the **decorator** pattern, which means that we will create a wrapper over another repository.

> **Decorator pattern**
>
> **Decorator** is a design pattern that allows you to add behavior to an object without subclassing it. The additional behavior is implemented in a wrapper class, which exposes the same members as the internal class. The decorator pattern allows you to easily replace the internal class without affecting other parts of your system. In a general case, the decorator may extend multiple internal classes, which wouldn't be possible with creating an inherited class, because multiple subclassing is not supported in C#.

The inner repository implementing the IRepository interface will be CustomersRepository, and we don't have to modify it. The outer repository (let's name it CustomersCachedRepository) will implement the same IRepository interface, but additionally, it will use the caching service to retrieve cached items.

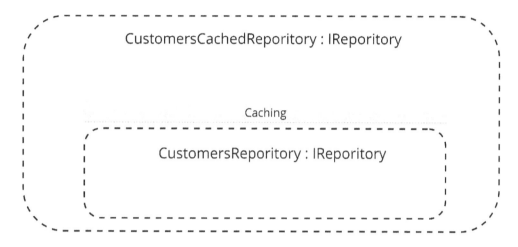

Figure 4.12 – Decorator pattern in repositories

To cache data, we will implement a caching service that will be responsible for adding and retrieving cached items. Additionally, the caching service will include APIs to maintain the cache validity after data updates. We will use these APIs in the caching repository and unit of work:

1. Create an ICacheService interface with the following methods:

    ```
    public interface ICacheService {
        bool TryGetValue(object key, out object? result);
        TItem Set<TItem>(object key, TItem value);
        void ClearCollectionCache(string collectionKey);

        void AddPendingAction(CollectionCacheUpdate pendingAction);
        void ClearCacheUpdateActions();
        void ExecuteCacheUpdateActions();
    }
    ```

    You can add this interface to the DataAccess folder to maintain the project structure.

2. Create a MemoryCacheService class and start implementing the ICacheService interface. Add the Cache field to keep the cache storage. As storage, we will use the MemoryCache class from the System.Runtime.Caching namespace. Add the TryGetValue and Set methods to get and set items in the cache. Add the ClearCollectionCache method to clear the collection cache:

MemoryCacheService.cs

```
public class MemoryCacheService : ICacheService {
    readonly MemoryCache Cache = new MemoryCache(new
MemoryCacheOptions());
    readonly TimeSpan CacheDuration = TimeSpan.FromMinutes(15);
    public bool TryGetValue(object key, out object result) {
        return Cache.TryGetValue(key, out result);
    }
    public TItem Set<TItem>(object key, TItem value) {
        return Cache.Set(key, value, CacheDuration);
    }
    public void ClearCollectionCache(string collectionKey) {
        Cache.Remove(collectionKey);
    }
}
```

The CacheDuration field specifies the cache duration: MemoryCache can automatically mark cached items as outdated within a certain time frame. This helps you avoid storing outdated data or too many entries.

3. We will need to execute postponed actions to update the cache when modifying data. This is required because when executing IRepository.AddAsync, IRepository.DeleteAsync, and IRepository.UpdateAsync methods, we don't know if the database will be updated when we call the DbContext.SaveChanges method. Create a CollectionCacheUpdate class to store information about pending update actions:

```
public class CollectionCacheUpdate(string collectionName,
Action<IList> updateAction) {
    public string CollectionKey { get; set; } = collectionName;
    public Action<IList> UpdateAction { get; set; } =
updateAction;
}
```

4. Implement the `AddPendingAction` and `ClearCacheUpdateActions` methods
    in the `MemoryCacheService` class. In `AddPendingAction`, add a pending
    action to the `PendingCacheUpdateActions` collection. Clear the collection
    in `ClearCacheUpdateActions`:

MemoryCacheService.cs

```
readonly List<CollectionCacheUpdate> PendingCacheUpdateActions =
new();

public void AddPendingAction(CollectionCacheUpdate
pendingAction) {
    PendingCacheUpdateActions.Add(pendingAction);
}
public void ClearCacheUpdateActions() {
    PendingCacheUpdateActions.Clear();
}
```

5. Implement the `ExecuteCacheUpdateActions` method. In
    `ExecuteCacheUpdateActions`, iterate through all actions in the
    `PendingCacheUpdateActions` collection and invoke `UpdateAction` for each item:

```
public void ExecuteCacheUpdateActions() {
    foreach (var ca in PendingCacheUpdateActions) {
        if (Cache.TryGetValue(ca.CollectionKey, out var
          cachedCollection))
            ca.UpdateAction((IList)cachedCollection);
    }
    PendingCacheUpdateActions.Clear();
}
```

Implement the singleton pattern in the MemoryCache class by adding a static `Instance` property:

```
public class MemoryCacheService : ICacheService {
    //…
    public static MemoryCacheService Instance { get; } = new();
}
```

A better technique would be to register `MemoryCacheService` in a dependency injection
container, but we will use a static property for simplicity.

6. Create a repository with caching support. Create a `CustomersCachedRepository` class with a constructor accepting an inner repository and a caching service. Additionally, create a `CollectionName` field to store the collection cache key:

CustomersCachedRepository.cs

```
public class CustomersCachedRepository(
    IRepository<Customer> innerRepository,
    ICacheService cacheService
) : IRepository<Customer> {
    protected readonly IRepository<Customer> InnerRepository =
        innerRepository;
    protected readonly ICacheService CacheService =
        cacheService;
    protected readonly string CollectionName =
        "customers";
}
```

7. IIn the `CustomersCachedRepository` class, implement the methods defined in the `IRepository` interface:

CustomersCachedRepository.cs

```
public async Task<IEnumerable<Customer>> GetAllAsync() {
    if (!CacheService.TryGetValue(CollectionName,
        out object customers))
    {
        customers = await InnerRepository.GetAllAsync();
        CacheService.Set(CollectionName, customers);
    }
    return (IEnumerable<Customer>)customers;
}
public async Task AddAsync(Customer item) {
    await InnerRepository.AddAsync(item);
    CacheService.AddPendingAction(new CollectionCacheUpdate(
        CollectionName,
        cachedList => cachedList.Add(item)
    ));
}
public async Task DeleteAsync(Customer item) {
    await InnerRepository.DeleteAsync(item);
    CacheService.AddPendingAction(new CollectionCacheUpdate(
        CollectionName,
        cachedList => cachedList.Remove(item)
```

```
            ));
        }
        public async Task UpdateAsync(Customer item) {
            await InnerRepository.UpdateAsync(item);
            CacheService.AddPendingAction(new CollectionCacheUpdate(
                CollectionName,
                cachedList =>
                {
                    int editedItemIndex = ((List<Customer>)cachedList).
    FindIndex(c => c.Id == item.Id);
                    cachedList[editedItemIndex] = item;
                }));
        }
        public async Task<Customer> GetByIdAsync(int id) {
            return await InnerRepository.GetByIdAsync(id);
        }
```

All methods except `GetByIdAsync` work with the inner repository and update the cache. Note that `AddAsync`, `DeleteAsync`, and `UpdateAsync` don't update the cache directly. Instead, they call `AddPendingAction` to add an update action that will be executed only when you save changes to the database.

8. Update `CrmUnitOfWork` so that it works with `CustomersCachedRepository` instead of `CustomerRepository`. Additionally, call the update actions of the cached service in the `SaveAsync` method:

```
public class CrmUnitOfWork : IDisposable, IUnitOfWork<Customer>
{
    readonly ICacheService CacheService = MemoryCacheService
      .Instance;
    //...
    public IRepository<Customer> Items =>
        customerRepository ??= new CustomersCachedRepository(new
          CustomerRepository(Context), CacheService);
    public async Task SaveAsync() {
        await Task.Run(() =>
        {
            try {
                Context.SaveChanges();
            }
            catch {
                CacheService.ClearCacheUpdateActions();
                throw;
            }
            CacheService.ExecuteCacheUpdateActions();
```

```
            });
        }
    }
```

Note that if the `SaveChanges` method raises an exception, it indicates that cache update actions are unnecessary. Therefore, we invoke `ClearCacheUpdateActions` within the catch block. It's crucial to use the `throw` operator to propagate the exception, enabling the validation logic to catch it and display a validation alert.

Now, you can run the project and set a breakpoint in the `CustomerRepository.GetAllAsync` method. You'll observe that this method is called only once, even when refreshing the collection of customers.

How it works...

In this recipe, we applied the decorator pattern to encapsulate an inner repository, which accesses data, within an outer repository responsible for caching items. Both the inner (`CustomersRepository`) and outer (`CustomersCachedRepository`) repositories implement the same `IRepository` interface. This allows us to easily switch one repository with another.

The caching repository uses a caching service (`MemoryCacheService`) to manage cached items. In addition to standard methods for retrieving and storing cached data (`TryGetValue`, `Set`), it supports deferred updates using methods such as `AddPendingAction`, `ExecuteCacheUpdateActions`, and `ClearCacheUpdateActions`. Deferred updates (of pending actions) enable us to execute cache updates only when `CrmUnitOfWork.SaveAsync` completes successfully. If `SaveAsync` fails due to a database error, these deferred updates are cleared to maintain data consistency. This approach enhances performance by minimizing unnecessary cache updates and ensures robust error handling in data operations.

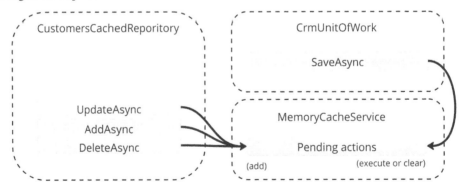

Figure 4.13 – Cache service pending actions

There's more...

In our example, we didn't load much data, so it's unlikely you will notice significant performance improvement. However, in a real-world application scenario, the benefits of caching would likely become more apparent.

To better visualize how caching enhances performance, you can simulate a long database operation by adding an artificial delay to the `CustomerRepository.GetAllAsync` method:

CustomersRepository.cs

```
public async Task<IEnumerable<Customer>> GetAllAsync() {
    await Task.Delay(3000);
    return await Task.Run(() => DbSet.ToList());
}
```

You'll observe that the initial loading of the collection takes longer due to the caching mechanism fetching data. However, subsequent refreshes are noticeably faster as they retrieve data from the cache.

Currently, our implementation always retrieves data from the cache. If you need to fetch fresh data in specific scenarios, you can extend the `CustomersCachedRepository.GetAllAsync` method by adding a Boolean parameter. When this parameter is set to `true`, clear the cache before fetching the data. This flexibility allows you to balance between performance optimization through caching and the requirement for up-to-date data in dynamic scenarios:

CustomersCachedRepository.cs

```
public async Task<IEnumerable<Customer>> GetAllAsync(bool fresh =
false) {
    if (fresh)
        CacheService.ClearCollectionCache(CollectionName);
    //...
}
```

You can call `GetAllAsync` with a parameter when a user explicitly refreshes the collection using the pull-to-refresh action.

Note that you need to modify the `IRepository` interface so that it includes a `GetAllAsync` method with a parameter.

Connecting to a remote web API service

For me, it's challenging to name even 10 applications on my phone that rely exclusively on local data without interacting with a server. Modern applications typically adopt a distributed architecture and frequently need to fetch data from remote services. In this recipe, we'll leverage the infrastructure we've built in previous topics to efficiently work with a web API service. You'll see how the patterns introduced earlier allow seamless switching of data retrieval logic while maintaining all other classes without modifications. This approach ensures flexibility and scalability in managing data access across different application scenarios.

Getting ready

In this recipe, we'll fetch data from a web API service. Creating a service is beyond the scope of this .NET MAUI cookbook, so I've prepared a starting project with a simple web API service to get you started: `https://github.com/PacktPublishing/.NET-MAUI-Cookbook/tree/main/Chapter04/c4-WebApiStart`.

Note that to run the web service, you need to have the **ASP.NET and web development** workload installed in Visual Studio:

Figure 4.14 – ASP.NET and web development workload

All UI and data access code is based on the *Implementing data caching for enhanced performance* recipe. Here's how the starting project differs from the one obtained in the previous recipe:

- **Web API service**: This is implemented in a separate project named `c4-WebApiServer`. For guidance on creating a service, refer to this tutorial: `https://learn.microsoft.com/en-us/aspnet/core/tutorials/first-web-api`.

- `WebApiHttpClient`: This is introduced to access the `HttpClient` instance, which is used to communicate with the web API service. This class utilizes device-specific APIs. This topic will be covered further in *Chapter 7, Understanding Platform-Specific APIs and Custom Handlers*. In a nutshell, `WebApiHttpClient` initializes an `HttpClient` instance with a custom message handler to pass the HTTPS certificate checks. This is required because we don't create a real SSL certificate. Additionally, `WebApiHttpClient` defines different base addresses for the Android and iOS platforms, because they use different addresses to access the local machine:

```
public static class WebApiHttpClient {
    public static HttpClient Instance =
    new (CustomHttpMessageHandler
      .GetMessageHandler() )      {
        Timeout = new TimeSpan(0, 0, 20)
    };
    static WebApiHttpClient() {
#if ANDROID
    Instance.BaseAddress = new Uri("https://10.0.2.2:7197/
api/");
    #else
        Instance.BaseAddress = new Uri("https://localhost:7197/
api/");
    #endif
    }
}
```

The port (`7197`) is defined in the `launchSettings.json` file of the `c4-WebApiServer` project.

`CustomHttpMessageHandler` is a partial class defined in three folders: `HttpCommunication`, `Platforms/Android`, and `Platforms/iOS`.

You can learn more about this by accessing a local web API service during development at `https://learn.microsoft.com/en-us/dotnet/maui/data-cloud/local-web-services`.

The complete project for this recipe is available at `https://github.com/PacktPublishing/.NET-MAUI-Cookbook/tree/main/Chapter04/c4-WebApiComplete`.

How to do it...

With the foundation laid in our previous recipes, transitioning to load data from a web API service requires minimal adjustments. Essentially, we'll replace `CustomerRepository` with `CustomerWebRepository` and make corresponding updates to `CrmUnitOfWork`. All existing logic for editing, validation, and caching will seamlessly continue to function without any modifications. This illustrates the flexibility and maintainability achieved through the unit of work, repository, and decorator patterns introduced in the earlier recipes:

1. Create a repository that works with a service. Create a `CustomerWebRepository` class in the `DataAccess` folder and define the `httpClient` field to store a `HttpClient` instance. Additionally, define the `CollectionName` variable and assign it to the `Customers` string. We will use this string to build the path to web API endpoints:

CustomerWebRepository.cs

```
public class CustomerWebRepository : IRepository<Customer> {
    readonly HttpClient httpClient = WebApiHttpClient.Instance;
    readonly string CollectionName = "Customers";
}
```

2. Implement the repository interface members. Implement the methods defined in the `IRepository` interface:

CustomerWebRepository.cs

```
public async Task<IEnumerable<Customer>> GetAllAsync() {
    var response = await httpClient.GetAsync(CollectionName);
    response.EnsureSuccessStatusCode();
    return await response.Content
      .ReadAsAsync<IEnumerable<Customer>>();
}
public async Task AddAsync(Customer item) {
    var response = await httpClient
      .PostAsJsonAsync(CollectionName, item);
    response.EnsureSuccessStatusCode();
}
public async Task DeleteAsync(Customer item) {
    var response = await httpClient
      .DeleteAsync($"{CollectionName}/{item.Id}");
    response.EnsureSuccessStatusCode();
}
public async Task<Customer> GetByIdAsync(int id) {
```

```
        var response = await httpClient.GetAsync($"{CollectionName}/
    {id}");
        response.EnsureSuccessStatusCode();
        return await response.Content.ReadAsAsync<Customer>();
    }
    public async Task UpdateAsync(Customer item) {
        var response = await httpClient
        .PutAsJsonAsync( $"{CollectionName}/{item.Id}",
            item);
        response.EnsureSuccessStatusCode();
    }
```

In each method, we access the web API service using the `httpClient` object. We call `EnsureSuccessStatusCode` to throw an exception if an operation fails. In case of an exception, a user will see an alert, which we implemented in the *Handling errors while saving data to a database* recipe.

3. Incorporate the web repository into the unit of work. Update the `CrmUnitOfWork` class to use `CustomerWebRepository` in `CustomersCachedRepository` as the first parameter. Remove the `Context` field and code from the `Dispose` method. Call `ExecuteCacheUpdateActions` and return `Task.CompletedTask` in the `SaveAsync` method:

    ```
    public class CrmUnitOfWork : IDisposable, IUnitOfWork<Customer>
    {
        readonly ICacheService CacheService = MemoryCacheService
          .Instance;
        IRepository<Customer> customerRepository;
        public IRepository<Customer> Items =>
            customerRepository ??= new CustomersCachedRepository(new
              CustomerWebRepository(), CacheService);
        public async Task SaveAsync() {
            CacheService.ExecuteCacheUpdateActions();
            await Task.CompletedTask;
        }
        public void Dispose() { }
    }
    ```

4. That's it! Now, you can run the project. Note that you need to start the web API service first and then start the .NET MAUI application:

I. If you are using Visual Studio, right-click the c4-WebApiServer project and select **Set as Startup Project**:

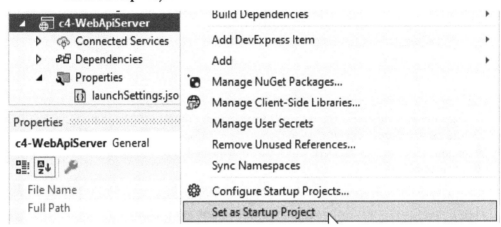

Figure 4.15 – Setting a startup project

II. After that, open the debug options dropdown and select **https**:

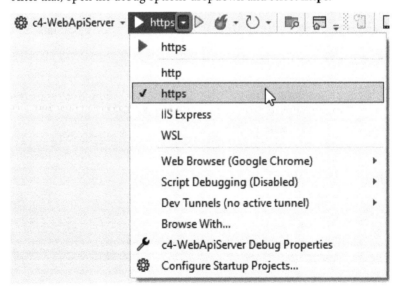

Figure 4.16 – Selecting the startup configuration

III.   Right-click c4-WebApiServer and select **Debug | Start New Instance**:

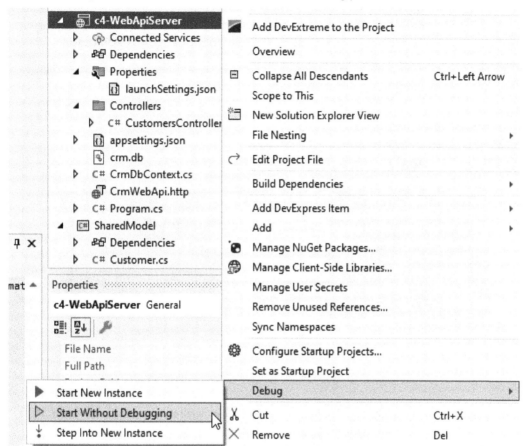

Figure 4.17 – Starting without debugging

IV.   Right-click c4-WebApiMauiClient and select the same action: **Debug | Start New Instance**.

How it works...

In this recipe, we adjusted the CrmUnitOfWork class to utilize CustomerRepository instead of CustomerWebRepository. Thanks to our loosely coupled architecture, the view model, caching, UI, and database validation logic remained unchanged.

In `CustomerWebRepository`, we employed `HttpClient` to interact with web API endpoints. It's crucial to understand that when working with a remote service, client-side classes do not communicate directly with `DbContext` and EF Core. These responsibilities are handled by the Web API server. Therefore, in `CrmUnitOfWork`, we no longer need to call `DbContext.SaveChanges`.

An important implication of this shift is that each create, update, or delete action now saves changes to the database without explicitly calling `DbContext.SaveChanges`.

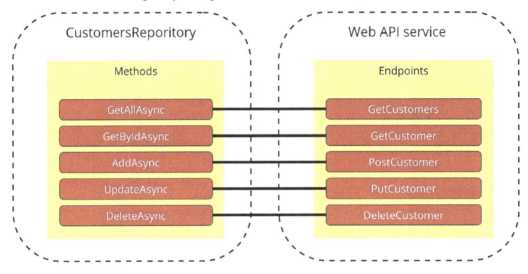

Figure 4.18 – Web API and repository communication

If your application works solely with a remote service, you can usually remove the unit of work layer from the client application without any negative consequences.

There's more...

Android and iOS emulators can access the local machine they are running on using the `10.0.2.2` and `localhost` addresses for Android and iOS, respectively. However, when debugging your application on a real device, accessing your machine directly is not straightforward unless your web API service is published and visible to other devices.

To address this, Visual Studio offers a feature called **dev tunnels**, which creates a debugging URL accessible to other devices. This allows you to debug applications running on real devices more effectively. We will use this technique in the next chapter.

In the meantime, you can learn how to configure dev tunnels in Visual Studio in the following help article: `https://learn.microsoft.com/en-us/connectors/custom-connectors/port-tunneling`.

When prototyping, developing, and testing your application, you can also use the DummyJSON service (`https://dummyjson.com/docs`), which allows you to load fake data in the JSON format. This is especially handy when the web API isn't ready yet, but you've already started working on the client side.

5
Authentication and Authorization

Long before the digital age, the concepts of **authentication** and **authorization** were already in play. The ancient Romans, as described by the Greek historian Polybius, used *watchwords* to control access to guarded areas. In modern realms, when automated systems are constantly executing thousands of operations on our behalf, proper access control is not just a necessity; it's the backbone of secure and efficient operations.

When diving into authentication and authorization, you'll come across a mix of terms that can be confusing since they're often used in similar contexts but have different meanings. To keep things clear, let's go over some of the key terms we'll be using in this chapter:

- **Authentication**: The process of verifying your identity. A basic example would be entering and checking your username and password. However, it can also involve more advanced methods such as fingerprint scanning, face recognition, or **two-factor authentication (2FA)**.

- **Authorization**: Once your identity is confirmed, the next step is figuring out what you're allowed to do. This is where authorization comes in. When a system decides if you can access certain information or perform specific actions, that's authorization in action.

- **Open Authorization (OAuth) 2.0**: An authorization standard that lets third-party apps access your resources without needing your username and password. For example, when you sign in to an app using Google or **Microsoft Entra ID** , OAuth 2.0 allows the app to access what it needs without exposing your credentials. If you're already logged in to Google, you're good to go. If not, you'll be redirected to Google to sign in.

- **OpenID Connect (OIDC)**: An authentication layer built on top of OAuth 2.0. While OAuth 2.0 manages only authorization, OIDC extends the flow and determines how a user is authenticated and what user information is provided. For example, Google authentication uses OIDC to obtain information about the user, authenticate them, and communicate with the client application.

The .NET environment provides several solutions that build upon the foundational concepts of authentication and authorization. With so many options, it's easy to feel overwhelmed, so here's a brief overview of .NET-based technologies related to these topics:

- **Microsoft Entra ID** (formerly known as **Azure AD**): This is a cloud-based **identity and access management** (**IAM**) service designed for organizations. It enables enterprise users to access external resources securely.

- **Microsoft Entra External ID** (successor to **Azure AD Business-to-Consumer** (**Azure AD B2C**)): A cloud-based solution that offers secure access for external users, including accounts from social identity providers such as Google or Facebook.

- **ASP.NET Core Identity**: This framework is designed for managing user authentication and authorization within ASP.NET Core applications. Since it's hosted on your machine, you have full control over the entire authentication and authorization flow. We will make extensive use of ASP.NET Core Identity in this chapter, so you'll become more familiar with it as you work through the recipes.

- **IdentityServer**: IdentityServer is an open source framework for implementing authentication and authorization in .NET applications using OIDC and OAuth 2.0. It's important to note that ASP.NET Core Identity is not built on IdentityServer, and you don't need IdentityServer to support social identity providers like such as Google or Facebook. IdentityServer is necessary when you need to implement your own OAuth-based authentication server. When using Google OAuth, this role is handled by Google's servers.

In this chapter, we will create an authentication server using ASP.NET Core Identity and connect it to a **.NET Multi-platform App UI** (**.NET MAUI**) client application. You'll learn how to configure ASP.NET Core Identity to handle both password-based and social identity provider (such as Google) authentication. We'll walk through building an application with a login form and **role-based access control** (**RBAC**), allowing different roles to perform distinct actions.

Additionally, you'll implement local session storage and fingerprint authentication to streamline the user login process. To round things off, we'll delve into the inner workings of authentication processes, which are crucial for avoiding common mistakes and enhancing security.

In this chapter, we'll be covering the following recipes:

- Creating an authentication service with ASP.NET Core Identity
- Building a client application connected to the authentication service
- Implementing role-based access rules on the server
- Accessing endpoints with role-based access in the client application
- Signing in with a Google account

- Managing secured sessions
- Implementing biometric authentication

Technical requirements

Most of the recipes in this chapter will utilize an ASP.NET Core service for authentication-related operations. To create and run an ASP.NET Core project on Windows, ensure that you have the **ASP. NET and web development** workload installed in Visual Studio. While this chapter primarily uses Visual Studio for Windows, you can also follow the recipes on macOS using VS Code. Although VS Code lacks some of the features available in Visual Studio, you can achieve similar results using the command line.

You can download all the projects created in this chapter from GitHub: `https://github.com/ PacktPublishing/.NET-MAUI-Cookbook/tree/main/Chapter05`

Creating an authentication service with ASP.NET Core Identity

Before the internet era, many applications relied on simple offline authentication mechanisms, where a username and password hash were stored locally. Although some applications still require offline login, most now handle authentication on the server side, which manages users and their permissions.

As noted in the chapter introduction, while there are cloud-based solutions with premium features, we will build our own authentication service using ASP.NET Core Identity. This approach will provide a thorough understanding of authentication and authorization mechanisms and allow us to tailor them to our needs.

In this recipe, we will set up a basic authentication service that enables user registration and password-based login through a browser. In the next recipe, we will develop a client .NET MAUI application that connects to this service.

Getting ready

As mentioned in the *Technical requirements* section of this chapter, you need to ensure that you have the ASP.NET and web development workload installed in Visual Studio. To verify which workloads are installed, follow these steps:

1. Open the Start menu in Windows.
2. Type `Visual Studio Installer`.
3. Click **Modify**.

The following workload should be checked:

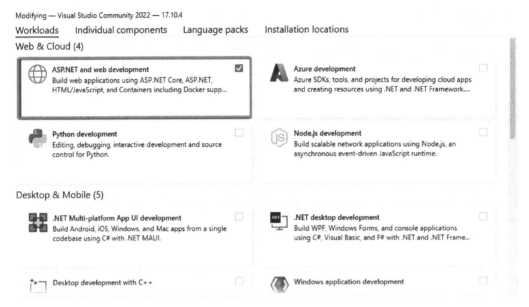

Figure 5.1 – ASP.NET and web development workload

For VS Code instructions, please refer to https://learn.microsoft.com/en-us/aspnet/core/tutorials/first-web-api?&tabs=visual-studio-code.

The code for this recipe is available at https://github.com/PacktPublishing/.NET-MAUI-Cookbook/tree/main/Chapter05/c5-AuthenticationService.

How to do it...

We'll begin by creating a standard ASP.NET Core Web API application and leverage the built-in solutions provided by ASP.NET Core Identity to integrate authentication capabilities. Finally, we'll test the service using **Swagger** in a browser.

> **Swagger**
>
> Swagger (also known as **OpenAPI**) is a set of tools that aids developers in designing, building, documenting, and testing RESTful APIs. It provides an automatically generated **user interface (UI)** that allows you to test a web service directly in your browser.

Let's begin:

1. Create a new ASP.NET Core Web API project:

    I.   Open Visual Studio and click **Create a new project**.

    II.   Type Web API in the search box, select **ASP.NET Core Web API**, and click **Next**.

    III. Enter the project name (for example, c5-AuthenticationService) and click **Next**.

    IV.   Uncheck all options except **Configure for HTTPS** and **Enable OpenAPI support**, then click **Create**. Using HTTPS ensures secure data transmission between client and server, while the OpenAPI option allows us to test the web service in a browser. Ensure that **Use controllers** is unchecked, as we will be using minimal APIs for a more modern and concise configuration. Click **Create**:

Minimal APIs

Minimal APIs in ASP.NET Core are a simplified approach to building HTTP APIs with minimal configuration and a lightweight syntax.

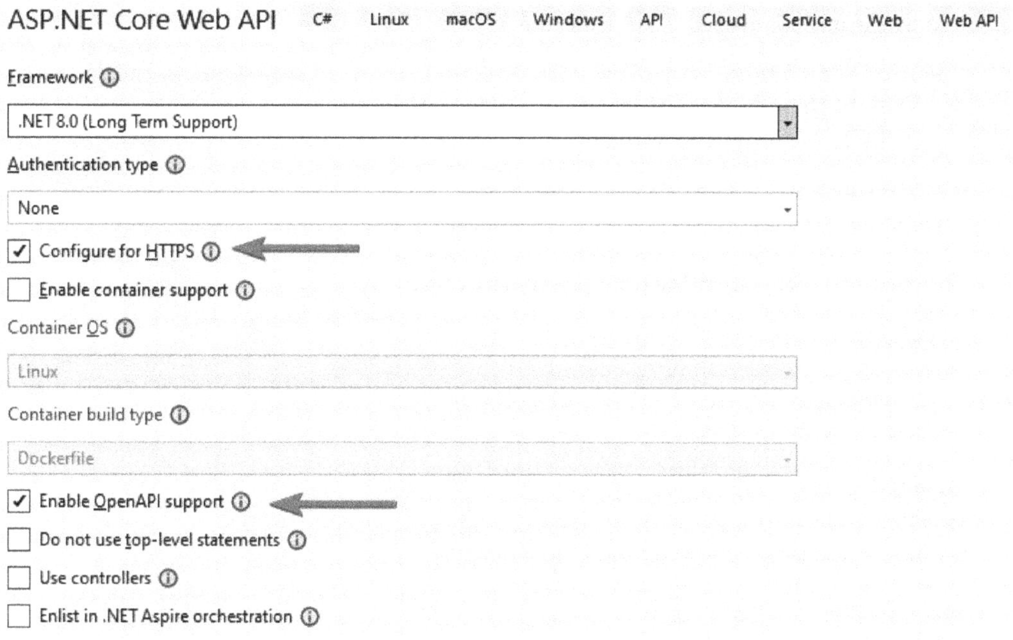

ASP.NET Core Web API   C#   Linux   macOS   Windows   API   Cloud   Service   Web   Web API

Framework ⓘ

.NET 8.0 (Long Term Support)

Authentication type ⓘ

None

☑ Configure for HTTPS ⓘ ◀━━━━━

☐ Enable container support ⓘ

Container OS ⓘ

Linux

Container build type ⓘ

Dockerfile

☑ Enable OpenAPI support ⓘ ◀━━━━━

☐ Do not use top-level statements ⓘ

☐ Use controllers ⓘ

☐ Enlist in .NET Aspire orchestration ⓘ

Figure 5.2 – ASP.NET Core Web API project options

2. Remove the default `weatherforecast` endpoint and `WeatherForecast` record definition from the `Program.cs` file:

```
//var summaries = new []
//{
    //…
//};
//app.MapGet ("/weatherforecast", () =>
//{
    //…
//})
//.WithName ("GetWeatherForecast")
//.WithOpenApi ();

//internal record WeatherForecast(DateOnly Date, int
TemperatureC, string? Summary) { …  }
```

3. Install the following NuGet packages:

-   `Microsoft.EntityFrameworkCore`: To use **Entity Framework Core (EF Core)** for storing data and managing authentication.

-   `Microsoft.EntityFrameworkCore.Sqlite`: For using SQLite as the database. Note that SQLite is recommended primarily for client-side use due to its limited scalability, security, and concurrency features.

-   `Microsoft.AspNetCore.Identity.EntityFrameworkCore`: Provides components to integrate ASP.NET Core Identity with EF Core.

4. Create a `User` class inheriting from `IdentityUser`:

```
public class User . IdentityUser
{
    public DateOnly BirthDate { get; set; }
}
```

In ASP.NET Core Identity, `IdentityUser` is the base class for application users managed by the system. It includes basic properties for user management, such as `UserName`, `PhoneNumber`, and `Email`, so there's no need to add them manually.

5. Create an `ApplicationDbContext` class inheriting from `IdentityDbContext`:

```
public class ApplicationDbContext :
  IdentityDbContext<User>
{
```

```
    public ApplicationDbContext(
    DbContextOptions<ApplicationDbContext> options
    ) : base(options) { }
}
```

The `ApplicationDbContext` class will handle database operations related to identity users.

6. In the `Program.cs` file, configure authentication by adding the following code before calling the `builder.Build()` method:

Program.cs

```
builder.Services.AddAuthentication()
    .AddBearerToken(IdentityConstants.BearerScheme);
builder.Services.AddIdentityCore<User>()
    .AddEntityFrameworkStores<ApplicationDbContext>()
    .AddApiEndpoints()
    .AddDefaultTokenProviders();
```

- `AddAuthentication` registers the services necessary for authentication in ASP.NET Core Identity.

- `AddBearerToken` configures the identity system to use bearer access tokens. A bearer token is a secret string used by a client to prove it has permission to access a resource. ASP.NET Core Identity supports the automatic generation of bearer tokens.

- `AddIdentityCore` adds and configures the identity system for the specified `User` type.

- `AddEntityFrameworkStores` informs the identity system to use the `ApplicationDbContext` class created in the previous step.

- `AddApiEndpoints` registers default endpoints for identity operations, such as `registration` and `login`.

- `AddDefaultTokenProviders` registers default token providers for generating and validating access tokens used in identity management.

7. Next, call `AddDbContext` to set up EF Core with SQLite for database operations:

```
builder.Services.AddDbContext<ApplicationDbContext>(options =>
    options.UseSqlite(@"Data Source=mydatabase.db"));
```

Although `AddEntityFrameworkStores<ApplicationDbContext>` was called previously, you still need to configure `ApplicationDbContext` separately.

8. Call `MapIdentityApi` just before `app.Run()` in the `Program.cs` file to set up routes for the registered identity endpoints, making them available to the client:

```
app.MapIdentityApi<User>();
```

9. Obtain an instance of `ApplicationDbContext` using a **service provider** (SP) and call `EnsureCreated` to create the database if it doesn't exist. Add this code before `app.Run()`:

```
using (var scope = app.Services.CreateScope())
{
    var dbContext = scope.ServiceProvider
      .GetRequiredService<ApplicationDbContext>();
    dbContext.Database.EnsureCreated();
}
```

10. Now, run the project. After running the project, a browser should open with a Swagger UI (thanks to the OpenAPI support added in *step 1*). Since `AddApiEndpoints` and `MapIdentityApi` were called in *steps 6* and *8*, you'll see basic endpoints for user management. To test registration and login:

I.   Expand the `/register` item and click **Try it out**:

Figure 5.3 – Registering with Swagger

II.   In the **Request body** section, enter an email and password for a new user and click **Execute**:

```
{
  "email": "test@test.com",
  "password": "123Password123!"
}
```

Note that passwords should contain lowercase and uppercase letters, digits, and special characters. If successful, you should see `Success` in the response description, indicating that the user has been created.

III. Now, you can log in using the specified credentials. Expand the `/login` item and click **Try it out**. Since bearer token authentication is used, select **false** for `useCookies` and `useSessionCookies`:

Figure 5.4 – Logging in with Swagger

IV. In the **Request body** section, enter the email and password specified earlier. Leave other parameters at their default values:

```
{
    "email": " test@test.com",
    "password": "123Password123!",
    "twoFactorCode": "string",
    "twoFactorRecoveryCode": "string"
}
```

In **Response body**, you should see text similar to the following:

```
{
    "tokenType": "Bearer",
    "accessToken": "CfDJ8ENrCbboN0tArI5SaUti2haO…",
    "expiresIn": 3600,
    "refreshToken": "CfDJ8ENrCbboN0tArI5SaUti2hY…"
}
```

Here is a description of the returned values:

- `tokenType` indicates the token type used. Since `AddBearerToken` was called, the type is `"Bearer"`.

- `accessToken` can be used to access protected endpoints.

- `expiresIn` denotes the duration (in seconds) for which the access token is valid. For example, a value of `3600` means the token is valid for 1 hour.

- `refreshToken` is a token used to obtain a new access token after the current one expires.

How it works...

The authentication server we created includes the following key components:

- **Endpoints**: These act as connectors between the server and the outside world. They handle incoming requests, invoke authentication logic if necessary, and return responses to clients. For instance, we used the register endpoint to create a new user and the login endpoint to authenticate and obtain an access token.

- **Middleware**: This is a chain of handlers that process a request. When an endpoint is called, ASP.NET Core processes it through multiple middleware components, each serving a specific function such as authentication or authorization. In addition to authentication-related middleware, ASP.NET Core apps include other layers, such as those for exception handling, cookie management, and session management.

- **Database**: In our scenario, an SQLite database stores information about application users, their roles, tokens, and other related data.

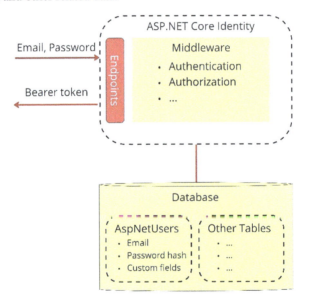

Figure 5.5 – ASP.NET Core Identity elements

When testing endpoints in the browser, we utilized the UI generated by Swagger (also known as OpenAPI). Swagger uses an OpenAPI specification to describe the structure of your API and generates a UI based on this description. Beyond testing, OpenAPI helps other developers understand the available endpoints and the parameters they require. This is particularly useful for API services accessed by other developers who need to understand the functionality your service provides.

There's more...

When you run an ASP.NET Core project, it operates on a local server that is not accessible from other devices unless you open ports for external connections and use a specific IP associated with your machine. Although Android and iOS emulators offer reserved addresses for accessing the host machine (for example, `https://10.0.2.2` for Android and `https://localhost` for iOS), the usage of these addresses may be inconvenient due to the following reasons:

- Since Android and iOS use different addresses to access the host machine, you need to write platform-specific code.

- Testing on real devices is challenging because connecting via USB does not automatically make the server accessible. You either need to include the device in your local network or make the service available from external networks.

- By default, ASP.NET Core applications do not provide a signed certificate. Android and iOS have built-in certificate checks that require a custom `HttpMessageHandler` class to use HTTPS instead of HTTP. HTTPS is necessary for Google OAuth, so we need it to test Google account authentication.

To address these issues, you can use dev tunnels, a feature available in .NET. Although we mentioned it in the previous chapter, we did not configure it at that time. This chapter will guide you through creating a tunnel using Visual Studio, which will be used in the following recipes.

> **macOS**
>
> macOS users can use the console `devtunnel` tool provided by .NET. Instructions can be found here: `https://github.com/PacktPublishing/.NET-MAUI-Cookbook/tree/main/Chapter05/c5-AuthenticationServiceAndClient#vs-code`. You need to create a persistent public tunnel with a preserved DNS name, which is crucial for working with Google OAuth due to its redirection steps.

1. In Visual Studio, right-click on the `c5-AuthenticationService` project and select **Set as Startup Project**:

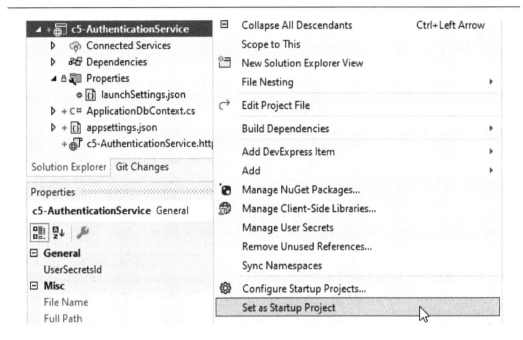

Figure 5.6 – Setting a startup project

2. Click the dropdown arrow next to the play (start debugging) button and select **Dev Tunnels | Create a Tunnel**:

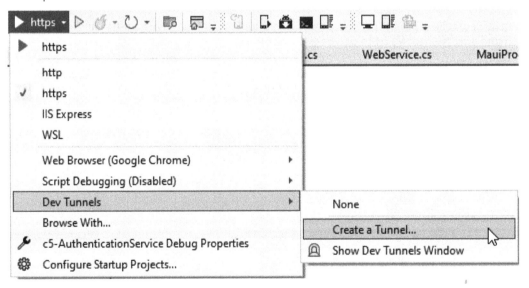

Figure 5.7 – Creating a new tunnel item

3. Log in to your account if you haven't already. You can use your Microsoft, GitHub, or Entra ID accounts. Enter a tunnel name, then select **Persistent** in the **Tunnel Type** field and **Public** in the **Access** field:

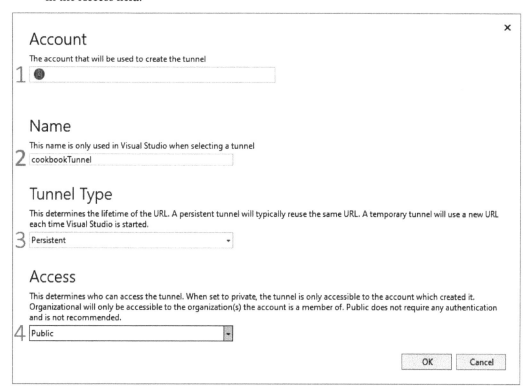

Figure 5.8 – Tunnel creation dialog

Note that Visual Studio may take 15-20 seconds to create the tunnel.

4. Run the project to activate the tunnel. A browser should open with a message informing you that you are about to connect to the tunnel. Click **Continue**. You should see the same Swagger window as before, but now the tunnel is accessible from the outside world. You can even connect to it from your phone by entering the address from the browser's URL string.

5. Open the **Dev Tunnels** window by selecting the **Debug** dropdown | **Dev Tunnels** | **Show Dev Tunnels Window**:

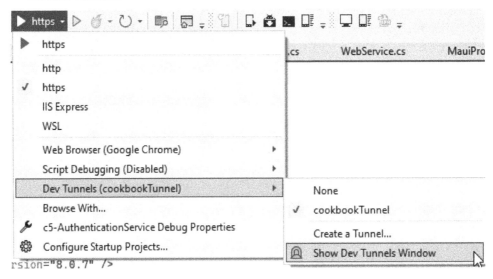

Figure 5.9 – Opening the Dev Tunnels window

6. Click the **Settings** icon and check **Use Tunnel Domain**. This operation might take 1-2 minutes:

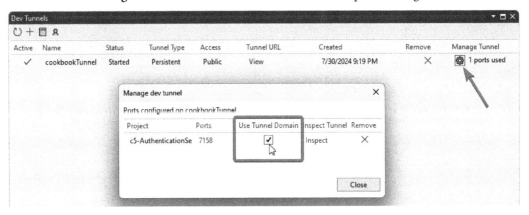

Figure 5.10 – Activating a tunnel domain

By default, a tunnel overrides the HTTP host header to localhost, which works for simple usage scenarios. However, this can cause issues with authentication processes involving redirections and URL checks. For example, during Google authentication, Google redirects your app to a URL registered in the Google Developer Console. It is crucial that this URL's base address matches the URL of your service. We will cover this topic in greater detail in the *Signing in with a Google account* recipe.

Building a client application connected to the authentication service

Once we have an authentication service, building a simple login form is straightforward. We can use the standard `HttpClient` class to send HTTP requests and receive responses.

We will create a simple login form with two editors and a **Log In** button that sends an email and password to the server. To maintain a structured code base, we will place all communication logic into a separate `WebService` class. The view model will act as an intermediary between the view and the service:

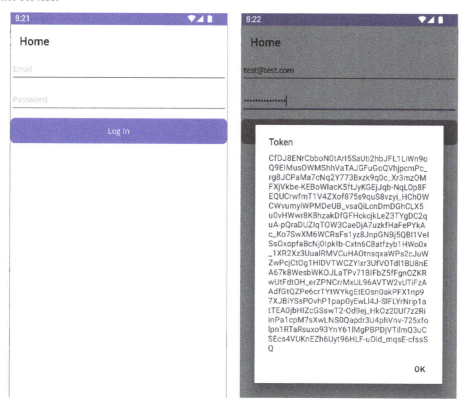

Figure 5.11 – Basic app with a login form

Note that when your service is hosted on your local machine, external devices cannot access it unless you create a tunnel. In this and other recipes, we will use the dev tunnel configured in the previous recipe in the *There's more…* section. This allows you to test your application from emulators and real devices even if they are not connected to your local network.

Getting ready

Start with the project you got after finishing the previous recipe (*Creating an authentication service with ASP.NET Core Identity*). This project is available at `https://github.com/PacktPublishing/.NET-MAUI-Cookbook/tree/main/Chapter05/c5-AuthenticationService`.

> **Important note**
> It's important that you complete the steps of the *There's more...* section of the previous recipe and configure dev tunnels to access the authentication service from your emulator or device.

The code for this recipe is available at `https://github.com/PacktPublishing/.NET-MAUI-Cookbook/tree/main/Chapter05/c5-AuthenticationServiceAndClient`.

How to do it...

Let's create a simple UI client to access the service created in the previous recipe:

1. Add a new .NET MAUI project to the solution that you obtained after following the previous recipe or downloading it from `https://github.com/PacktPublishing/.NET-MAUI-Cookbook/tree/main/Chapter05/c5-AuthenticationService`. Right-click the solution in **Solution Explorer** and select **Add | New Project**.

2. Replace the default elements in `MainView` with a vertical stack panel containing an email and password entry, along with a button to trigger the login action:

MainView.xaml

```
<VerticalStackLayout Spacing="10">
    <Entry Placeholder="Email"
           Text="{Binding Email}"/>
    <Entry Placeholder="Password"
           Text="{Binding Password}"
           IsPassword="True"/>
    <Button Text="Log In"
            Command="{Binding LogInCommand}"/>
</VerticalStackLayout>
```

Remove unnecessary code from the `MainPage.xaml.cs` file and leave only the page constructor.

3. Add the `CommunityToolkit.Mvvm` NuGet package. This package allows the use of autogenerated properties and commands.

4. Define a `MainViewModel` class with `Email` and `Password` properties and a `LogInAsync` command:

```
public partial class MainViewModel : ObservableObject
{
    [ObservableProperty]
    string email;
    [ObservableProperty]
    string password;
    [RelayCommand]
    async Task LogInAsync()
    {
    }
}
```

5. Assign `BindingContext` in `MainView.xaml` to `MainViewModel`:

```
xmlns:local="clr-namespace:c5_AuthenticationClient"
<ContentPage.BindingContext>
    <local:MainViewModel/>
</ContentPage.BindingContext>
```

6. Create a `WebService` class. This class will handle all server communication. Instantiate `HttpClient` and assign it to a field. Set the base address using your dev tunnel URL:

```
public class WebService
{
    static string baseAddress = "[Your Dev Tunnel URL]";
    HttpClient httpClient = new HttpClient()
      { BaseAddress = new Uri(baseAddress) };
    public static WebService Instance { get; } = new();
}
```

Make sure that you configured a tunnel as described in the *There's more…* section of the previous recipe. As a base address, use your dev tunnel URL. You can find it in a browser URL string after running your ASP.NET Core server app. Make sure that you have a slash at the end of your base address URL (for example, `https://xxxxxxxx-1111.asse.devtunnels.ms/`). If your ASP.NET Core server app is run on localhost, set `c5-AuthenticationService` as the startup project and select your previously created tunnel in the **Dev Tunnels** pop-up menu under the **Debug** dropdown:

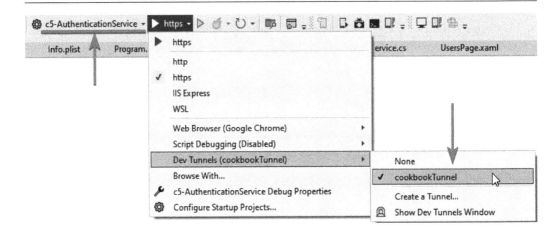

Figure 5.12 – Selecting an existing tunnel

7. Add the RequestTokenAsync and SetAuthHeader methods to the WebService class. RequestTokenAsync posts data to a specified URL and deserializes the response into BearerTokenInfo. SetAuthHeader sets the authorization header for subsequent requests. This will include the token in all further requests, which allows us to access protected endpoints:

```
async Task<BearerTokenInfo> RequestTokenAsync(string
  url, object postContent)
{
    HttpResponseMessage response = await
      httpClient.PostAsync(url, new StringContent(
        JsonSerializer.Serialize(postContent),
        Encoding.UTF8,
        "application/json")
      );
    response.EnsureSuccessStatusCode();
    BearerTokenInfo tokenInfo = await response.Content
      .ReadFromJsonAsync<BearerTokenInfo>();
    tokenInfo.TokenTimestamp = DateTime.UtcNow;
    SetAuthHeader(tokenInfo.AccessToken);
    return tokenInfo;
}
public void SetAuthHeader(string token)
{
    httpClient.DefaultRequestHeaders.Authorization =
      new AuthenticationHeaderValue("Bearer", token);
}
```

Setting `TokenTimestamp` to `DateTime.UtcNow` will allow us to save the time when we obtained the token. This will allow us to determine when we need to refresh the token.

8. Simplify the usage of the `RequestTokenAsync` method by wrapping it in the `Authenticate` method:

```
public async Task<BearerTokenInfo> Authenticate(string
    email, string password)
{
    return await RequestTokenAsync("login/",
      new { email, password });
}
```

9. Create a `BearerTokenInfo` class. We will use this `BearerTokenInfo` class to store the access and refresh tokens, the token timestamp, and the expiration period:

```
public class BearerTokenInfo
{
    public string AccessToken { get; set; }
    public int ExpiresIn { get; set; }
    public string RefreshToken { get; set; }
    public DateTime? TokenTimestamp { get; set; }
}
```

10. Add a `webService` field to `MainViewModel` and implement the `LogInAsync` method. In `LogInAsync`, call `Authenticate` and display a message to a user with the obtained token. If an exception is raised, display its text in a `catch` block:

MainViewModel.cs

```
public partial class MainViewModel : ObservableObject
{
    WebService webService = WebService.Instance;
    [RelayCommand]
    async Task LogInAsync()
    {
        try
        {
            BearerTokenInfo tokenInfo =
              await webService.Authenticate(Email,
                Password);
            await Shell.Current.DisplayAlert(
              "Token", tokenInfo.AccessToken, "OK");
        }
        catch (Exception ex)
```

```
            {
                await Shell.Current.DisplayAlert("Error",
                    ex.Message, "OK");
            }
        }
    }
```

Now, you can run the project. Start the service project first (ensure your dev tunnel is activated). Then, start the client .NET MAUI app and enter the email and password you registered in the previous recipe (email: test@test.com; password: 123Password123!).

How it works...

We implemented all logic related to server communication in a WebService class. One of its main methods is RequestTokenAsync, which sends a POST request to the server and deserializes a token from the response. The server returns the token as a JSON string with the following format:

```
{
    "tokenType": "Bearer",
    "accessToken": "CfDJ8ENrCbboN0tArI5SaUti2haO…",
    "expiresIn": 3600,
    "refreshToken": "CfDJ8ENrCbboN0tArI5SaUti2hY…"
}
```

We can use the ReadFromJsonAsync method and create a BearerTokenInfo instance directly from the JSON string because the BearerTokenInfo class properties have similar names to attributes in the retrieved JSON:

```
BearerTokenInfo tokenInfo = await response.Content
    .ReadFromJsonAsync<BearerTokenInfo>(),
```

After obtaining the token, we assign it to the default authorization header of HttpClient to access protected endpoints in further recipes:

```
httpClient.DefaultRequestHeaders.Authorization =
    new AuthenticationHeaderValue("Bearer", token);
```

The first parameter in the AuthenticationHeaderValue constructor specifies the authentication scheme. We pass "Bearer" to the constructor because we are using bearer tokens.

There's more…

In the `MainViewModel.LogInAsync` method, we use a `try/catch` block with general exception handling when calling `WebService.Authenticate`:

```
async Task LogInAsync() {
    try {
        await webService.Authenticate(Email, Password);
        await Shell.Current.GoToAsync(nameof(UsersPage));
    }
    catch (Exception ex) {
        await Shell.Current.DisplayAlert("Error",
            ex.Message, "OK");
    }
}
```

While this approach allows us to handle all types of errors, typically, it is better to avoid showing raw errors to the user. A more refined technique is to catch specific exception types and check their properties, as in the following example:

```
catch (HttpRequestException e) when (e.StatusCode ==
    HttpStatusCode.BadRequest) {
    //…
}
catch (HttpRequestException e) when (e.StatusCode ==
    HttpStatusCode.NotFound) {
    //…
}
```

Implementing role-based access rules on the server

In applications, RBAC is essential for managing different levels of permissions and access. This approach allows for varying capabilities based on user roles, such as differentiating between administrators and standard users. ASP.NET Core Identity provides built-in support for managing user roles and configuring access rules.

In this recipe, we will implement several endpoints with different access rules to demonstrate RBAC:

- `/users`: Returns all users registered in the system. Accessible only to authenticated users.

- `/users/delete/{email}`: Deletes a user with the specified email. Accessible only to admin users.

- /users/candelete: Determines if a user can delete other users. Accessible to all users but returns true only for admin users.

- /me: Returns information about the currently authenticated user. Accessible only to authenticated users.

We will also populate our database with predefined users assigned different roles for testing purposes in Swagger.

Getting ready

Start with the project you completed in the previous recipe (*Building a client application connected to the authentication service*). This project is available at https://github.com/PacktPublishing/.NET-MAUI-Cookbook/tree/main/Chapter05/c5-AuthenticationServiceAndClient.

The code for this recipe is available at https://github.com/PacktPublishing/.NET-MAUI-Cookbook/tree/main/Chapter05/c5-RoleBasedAccessPart1.

How to do it...

Let's create two roles, Admin and User, and assign corresponding policies to them (AdminPolicy and UserPolicy). After that, create different endpoints available either to admins or all users. When an authenticated user makes a request, ASP.NET Core Identity will automatically check a user role and decide if access is allowed:

1. First, add role management services to your application. This involves calling the AddRoles method in conjunction with AddIdentityCore:

    ```
    builder.Services.AddIdentityCore<User>().
    AddRoles<IdentityRole>()
        .AddEntityFrameworkStores<ApplicationDbContext>()
        .AddApiEndpoints()
        .AddDefaultTokenProviders();
    ```

    Note that AddIdentityCore should already be present since we added it in the *Creating an authentication service with ASP.NET Core Identity* recipe. AddIdentityCore adds the services that are important for user-management actions, such as user creation and password management, while AddRoles allows us to additionally introduce and manage user roles.

2. Add an AddAuthorization call and create admin and user policies and roles in the following manner:

    ```
    builder.Services.AddAuthorization(options =>
    {
        options.AddPolicy("AdminPolicy", policy =>
    ```

```
        policy.RequireRole("Admin"));
    options.AddPolicy("UserPolicy", policy =>
        policy.RequireRole("User"));
});
```

3. Let's create our first protected endpoint that returns all users in the system. To allow accessing it only for authenticated users, you need to add a `RequireAuthorization` call at the end:

```
app.MapGet("/users", async (
    UserManager<User> userManager) =>
    {
        var users = await userManager.Users
            .Select(u => new
            {
                u.Email,
                u.BirthDate
            })
            .ToListAsync();
        return Results.Ok(users);
    }).RequireAuthorization();
```

In the endpoint body, we use the `UserManager` object to access the storage of users. Since we don't need to return all information about users (such as their hashed passwords), we create a new anonymous object with only `Email` and `BirthDate` properties. The `userManager` parameter is automatically injected by the **dependency injection** (**DI**) system provided by ASP.NET Core.

4. Add a delete endpoint by calling `MapDelete`. Let's make this endpoint available only to admins. To do this, call `RequireAuthorization` with `"AdminPolicy"` as a parameter:

```
app.MapDelete("/users/delete/{email}", async (
    string email,
    UserManager<User> userManager,
    HttpContext httpContext) =>
    {
        var user =
            await userManager.FindByEmailAsync(email);
        if (user == null)
        {
            return Results.NotFound();
        }
        var result =
            await userManager.DeleteAsync(user);
        if (result.Succeeded)
        {
```

```
            return Results.Ok();
        }
        return Results.Problem("Failed to delete the user.");
    }).RequireAuthorization("AdminPolicy");
```

In the endpoint, we try to find a user by an associated email and delete the user from the system by calling `UserManager.DeleteAsync`.

5. Let's create an endpoint that will return `true` or `false` depending on whether the delete action is allowed. This will help us determine if the delete operation is available in advance before trying to execute it:

```
app.MapGet("/users/candelete", async (
    HttpContext httpContext,
    IAuthorizationService authorizationService) =>
    {
        var authResult =
            await authorizationService.AuthorizeAsync(
                httpContext.User, "AdminPolicy");
        return Results.Ok(authResult.Succeeded);
    });
```

The `HttpContext.User` property contains information about the current user who executed the request. `AuthorizeAsync` checks if the user meets the specified policy. Unlike `RequireAuthorization`, the `AuthorizeAsync` method allows you to implement more complex logic during the authorization check and execute specific actions if required.

6. Create a simple endpoint that returns information about the currently logged-in user. We will use the `ClaimsPrincipal` object to get the current user email and then call `UserManager.FindByEmailAsync` to find the `User` object in storage to get access to all user properties:

```
app.MapGet("/me", async (ClaimsPrincipal principal,
    UserManager<User> userManager) =>
{
        string userEmail = principal.Claims.First(c =>
            c.Type == ClaimTypes.Email).Value;
        User currentUser =
            await userManager.FindByEmailAsync(userEmail);
        return Results.Ok(new
        {
            currentUser.Email,
            currentUser.BirthDate
        });
}).RequireAuthorization();
```

7. We will need to create new users in our system, so create a separate `UserManagerExtensions` class and incorporate logic related to user creation in the `CreateUserWithRoleAsync` method. This method will accept a `RoleManager` object and a role name to create users with roles. Additionally, it will use information about the created user: email, password, and birth date.

Before creating a user, check if it already exists by calling `FindByEmailAsync`. After that, call `CreateAsync`. In a general case, users can be created without a password (for example, if Google OAuth is used), so we will check the `password` parameter and call another `CreateAsync` overload if the password is empty. To create and assign a role to a user, it's sufficient to call the `RoleManager.CreateAsync` and `UserManager.AddToRoleAsync` methods:

```
public static class UserManagerExtensions
{
    public static async Task<IResult>
      CreateUserWithRoleAsync(
        this UserManager<User> userManager,
        RoleManager<IdentityRole> roleManager,
        string email,
        string password,
        DateOnly birthDate,
        string roleName)
    {
        User user =
          await userManager.FindByEmailAsync(email);
        if (user != null)
            Results.BadRequest("A user with this email already
exists");
        user = new User { UserName = email,
          Email = email, BirthDate = birthDate };
        IdentityResult result = null;
        if (string.IsNullOrEmpty(password))
            result =
              await userManager.CreateAsync(user);
        else
            result =
              await userManager.CreateAsync(user,
                password);
        if (result.Succeeded)
        {
            if (!await roleManager.RoleExistsAsync(
                roleName))
            {
                await roleManager.CreateAsync(
                  new IdentityRole(roleName));
            }
```

```
        await userManager.AddToRoleAsync(user,
          roleName);
        return Results.Ok("User registered successfully");
    }
    return Results.BadRequest(result.Errors);
  }
}
```

8. To populate your database with users, locate the code where you call the `EnsureCreated` method and use the `CreateUserWithRoleAsync` method created in the previous step:

Program.cs

```
using (var scope = app.Services.CreateScope())
{
    var services = scope.ServiceProvider;
    var dbContext = services
      .GetRequiredService<ApplicationDbContext>();
    dbContext.Database.EnsureCreated();
    var userManager = services
      .GetRequiredService<UserManager<User>>();
    var roleManager = services
      .GetRequiredService<RoleManager<IdentityRole>>();
    await userManager.CreateUserWithRoleAsync(
        roleManager,
        "admin@cookbook.com",
        "123Password123!",
        new DateOnly(1991,4,20),
        "Admin");
    for (int i = 1; i < 10; i++)
    {
        await userManager.CreateUserWithRoleAsync(
            roleManager,
            $"user{i}@cookbook.com",
            "123Password123!",
            new DateOnly(2000, 1, i),
            "User");
    }
}
```

9. Next, configure Swagger for authorization. Modify the `AddSwaggerGen` method to enable authorization capabilities in Swagger:

```
builder.Services.AddSwaggerGen(c =>
{
    c.SwaggerDoc("v1", new OpenApiInfo
    {
        Title = "WebAPI API",
        Version = "v1",
    });
    c.AddSecurityDefinition("Bearer", new
      OpenApiSecurityScheme()
    {
        Type = SecuritySchemeType.Http,
        Name = "Bearer",
        Scheme = "bearer",
        BearerFormat = "Bearer",
        In = ParameterLocation.Header
    });
    c.AddSecurityRequirement(new OpenApiSecurityRequirement()
        {
            {
                new OpenApiSecurityScheme() {
                    Reference = new OpenApiReference() {
                    Type = ReferenceType.SecurityScheme,
                    Id = "Bearer"}},
                new string[0]
            },
        });
});
```

The `SwaggerDoc` method defines a Swagger document with a specific title and version. `AddSecurityDefinition` defines a security scheme that Swagger will use to document the authentication methods. `AddSecurityRequirement` specifies the security requirements applied to all operations in the API. In our case, it enforces the use of the `Bearer` token authentication security scheme.

10. You can test our endpoints in Swagger as follows:

I.   Run the application, expand the `/login` item, and click **Try it out**. Set `useCookies` and `useSessionCookies` to `false` and type `user1@cookbook.com` as an email and `123Password123!` as a password:

Figure 5.13 – Invoking a login action in Swagger

II.   Copy the accessToken value from the **Response body** section:

Figure 5.14 – Access token in Swagger

III. Click the **Authorize** button in the top-right corner of the page and paste the copied token into the **Value** field. Click **Authorize**:

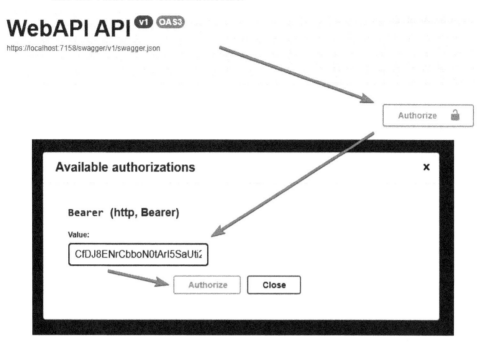

Figure 5.15 – Authorizing in Swagger

IV. Expand the /me item in the main list of endpoints, click **Try it out**, and then **Execute**. You should see information about the current user in the **Response body** section.

V. Expand the /users/delete/{email} item, click **Try it out**, enter user2@cookbook.com into the Email **field**, and click **Execute**. You should see a 401 error, which means that the current user cannot access this endpoint.

VI. Repeat all these steps, starting with the login endpoint, but now use admin@cookbook.com as an email in the **Request body** section. After getting the token and authorizing it as an admin user, you should be able to delete a user using the users/delete/{email} endpoint.

How it works...

Let's summarize the main APIs we used to implement authorization and user management in our service:

- AddRoles to configure role management services
- AddAuthorization to configure authorization

- `AddPolicy` to add admin and user policies

- `RequireAuthorization` to let ASP.NET Core Identity know that an endpoint requires authorization and a specified policy

- `IAuthorizationService`, whose `AuthorizeAsync` method we used to dynamically check if a user meets a policy and can perform a certain action in our endpoint

- `RoleManager` to create roles and assign them to users via the `CreateAsync` and `AddToRoleAsync` methods

- `UserManager` to create and return application users

ASP.NET Core Identity handles all underlying tasks related to authorization automatically. This includes validating access tokens in API requests, associating them with users, and checking if a user's role meets the access requirements specified in an endpoint.

Configuring Swagger in the `AddSwaggerGen` method adds an **Authorize** button to the Swagger UI. This feature allows you to test and debug access rules directly in the browser before creating a client application.

There's more...

When creating a policy, we added only one requirement to it – that a user should have the `Admin` role:

```
options.AddPolicy("AdminPolicy", policy => policy.
RequireRole("Admin"));
```

However, you can easily create more complex policies involving multiple requirements. For example, the following code creates a policy requiring that a user must have a `Level` claim type whose value is `Zero`:

```
options.AddPolicy("AdminZeroPolicy", policy =>
{
    policy.RequireRole("Admin");
    policy.RequireClaim("Level", "Zero");
});
```

You can add a custom claim to a user by defining a corresponding property in the `User` class:

```
public class User : IdentityUser
{
    public string Level { get; set; }
}
```

For more complex rules, you can create an `AuthorizationHandler` descendant and override the `HandleRequirementAsync` method. Additionally, it's necessary to create a class implementing the `IAuthorizationRequirement` interface to further register it in a policy requirement:

```
public class CustomRequirement(string someParameter) :
IAuthorizationRequirement {
    public string SomeParameter { get; } = someParameter;
}
public class CustomRequirementHandler :
  AuthorizationHandler<CustomRequirement> {
    protected override Task
      HandleRequirementAsync(AuthorizationHandlerContext
        context, CustomRequirement requirement) {
          if (...) {
            context.Succeed(requirement);
          }
          else {
            context.Fail();
          }
          return Task.CompletedTask;
        }
}
```

To allow or prohibit an action, call `Succeed` or `Fail` methods correspondingly. To use the custom requirement in a policy, add it to the `Requirements` collection and register `CustomRequirementHandler` in a DI container:

```
builder.Services.AddAuthorization(options =>
{
    options.AddPolicy("CustomPolicy", policy =>
        policy.Requirements.Add(new
          CustomRequirement("Some Value")));
});
builder.Services.AddSingleton<IAuthorizationHandler,
  CustomRequirementHandler>();
```

Accessing endpoints with role-based access in the client application

How to access a secured endpoint from a client app? How to determine if a certain action is available to the current user and enable corresponding UI elements? We will address these questions in this recipe.

We'll build upon the application from the previous recipe. After a user logs in, their email will be displayed in the window title. We will also load data from an endpoint that is accessible only to authenticated users. Additionally, we'll add a **Delete** button that will be visible only to users with the Admin role.

Getting ready

Start with the project you completed in the previous recipe (*Implementing role-based access rules on the server*). This project is available at https://github.com/PacktPublishing/.NET-MAUI-Cookbook/tree/main/Chapter05/c5-RoleBasedAccessPart1.

The code for this recipe is available at https://github.com/PacktPublishing/.NET-MAUI-Cookbook/tree/main/Chapter05/c5-RoleBasedAccessPart2.

To test the app, you need to update the WebService.baseAddress field (c5-AuthenticationClient/Model/WebService) so that it includes your dev tunnel address and run the ASP.NET Core project before the .NET MAUI project.

How to do it...

In this recipe, we will add methods to the WebService class to consume protected web API endpoints. After that, we will create a view model and view to present data after the login screen.

Let's start with adjusting WebService:

1. Navigate to the c5-AuthenticationClient project within the solution you obtained from the previous recipe or downloaded from https://github.com/PacktPublishing/.NET-MAUI-Cookbook/tree/main/Chapter05/c5-RoleBasedAccessPart1. Add a new class named User to the project. This class should include only the properties returned by the users endpoint that was created in the previous recipe:

    ```
    public class User
      {
          public string Email { get; set; }
          public DateOnly BirthDate { get; set; }
      }
    ```

2. In the `WebService` class, create a `GetUsersAsync` method to request a list of users. Use the standard `GetAsync` method available in `HttpClient` to make the request. Once you receive the response, deserialize the collection using the `JsonSerializer` class:

WebService.cs

```
public async Task<IEnumerable<User>> GetUsersAsync()
{
    HttpResponseMessage response =
      await httpClient.GetAsync("users");
    response.EnsureSuccessStatusCode();
    string json =
      await response.Content.ReadAsStringAsync();
    return JsonSerializer.Deserialize<List<User>>(
      json, new JsonSerializerOptions
    {
        PropertyNameCaseInsensitive = true
    });
}
```

3. Add a method to delete a user by their email address. To do this, call the `users/delete/{email}` endpoint using the `HttpClient.DeleteAsync` method:

WebService.cs

```
public async Task DeleteUserAsync(string email)
{
    var response = await
      httpClient.DeleteAsync($"users/delete/{email}");
        response.EnsureSuccessStatusCode();
}
```

4. Let's add a method to check if the currently authenticated user is allowed to delete other users. To do this, call the `users/candelete` endpoint:

WebService.cs

```
public async Task<bool> CanDeleteUsersAsync()
{
    HttpResponseMessage response =
      await httpClient.GetAsync("users/candelete");
    response.EnsureSuccessStatusCode();
    string json =
      await response.Content.ReadAsStringAsync();
```

```
        return JsonSerializer.Deserialize<bool>(json);
}
```

5. Create a method to obtain information about the currently logged-in user:

WebService.cs

```
public async Task<User> GetCurrentUserAsync()
{
    HttpResponseMessage response =
      await httpClient.GetAsync("me");
    response.EnsureSuccessStatusCode();
    string json =
      await response.Content.ReadAsStringAsync();
    return JsonSerializer.Deserialize<User>(json,
      new JsonSerializerOptions
    {
        PropertyNameCaseInsensitive = true
    });
}
```

6. Next, let's use these methods in your view models. Create a `UsersViewModel` class that includes the following properties: `Users`, `LoggedInUser`, and `AllowDelete`. Additionally, create a field to store an instance of the `WebService` class:

UsersViewModel.cs

```
public partial class UsersViewModel : ObservableObject
{
    [ObservableProperty]
    ObservableCollection<User> users;

    [ObservableProperty]
    User loggedInUser;

    [ObservableProperty]
    [NotifyCanExecuteChangedFor(nameof(DeleteUserCommand))]
    bool allowDelete;
    WebService service = WebService.Instance;
}
```

7. Create a command to delete a user. In this command, call the `WebService.DeleteUserAsync` method and pass the user's email as a parameter:

UsersViewModel.cs

```
[RelayCommand(CanExecute = nameof(CanDeleteUser))]
async Task DeleteUser(User user)
{
    try
    {
        await webService.DeleteUserAsync(user.Email);
        Users.Remove(user);
    }
    catch (Exception ex)
    {
        await Shell.Current.DisplayAlert("Error",
          ex.Message, "OK");
    }
}
bool CanDeleteUser() => AllowDelete;
```

8. Create an `Initialize` command to perform the following tasks:

- Load a collection of users

- Determine if the delete action is available for the current user

- Retrieve information about the currently logged-in user:

UsersViewModel.cs

```
[RelayCommand]
async Task Initialize()
{
    Users = new ObservableCollection<User>(
      await service.GetUsersAsync());
    AllowDelete =
      await webService.CanDeleteUsersAsync();
    LoggedInUser =
      await webService.GetCurrentUserAsync();
}
```

9. Add the `CommunityToolkit.Maui` NuGet package. We will need it to use the `EventToCommand` behavior. Don't forget to call `UseMauiCommunityToolkit` in the `MauiProgram.CreateMauiApp` class.

10. Create a content page named `UsersPage` and bind its title to the current user email. Additionally, call the `Initialize` command when the view is appearing using `EventToCommand`:

ViewModels.xaml

```
<ContentPage ...
xmlns:vm="clr-namespace:MauiApp1.ViewModels"
xmlns:tk="http://schemas.microsoft.com/dotnet/2022/maui/toolkit"
Title="{Binding LoggedInUser.Email, StringFormat='Hi, {0}'}">
    <ContentPage.Behaviors>
        <tk:EventToCommandBehavior
        EventName="Appearing"
        Command="{Binding InitializeCommand}"/>
    </ContentPage.Behaviors>
    <ContentPage.BindingContext>
        <vm:UsersViewModel/>
    </ContentPage.BindingContext>
```

11. Add a `CollectionView` element and bind it to the `Users` property. Create a `DataTemplate` instance in page resources to represent a user in the collection. Let's add a button to each item to be able to delete a user:

ViewModels.xaml

```
<ContentPage.Resources>
    <DataTemplate x:Key="userTemplate">
        <Grid ColumnDefinitions="*,*, 70" Padding="5">
            <Label Text="{Binding Email}"/>
            <Label Text="{Binding BirthDate}"
                    Grid.Column="1"/>
            <Button Text="Del"
            Command="{Binding
              Path=BindingContext.DeleteUserCommand,
              Source={RelativeSource Mode=
              FindAncestor, AncestorType={x:Type
                CollectionView}}}"
            CommandParameter="{Binding}"
            Grid.Column="2"/>
        </Grid>
    </DataTemplate>
</ContentPage.Resources>
<CollectionView ItemsSource="{Binding Users}"
                ItemTemplate="{StaticResource userTemplate}"/>
```

12. In the `AppShell` class, register a route for `UserPage` so that we can navigate to it:

```
public AppShell()
{
    InitializeComponent();
    Routing.RegisterRoute(nameof(UsersPage), '
      typeof(UsersPage));
}
```

13. Modify the `MainViewModel.LogInAsync` method to navigate to `UsersPage` after authenticating:

MainViewModel.cs

```
async Task LogInAsync()
{
    try
    {
        BearerTokenInfo tokenInfo =
          await WebService.Instance.Authenticate(
            Email, Password);
        await Shell.Current.GoToAsync(
          nameof(UsersPage));
    }
    catch (Exception ex)
    {
        await Shell.Current.DisplayAlert("Error",
          ex.Message, "OK");
    }
}
```

Now, you can run and test the application. Make sure to activate the dev tunnel configured before and run the server application first. After that, run the .NET MAUI app. You can enter different credentials to test different roles. For example, to test `Admin`, type `admin@cookbook.com` as an email and `123Password123!` as a password. You should see that you can delete users. If you log in using the `user1@cookbook.com` email, the **Delete** button should be disabled.

How it works...

To access protected endpoints, our client app uses a token obtained during authentication. This is achieved with the following code in the `WebService` class:

```
httpClient.DefaultRequestHeaders.Authorization =
  new AuthenticationHeaderValue("Bearer", token);
```

We added this code when we implemented the *Building a client application connected to the authentication service* recipe. Since we're using a single `HttpClient` instance, the default authorization header is automatically included in all subsequent requests. This allows the server to identify users and determine if a request is authorized.

The following diagram illustrates our application structure:

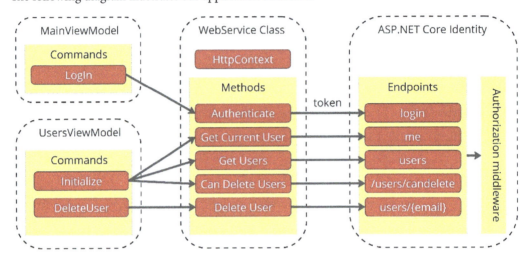

Figure 5.16 – Structure of the created application with authorization

Signing in with a Google account

Have you ever found an interesting web service but closed the browser page as soon as you realized you'd need to go through the entire registration process to use it? On the other hand, if the service offers single-click sign-up options, such as using your Google or Facebook account, you're more likely to continue using it, right?

Signing in and signing up are among the first actions your app users will take, so it's important to make this process as easy as possible by offering social identity authentication options.

In this recipe, we'll implement Google-based authentication. We'll add an endpoint to ASP.NET Core Identity that will start a Google authentication flow and create a new user if they haven't registered before. Additionally, we'll develop the client-side UI for user authentication in our .NET MAUI app.

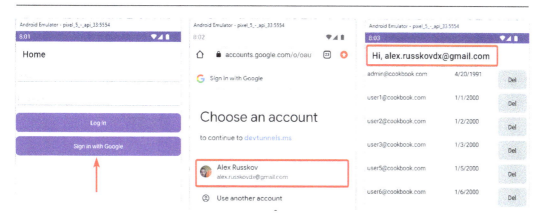

Figure 5.17 – Google sign-in

Getting ready

Start with the project you completed in the previous recipe (*Accessing endpoints with role-based access in the client application*). This project is available at `https://github.com/PacktPublishing/.NET-MAUI-Cookbook/tree/main/Chapter05/c5-RoleBasedAccessPart2`.

The code for this recipe is available at `https://github.com/PacktPublishing/.NET-MAUI-Cookbook/tree/main/Chapter05/c5-GoogleAuth`.

How to do it...

This recipe consists of three main parts:

- Configuring the Google Developer Console. Before you can use Google OAuth, you'll need to specify some basic settings related to your project.

- Adjusting an ASP.NET Core Identity service for the Google authentication flow. We'll add middleware that knows how to work with Google OAuth.

- Incorporating `WebAuthenticator` into the .NET MAUI project. `WebAuthenticator` is a default component that implements a browser-based authentication flow for OAuth providers.

Let's begin:

1. Open the Google Developer Console in your browser using the following URL: `https://console.cloud.google.com/`. If you don't have a Google account, create one. Once logged in, click **Select a project** in the top-left corner:

Figure 5.18 – Select a project menu in the Google Developer Console

2. In the opened dialog, click the **NEW PROJECT** button:

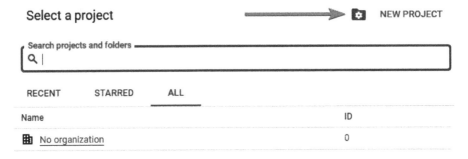

Figure 5.19 – NEW PROJECT button

3. Enter a name for your project. You can leave the **Location** field set to **No organization**:

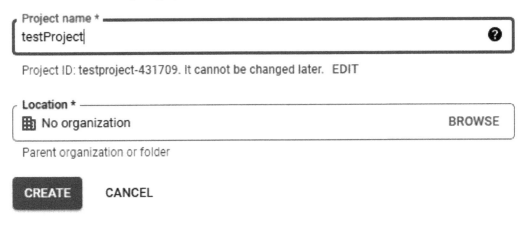

Figure 5.20 – New project details

4. Select the newly created project from the dropdown menu in the top-left corner:

Figure 5.21 – Selecting a created project

5. In the search field, type `credentials` and select **Credentials** under the **APIs & Services** category:

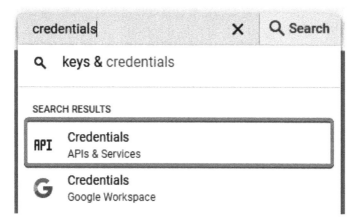

Figure 5.22 – Credentials in search

6. Click the **CREATE CREDENTIALS** button and select **OAuth client ID**:

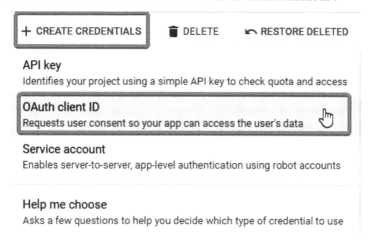

Figure 5.23 – New credentials (OAuth client ID)

7. You'll be prompted to create a consent screen. The information you configure on this screen will be displayed when a user signs in for the first time using their Google account. Select the **External** user type:

Figure 5.24 – User type in consent screen settings

8. On the next screen, enter your full application URL provided by dev tunnels in all the **App domain** fields. In the **Authorized domains** section, click **ADD DOMAIN** and enter devtunnels.ms:

Figure 5.25 – Registering authorized domains

You can leave other settings in their default state.

9. Return to the **Credentials** tab and click **CREATE CREDENTIALS** again (as in *step 6*). Select the **Web Application** type. In the **Authorized redirect URIs** section, click **ADD URI** and enter a URI that contains the dev tunnel base address and the signin-google endpoint. This endpoint is automatically created by ASP.NET Core Identity when the Google module is used:

Figure 5.26 – Registering authorized redirect URIs

10. Complete the other fields and click **Create**. You should see a dialog indicating that your OAuth client has been created:

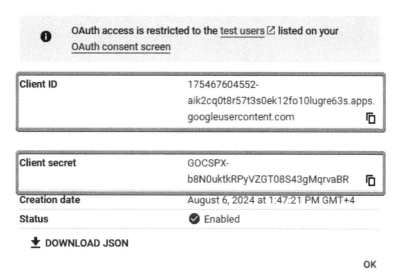

Figure 5.27 – Client ID and client secret

Save the **Client ID** and **Client secret** values to a text file or download the JSON. We will use these values later when configuring our ASP.NET Core Identity service.

11. Navigate to the `c5-AuthenticationService` project in the `c5-GoogleAuth` solution and add the `Microsoft.AspNetCore.Authentication.Google` NuGet package. This package contains core parts and middleware required for Google authentication.

12. Update your authentication configuration by adding the `AddCookie` and `AddGoogle` methods. In the options used with `AddGoogle`, specify the *client ID and client secret* strings that you obtained in *step 10*:

```
builder.Services.AddAuthentication(options =>
{
    options.DefaultSignInScheme =
        IdentityConstants.BearerScheme;
    options.DefaultAuthenticateScheme =
        IdentityConstants.BearerScheme;
    options.DefaultScheme =
        IdentityConstants.BearerScheme;
})
    .AddCookie(CookieAuthenticationDefaults
        .AuthenticationScheme)
    .AddGoogle(options =>
    {
        options.ClientId = "[Client ID from Step 10]";
        options.ClientSecret = "[Client Secret from Step 10]";
        options.SignInScheme =
            CookieAuthenticationDefaults
            .AuthenticationScheme;
    }).AddBearerToken(IdentityConstants.BearerScheme);
```

We'll need the cookie authentication scheme because the Google authentication middleware relies on it.

13. Next, add an endpoint that the mobile application will use to start the Google authentication flow. This endpoint will be called from the client application when a user taps **Sign in with Google**. Set the `AuthenticationProperties.RedirectUri` property to a URL where the user will be redirected after signing in with Google. We'll create the corresponding endpoint in the next step. Call the `Challenge` method to initiate the Google authentication flow. When `Challenge` is called, the user will be redirected to the Google authentication page, where they can select their Google account:

```
app.MapGet("/mauth/google", (HttpContext httpContext) =>
{
    var props = new AuthenticationProperties {
        RedirectUri = "mauth/google/callback" };
    return Results.Challenge(props, new List<string> {
        GoogleDefaults.AuthenticationScheme });
});
```

Note that `RedirectUri` is different from the authorized redirect URI we set up in the Google Developer Console (which we configured as `signin-google`). `RedirectUri` will come into play after visiting the default `signin-google` endpoint created by the middleware. Multiple redirections might seem a bit confusing now, but we'll clarify it in the *How it works...* section.

14. Add an endpoint that the Google middleware will automatically call as the final step in its authentication flow. This is the endpoint we specified as `RedirectUri` in the previous step. Use this endpoint to authenticate a user with the cookie scheme and create a corresponding identity user by calling `CreateUserWithRoleAsync` (which we set up in the *Implementing role-based access rules on the server* recipe):

```
app.MapGet("/mauth/google/callback", async (
    HttpContext context,
    UserManager<User> userManager,
    RoleManager<IdentityRole> roleManager) =>
{
    var authResult =
      await context.AuthenticateAsync(
        CookieAuthenticationDefaults
        .AuthenticationScheme);
    if (!authResult.Succeeded)
    {
        return Results.Redirect("myapp://");
    }
    var email = authResult.Principal.FindFirstValue(
      ClaimTypes.Email);
    await userManager.CreateUserWithRoleAsync(
      roleManager, email, null,
      new DateOnly(2000, 1, 1), "User");
    //…
});
```

15. Afterward, sign in the user to generate and get an access token. The `SignInAsync` method writes the token to the response body of the `HttpContext` object. To read it, assign a memory stream to the response body before calling `SignInAsync`, and then read the stream:

```
app.MapGet("/mauth/google/callback", async (…) =>
{
    //…
    using var responseBody = new MemoryStream();
    context.Response.Body = responseBody;
    await context.SignInAsync(
      IdentityConstants.BearerScheme,
        new ClaimsPrincipal(
          authResult.Principal.Identity));
```

```
context.Response.Body.Seek(0, SeekOrigin.Begin);
var responseText = await new
  StreamReader(context.Response.Body)
    .ReadToEndAsync();
JsonNode tokenData = JsonSerializer
    .Deserialize<JsonNode>(responseText);
});
```

16. Read the `accessToken`, `refreshToken`, and `expiresIn` values from the JSON obtained from the stream:

```
app.MapGet("/mauth/google/callback", async (…) =>
{
    //…
    string token = tokenData["accessToken"]
      .GetValue<string>();
    string refreshToken = tokenData["refreshToken"]
      .GetValue<string>();
    int expiresIn = tokenData["expiresIn"]
      .GetValue<int>();
    var redirectUrl = $"myapp://?access_token={token}&refresh_
      token={refreshToken}&expires_in={expiresIn}";
    return Results.Redirect(redirectUrl);
});
```

17. Go to the `c5-AuthenticationClient` project within the `c5-GoogleAuth` solution and add a **Sign in with Google** button to the main page. Bind this button to `GoogleSignInCommand`:

MainPage.xaml

```
<VerticalStackLayout Spacing="10">
    …
    <Button Text="Sign in with Google"
    Command="{Binding GoogleSignInCommand}"/>
</VerticalStackLayout>
```

You can find Google guidelines related to the signing-in UI on the following page: https://developers.google.com/identity/branding-guidelines.

18. In the `WebService` class, create a method that uses `WebAuthenticator` to access the `mauth/google` endpoint, which was created in *step 13*:

```
public async Task GoogleAuthAsync()
{
    WebAuthenticatorResult authResult =
      await WebAuthenticator.Default
        .AuthenticateAsync(
          new Uri($"{baseAddress}mauth/google"),
          new Uri("myapp://")
        );
    BearerTokenInfo tokenInfo = new BearerTokenInfo
    {
        AccessToken = authResult.AccessToken,
        RefreshToken = authResult.RefreshToken,
        ExpiresIn = int.Parse(
          authResult.Properties["expires_in"]),
        TokenTimestamp = DateTime.UtcNow
    };
    SetAuthHeader(tokenInfo.AccessToken);
}
```

The `WebAuthenticator` component handles authentication in a browser when `AuthenticateAsync` is called. You can obtain the access and refresh tokens using the `AccessToken` and `RefreshToken` properties. To get the `expires_in` value, use the `Properties` dictionary. This is necessary because the default `WebAuthenticatorResult.ExpiresIn` property has a `DateTimeOffset` type, but we passed a string there.

19. Create a `GoogleSignInAsync` command in the `MainViewModel` class and invoke `WebService.GoogleAuthAsync`. Handle any potential exceptions using `try/catch` blocks:

```
[RelayCommand]
async Task GoogleSignInAsync()
{
    try
    {
        await webService.GoogleAuthAsync();
        await Shell.Current.GoToAsync(nameof(UsersPage));
    }
    catch (Exception ex) when (!(ex is TaskCanceledException))
    {
        await Shell.Current.DisplayAlert("Sign in failed",
          ex.Message, "OK");
    }
}
```

Note that we excluded the TaskCanceledException exception type because this exception occurs when a user closes the browser window opened by WebAuthenticator.

20. Now, we need to inform WebAuthenticator that it should navigate back to the application when a user is redirected to the myapp:// address. For Android, go to the Platforms/Android folder in your project, add a class named WebAuthCallbackActivity, and inherit from WebAuthenticatorCallbackActivity. Create a const string field named CALLBACK_SCHEME and assign the Activity and IntentFilter attributes to the WebAuthCallbackActivity class:

```
namespace c5_AuthenticationClient.Platforms
{
    [Activity(NoHistory = true, LaunchMode =
      LaunchMode.SingleTop, Exported = true)]
    [IntentFilter(new[] {
      Android.Content.Intent.ActionView },
      Categories = new[] {
        Android.Content.Intent.CategoryDefault,
        Android.Content.Intent.CategoryBrowsable },
      DataScheme = CALLBACK_SCHEME)]
    public class WebAuthCallbackActivity :
      Microsoft.Maui.Authentication
      .WebAuthenticatorCallbackActivity
    {
        const string CALLBACK_SCHEME = "myapp";
    }
}
```

> **Important note**
>
> The namespace where WebAuthCallbackActivity is defined should only include your main namespace (c5_AuthenticationClient) followed by the Platforms suffix. *There should not be an* Android *part after* Platforms.

21. For iOS, go to the Platforms/iOS/Info.plist file in **Solution Explorer**, right-click on it, and select **Open With | XML (Text) Editor**. Then, add the following key:

```
<dict>
    <!--other keys above-->
    <array>
        <dict>
            <key>CFBundleURLName</key>
            <string>My App</string>
```

```
<key>CFBundleURLSchemes</key>
        <array>
            <string>myapp</string>
        </array>
        <key>CFBundleTypeRole</key>
        <string>Editor</string>
    </dict>
  </array>
</dict>
```

That's it! Now, you can test your project. As usual, make sure to activate your dev tunnel and run the server app first. One of the most common errors during Google OAuth testing is `redirect_uri_mismatch`. If you encounter this error, check the *There's more...* section for potential causes and solutions.

How it works...

As you may have noticed, the entire OAuth flow involves a series of redirects, which can be confusing when you're first learning about it. These redirects occur because the authentication process is actually delegated to a third-party server – in our case, Google's servers. However, the whole process becomes much easier to understand when we visualize it:

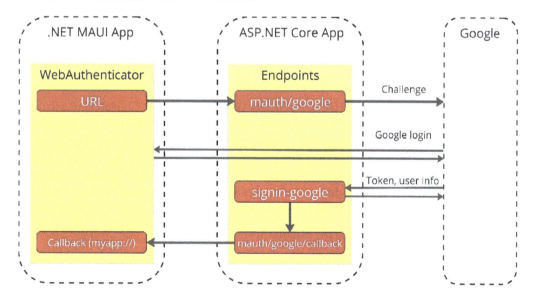

Figure 5.28 – Google sign-in flow

Here's a detailed breakdown of the preceding diagram:

1. In the .NET MAUI application, we create a `WebAuthenticator` component with a URL and a callback URL. When we call `WebAuthenticator.AuthenticateAsync`, it opens a browser window with the `mauth/google` endpoint, which was created in our ASP.NET Core server.

2. The `mauth/google` endpoint triggers the Google authentication scheme. The Google authentication middleware in our ASP.NET Core app then initiates the Google authentication flow.

3. The user is redirected to a Google page where Google displays a consent and login screen.

4. If the user successfully signs in to a Google account or already has an active session, Google calls the `signin-google` endpoint. This is the default endpoint created by the middleware when we call `AddGoogle` during service configuration.

5. The `signin-google` endpoint handles all the OAuth-related logic behind the scenes, including exchanging a secret code for a token from Google, among other operations.

6. Once the sign-in process is complete, the middleware redirects the user to our `mauth/google/callback` endpoint, which we specified in the `AuthenticationProperties.RedirectUri` parameter.

There's more...

As described in the *How it works...* section, the OAuth flow involves redirecting to the OAuth authentication server (Google's server) and then back to your application. Because of this flow, you might frequently encounter the `redirect_uri_mismatch` error if you overlook small but important steps:

*   **Configuring authorized redirect URIs in the Google Developer Console**: For security reasons, Google requires that when a user is authenticated, they are redirected to one of the URIs registered in advance. If you forget to update the authorized redirect URI after changing the address used by your server, you'll run into the `redirect_uri_mismatch` error. Keep in mind that if you are running multiple ASP.NET Core apps using different ports, the dev tunnels feature will create different addresses for each app. It's crucial to ensure that the address currently used by your debugged project is registered in the Google Developer Console.

*   **Configuring the tunnel to keep the original host header**: By default, when you use a tunnel, it replaces the host header with localhost. The host header specifies the domain name that the client is trying to communicate with, which allows the server to distinguish between different websites hosted on the same IP address. When the host header is replaced with localhost, the resulting redirect URI – taking into account the host header – will not match the URI registered in the Google Developer Console. To fix this issue, make sure you enable the **Use Tunnel Domain** option, as shown in *Figure 5.10*.

Managing secured sessions

Do you want your users to log in every time they start the application? Even with Google OAuth support, it can be inconvenient to authenticate repeatedly. To address this and maintain application security, a common approach is to implement sessions.

.NET MAUI provides an API for accessing local secured storage, which can store user-session information. We'll use this storage to save the access token, allowing access to protected APIs without frequent authentication.

Additionally, we'll implement token refresh functionality to request a new access token when it expires. We'll also create a logout feature that removes the token from storage and clears the authorization header from the `HttpClient` object.

Getting ready

Start with the project you completed in the previous recipe (*Signing in with a Google account*). This project is available at `https://github.com/PacktPublishing/.NET-MAUI-Cookbook/tree/main/Chapter05/c5-GoogleAuth`.

The code for this recipe is available at `https://github.com/PacktPublishing/.NET-MAUI-Cookbook/tree/main/Chapter05/c5-SessionManagement`.

How to do it...

Let's create a `SessionService` class to handle all session-related tasks. This service will save token information to secure storage and check if an existing token has expired. We'll extend the `WebService` class by adding a `RefreshTokenAsync` method for requesting a new token. On the view side, we'll perform a session check when showing the view and add a **Log Out** button to allow users to switch accounts.

1. Start by creating a new `SessionService` class. Add a `StorageKey` field to store the key used to access the token in secured storage. Also, include a static property to hold the current instance of the service and a property to retrieve the token from storage:

SessionService.cs

```
public class SessionService
{
    static string StorageKey = "TokenInfo";
    public static SessionService Instance { get; } = new();
    public BearerTokenInfo TokenInfo { get; private set; }
}
```

2. Add the `SaveTokenToStorage` method to save a token to secure storage. You can simply call the `SecureStorage.SetAsync` method to save the token. Also, create a method to remove the token, which we'll use for the logout action:

SessionService.cs

```csharp
public async Task SaveTokenToStorage(BearerTokenInfo token)
{
    string tokenInfoString =
      JsonSerializer.Serialize(token);
    await SecureStorage.Default.SetAsync(StorageKey,
      tokenInfoString);
    TokenInfo = token;
}
public void ClearTokenStorage()
{

    SecureStorage.Default.Remove(StorageKey);
    TokenInfo = null;
}
```

3. Create a `TokenExistsAsync` method to check if the secure storage contains a token. Since we previously used `JsonSerializer` to serialize the token, use the same class to deserialize it when checking for its existence:

SessionService.cs

```csharp
public async Task<bool> TokenExistsAsync()
{
    if (TokenInfo != null)
        return true;
    string tokenString = await SecureStorage.Default
      .GetAsync(StorageKey);
    if (string.IsNullOrEmpty(tokenString))
        return false;
    TokenInfo =
      JsonSerializer.Deserialize<BearerTokenInfo>(
        tokenString);
    return true;
}
```

4. Create a TokenExpired method to check if the token has expired, and a UseExistingSession method that combines all the previous methods. In UseExistingSession, first check if a token exists. If it does, verify if it's expired, and if necessary, refresh the token using the WebService class:

SessionService.cs

```
public bool TokenExpired()
{
    return (DateTime.UtcNow -
      TokenInfo.TokenTimestamp.Value).TotalSeconds >
      TokenInfo.ExpiresIn;
}
public async Task<bool> UseExistingSession()
{
    if (await TokenExistsAsync())
    {
        if (TokenExpired())
        {
            TokenInfo = await WebService.Instance
              .RefreshTokenAsync(
              TokenInfo.RefreshToken);
        }
        else
          WebService.Instance
          .SetAuthHeader(TokenInfo.AccessToken);
        return true;
    }
    return false;
}
```

Note that the WebService.RefreshTokenAsync method doesn't exist yet, so we'll create it in the next step.

5. Go to the WebService class and create a RefreshTokenAsync method. In this method, you'll need to call RequestTokenAsync and pass the refresh/ endpoint name along with the refresh token as parameters:

```
public async Task<BearerTokenInfo>
  RefreshTokenAsync(string refreshToken)
{
    return await RequestTokenAsync("refresh/",
      new { refreshToken });
}
```

6. Update the `WebService.RequestTokenAsync` method to call `SessionService.SaveTokenToStorage` before returning the token:

WebService.cs

```
async Task<BearerTokenInfo> RequestTokenAsync(
  string url, object postContent)
{
    //...
    SetAuthHeader(tokenInfo.AccessToken);
    await SessionService.Instance
      .SaveTokenToStorage(tokenInfo);
    return tokenInfo;
}
```

Note that we use static service instances for simplicity. For a clearer architecture, consider registering and injecting services using DI.

7. Update the `WebService.GoogleAuthAsync` method to also call `SaveTokenToStorage` here:

WebService.cs

```
public async Task GoogleAuthAsync ()
{
    //...
    SetAuthHeader(tokenInfo.AccessToken);
    await SessionService.Instance
      .SaveTokenToStorage(tokenInfo);
}
```

8. Create a `ResetAuthHeader` method to reset the authorization header. This method will be called during the logout operation:

WebService.cs

```
public void ResetAuthHeader()
{
    httpClient.DefaultRequestHeaders.Authorization =
      null;
}
```

9. In the `MainViewModel` class, add a `SessionLogIn` command, which will be invoked when the main page appears:

MainViewModel.cs

```
public partial class MainViewModel : ObservableObject
{
    //...
    SessionService sessionService = SessionService
      .Instance;
    [RelayCommand]
    async Task SessionLogInAsync()
    {
        if (await sessionService.UseExistingSession())
        {
            await Shell.Current
              .GoToAsync(nameof(UsersPage));
        }
    }
}
```

10. To invoke the `SessionLogInCommand` when the page appears, use `EventToCommandBehavior` on your main page:

MainPage.xaml

```
<ContentPage.Behaviors>
    <tk:EventToCommandBehavior
    EventName="Appearing"
    Command="{Binding SessionLogInCommand}"/>
</ContentPage.Behaviors>
```

11. In the `UsersViewModel` class, add a `sessionService` field to store the session service. Implement the LogOut command to clean up the token storage and the authentication header:

```
public partial class UsersViewModel : ObservableObject
{
    //...
    SessionService sessionService = SessionService
      .Instance;
    [RelayCommand]
    async Task LogOut()
    {
        sessionService.ClearTokenStorage();
```

```
                webService.ResetAuthHeader();
                await Shell.Current.GoToAsync("..");
        }
    }
```

12. Finally, add a button to the page toolbar to invoke the logout action:

UsersPage.xaml

```
<ContentPage.ToolbarItems>
    <ToolbarItem Text="Log Out"
                         Command="{Binding LogOutCommand}"/>
</ContentPage.ToolbarItems>
```

Now, you can run the project and test it. Make sure to enable the dev tunnel and run the ASP.NET Core application first. To test the session, log in using either your email and password or your Google account, then close and reopen the application. You should notice that you won't need to log in again during the second run.

How it works...

To summarize the implemented session flow, check out the following diagram:

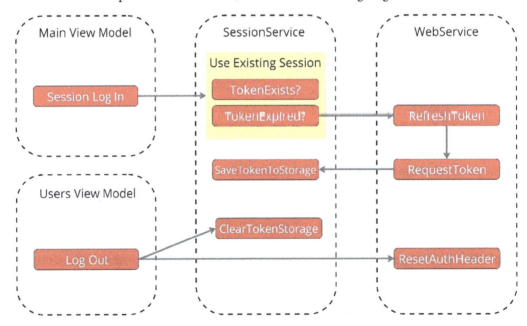

Figure 5.29 – Session management flow

Here's a summary of the implemented session flow:

1. When a user opens the main page, the `SessionLogIn` command is triggered. This command uses `SessionService` to check if a session exists and if it's still valid.

2. If a token exists and hasn't expired, the user is navigated to `UsersPage`. If the token has expired, `SessionService` refreshes the token using the `WebService` object.

3. After the token is refreshed, it is saved to storage.

4. On `UsersPage`, the `LogOut` command can be invoked. This command clears the token, resets the authentication header in `HttpClient` using the `WebService.ResetAuthHeader` method, and navigates the user to the main page.

With this structure, view models don't directly interact with session storage or the ASP.NET Core server. Instead, all logic is handled by separate service classes, helping to keep the code base cleaner.

There's more...

If you've tested signing in with Google, you might have noticed that you can only choose a user during the initial login. Even if you use the **Log Out** action, the next time you tap **Sign in with Google**, you'll be logged in with the previously selected user. This can be an issue if you have multiple Google accounts and need to switch between them.

Although the `WebAuthenticator` component doesn't provide APIs to clear Google session cookies, you can force the user to log in again by passing a `prompt` parameter when calling `Results.Challenge` in the `mauth/google` endpoint:

```
app.MapGet("/mauth/google", (
    HttpContext httpContext,
    bool forceLogin) =>
{
    var props = new AuthenticationProperties {
        RedirectUri = "mauth/google/callback" };
    if (forceLogin)
        props.Items["prompt"] = "login";
    return Results.Challenge(props, new List<string> {
        GoogleDefaults.AuthenticationScheme });
});
```

Note that we added `forceLogin` to the endpoint to determine if the `prompt` parameter should be set. You need to specify `forceLogin` when using the `mauth/google` endpoint in `WebAuthenticator`:

```
WebAuthenticatorResult authResult =
    await WebAuthenticator.Default.AuthenticateAsync(
        new Uri($"{baseAddress}mauth/google?forceLogin=true"),
        new Uri("myapp://"));
```

Implementing biometric authentication

Given that you've implemented login sessions, it's crucial to ensure that your device remains secure against unauthorized use. Otherwise, any person who takes your device can open and use your app with an active session. Fingerprint authentication is an effective solution for this.

While most devices already require a fingerprint or PIN to unlock them, you might want to add an extra layer of security to ensure that someone can't access a protected app even with an unlocked phone. This is especially important for apps dealing with sensitive information or high-security risks, such as banking apps.

In this recipe, we'll use the `Plugin.Maui.Biometric` library to implement fingerprint recognition. This library utilizes the device's built-in fingerprint recognition capabilities to verify the user's identity. We'll configure the app to support fingerprint recognition and trigger a fingerprint check with a button tap.

Getting ready

To follow the steps described in this recipe, we just need to create a blank .NET MAUI application.

The code for this recipe is available at `https://github.com/PacktPublishing/.NET-MAUI-Cookbook/tree/main/Chapter05/c5-BiometricAuth`.

How to do it...

This time, we'll start with a fresh .NET MAUI application since we don't need the server part or other modules. We'll focus on implementing fingerprint authentication by triggering it with a button click and displaying a message indicating whether the authentication succeeded.

1. Install the `Plugin.Maui.Biometric` NuGet package, which includes the `BiometricAuthenticationService` class responsible for biometric authentication.

2. Navigate to the `Platforms/Android/AndroidManifest.xml` file in **Solution Explorer**, right-click it, and select **Open With | XML (Text) Editor**. Add the USE_BIOMETRIC permission request:

   ```
   <uses-permission android:name=
     "android.permission.USE_BIOMETRIC" />
   ```

3. For iOS, navigate to the `Platforms/iOS/Info.plist` file in **Solution Explorer**, right-click it, and select **Open With | XML (Text) Editor**. Add the `NSFaceIDUsageDescription` key:

```
<key>NSFaceIDUsageDescription</key>
<string>This permission is required to use face and fingerprint
  authentication</string>
```

4. Add a button to the main page that will invoke a fingerprint check:

```
<Button x:Name="CounterBtn"
        Text="Test Fingerprint"
        Clicked="OnCounterClicked"
        VerticalOptions="Center"/>
```

5. Add a `Clicked` event handler:

```
private async void OnCounterClicked(object sender,
  EventArgs e)
{
    var result =
      await BiometricAuthenticationService.Default
        .AuthenticateAsync(new AuthenticationRequest()
    {
        Title = "Some title",
        NegativeText = "Cancel authentication"
    }, CancellationToken.None);

    if (result.Status == BiometricResponseStatus
        .Success)
    {
        await DisplayAlert("Success", "System user fingerprint
          is recognized", "OK");
    }
    else
    {
        await DisplayAlert("Rejected", "Couldn't authenticate",
          "OK");
    }
}
```

6. Now, you can test the application. Keep in mind that you need to add a fingerprint to the system to test it. The process can vary depending on the platform, but generally, the easiest way is to go to the device settings and search for `fingerprint`. If you're using an Android emulator, you can use fingerprint emulation, as shown in the following screenshot:

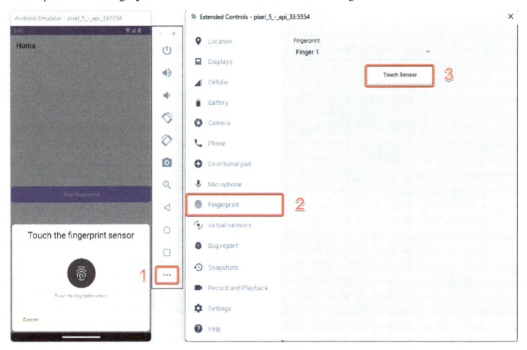

Figure 5.30 – Fingerprint in Android emulator

How it works...

The `BiometricAuthenticationService` class is used to invoke the device's fingerprint check and retrieve the result. It's important to note that you cannot register a custom fingerprint; you can only use one that's already registered in the system. Since the fingerprint check uses the device's biometric APIs, the appearance of the fingerprint dialog may vary depending on the platform.

The device biometric APIs require specific permissions, which is why we updated the `AndroidManifest.xml` and `Info.plist` files for Android and iOS, respectively.

There's more...

In this recipe, we accessed `BiometricAuthenticationService` using a static instance stored in the `Default` property:

```
BiometricAuthenticationService.Default.AuthenticateAsync(…)
```

If you're using DI, you can register the biometric service as an `IBiometric` interface and inject it into other classes in your app:

MauiProgram.cs

```
builder.Services.AddSingleton<IBiometric>(
    BiometricAuthenticationService.Default);
```

MainPage.xaml.cs

```
IBiometric BioAuth;
public MainPage(IBiometric bioAuth)
{
    BioAuth = bioAuth;
    InitializeComponent();
}
private async void OnCounterClicked(object sender,
  EventArgs e)
{
    var result = await BioAuth.AuthenticateAsync(...)
    //...
}
```

6

Real-Life Scenarios: AI, SignalR, and More

One day, I asked a developer why he hadn't considered using AI to automate document processing in his app. He thought it was a great idea but felt it was too complicated and time-consuming. He was amazed when I showed him how he could achieve it in just a day with existing technologies.

We're living in a time when technology is evolving rapidly. Some tools have been around for a while, and others, while emerging, are already making a big impact. While these technologies might seem complex at first, most of the hard work has already been done. Our job is to integrate them into our projects. Many of these tools weren't specifically designed for .NET MAUI, so knowing how to use them effectively is key.

In this chapter, we'll dive into AI capabilities for creating a smart assistant and for processing images. We'll explore cloud-based, server-side, and local models, giving you the flexibility to choose the best fit for your app. We'll also set up real-time data updates between the server and client using **SignalR**. Plus, we'll cover building simple apps for common tasks, such as uploading files to the server and handling local push notifications.

In this chapter, we'll be covering the following recipes:

- Creating an AI assistant that enhances text with OpenAI
- Building a chat bot with Ollama deployed to a self-hosted server
- Detecting a with a local ONNX model deployed on the device
- Sending real-time updates from the server using SignalR
- Uploading large files in chunks to a server
- Sending local push notifications
- Synchronizing data between offline and online databases

Technical requirements

Some of the recipes in this chapter will use an ASP.NET Core service for authentication-related tasks. To set up and run an ASP.NET Core project on Windows, make sure you have the ASP.NET and web development workload installed in Visual Studio.

You can download all the projects created in this chapter from GitHub: `https://github.com/PacktPublishing/.NET-MAUI-Cookbook/tree/main/Chapter06`.

Creating an AI assistant that enhances text with OpenAI

How many people have you met who weren't impressed by ChatGPT the first time they used it? AI technologies are advancing at an incredible rate, and you have a significant advantage if you understand which tasks they can handle and how to integrate them effectively into your app.

Connecting to cloud-based AI services, such as OpenAI or Azure, is the easiest way to leverage AI features. These services provide a range of capabilities for processing text, images, audio, and other types of data. Here are some classic examples of what you can achieve with these services:

- Chatbots
- Text moderation and fine-tuning
- Question categorization
- Object detection
- Audio-to-text conversion

To tap into these features, you only need to call a few functions that interact with the cloud service. We'll explore this technique by building a simple application that uses OpenAI functions to correct grammar errors in text entered by a user.

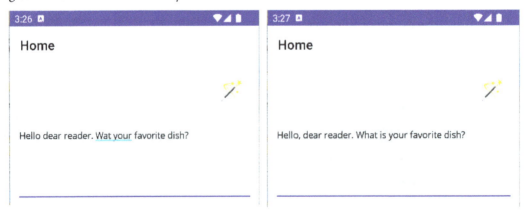

Figure 6.1 – OpenAI text correction demo: Before correction (left) and after correction (right)

Getting ready

To follow the steps in this recipe, you'll need an OpenAI account. If you've already set one up and tried out the paid features, you might need to add a small amount to your balance (around $5) to continue using OpenAI services. We'll go over the details of this process in the *How to do it...* section.

The code for this recipe is available at `https://github.com/PacktPublishing/.NET-MAUI-Cookbook/tree/main/Chapter06/c6-OpenAITextAssistant`.

How to do it...

We'll start by registering an OpenAI account and getting an API key to access OpenAI services. Next, we'll build a simple .NET MAUI app that connects to OpenAI. The app will include an editor where you can type text and a button that sends the text to OpenAI to fix grammar errors. Follow these steps:

1. First, create an OpenAI account if you don't already have one. Go to `https://platform.openai.com/` and click **Sign Up**, which is located in the top-right corner.

2. Once signed in, open the **Dashboard** tab, then click on **API Keys**. Verify your phone number and click **Create new secret key**:

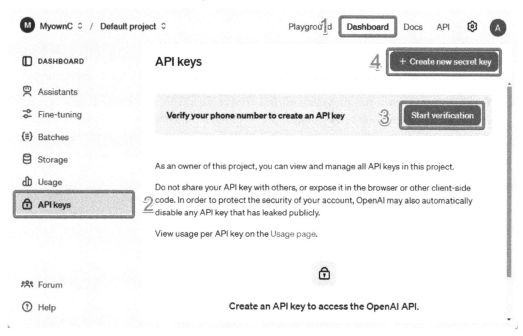

Figure 6.2 – The OpenAI Dashboard menu

3.   In the dialog, enter the key name and click **Create secret key**:

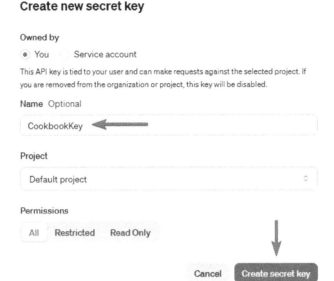

Figure 6.3 – Creating a secret key in OpenAI

Save the provided key to a text file or another secure location so you can use it later in your project.

4.   Next, check if OpenAI has provided any free trial credits. Go to the **Usage** page in the left navigation menu and look at the donut chart on the right. If it's empty and you don't see any links to activate free credits, it means credits haven't been assigned. This might happen if you created an account before, even with a different email or phone number.

Figure 6.4 – OpenAI usage limit

If you haven't received any credits, you'll need to purchase some. In the top-right corner, click **Settings**, then **Billing | Add Payment Methods**. After adding a payment method, add at least $5 to your balance. Once you've done that, your API key should be ready to use. Now, let's move on to creating a .NET MAUI app.

5. Create a new .NET MAUI application and add the following NuGet packages:

   - `CommunityToolkit.Mvvm`: Add this to use automatically generated view models

   - `OpenAI`: Add this to connect to OpenAI services

6. Create a `MainViewModel` class with a property to store text typed by a user:

MainViewModel.cs

```
public partial class MainViewModel : ObservableObject
{
    [ObservableProperty]
    string letterText;
}
```

7. Add a field to store the OpenAI chat client. Use the AI model name and your API key from *step 3* as parameters. For this example, we'll use `gpt-3.5-turbo` since it works faster and uses fewer resources:

MainViewModel.cs

```
public partial class MainViewModel : ObservableObject
{
    //...
    ChatClient aiClient = new(model: "gpt-3.5-turbo",
      "[Your API Key from Step 3]");
}
```

8. Create a method to send a request to OpenAI and handle the response. In this method, call `CompleteChatAsync` with the list of messages as a parameter:

```
[RelayCommand]
async Task FixErrorsAsync()
{
    try
    {
        ChatCompletion completion = await aiClient
            .CompleteChatAsync(new List<ChatMessage> {
            new SystemChatMessage($"You are an assistant
correcting text"),
```

```
                new UserChatMessage($"Fix grammar errors:
{LetterText}")
    });
        LetterText = completion.Content[0].Text;
    }
    catch (Exception ex)
    {
        await Shell.Current.DisplayAlert("Error",
            ex.Message, "OK");
    }
}
```

The OpenAI chat API supports *system*, *user*, and *assistant* messages. A system message sets general instructions for the AI model and can be specified once for the entire chat. User messages contain specific prompts or requests. In our case, a user message will ask the model to correct grammar errors in the provided text. Along with user messages, you can also include assistant messages, which are previous replies from the AI model. This will provide the model access to the chat history to reply based on your previous conversation. For example, if you first ask about Paris, and then you ask, "What is the weather there?", the AI model will understand that you are talking about Paris. This is a useful feature, but we won't need it in our scenario.

9. Now, you can implement the UI and bind it to the view model. In the `MainPage` class, add the `Entry` and `Button` elements to let the user type text and activate the AI assistant to correct grammar errors:

```
xmlns:vm="clr-namespace:c6_OpenAITextAssistant"
<ContentPage.BindingContext>
    <vm:MainViewModel/>
</ContentPage.BindingContext>
<Grid Padding="10">
    <Entry Text="{Binding LetterText}"
            Placeholder="Type your letter"
            HeightRequest="200"
            Background="AliceBlue"
            VerticalOptions="Start"/>
    <Button Text="&#x1FA84;"
            FontSize="30"
            Command="{Binding FixErrorsCommand}"
            VerticalOptions="Start"
            HorizontalOptions="End"
            BackgroundColor="Transparent"/>
</Grid>
```

In the preceding code snippet, 🪄 represents the Unicode for a magic wand image. You can remove any unnecessary default code from the `MainPage.xaml` and `MainPage.xaml.cs` files.

Now, run and test the project. Type any text into the entry field and press the magic wand button. You should see the corrected text within a few seconds. If your API key is invalid or you don't have enough credits, an error message will appear in a message box.

How it works...

When working with OpenAI services, most of the heavy lifting is handled by OpenAI and the client library. Here are the main components you'll use and adjust in your app:

- `ChatClient`: This is the entry point for chat-related requests to OpenAI. When creating `ChatClient`, you provide an API key and specify which AI model to use (in our case, `gpt-3.5-turbo`, but you can find all available models in the documentation: `https://platform.openai.com/docs/models`). `ChatClient` manages connection tasks and provides the API for making requests to OpenAI.

- `ChatMessage`: This represents a message sent to the chat. You can include multiple messages in a single chat request. There are three types of messages: system, user, and assistant. A system message provides general instructions for the AI model (you can use only one system message). User messages are your requests, and assistant messages are the AI model's previous responses. You can use multiple assistant and user messages to simulate a chat history, which may influence the model's responses.

- `ChatCompletion`: This contains the response from the chat assistant. It may include multiple response variants and additional metadata.

There's more...

In this recipe, we generated the entire response all at once and then retrieved it from OpenAI. If the generated text is too large, it can take some time to produce, which might cause delays in the UI. One way to address this is to use streaming completions, which send the generated text in smaller pieces. For streaming completions, use `CompleteChatStreamingAsync` instead of `CompleteChatAsync`, and iterate through the collection of returned `StreamingChatCompletionUpdate` objects in an asynchronous loop:

```
AsyncCollectionResult<StreamingChatCompletionUpdate>
   updates = aiClient.CompleteChatStreamingAsync(
         new SystemChatMessage($"You are an assistant correcting
   text"),
         new UserChatMessage($"Fix grammar errors in the following
   text: {LetterText}"));
```

```
LetterText = null;
await foreach (StreamingChatCompletionUpdate update
    in updates)
{
    foreach (ChatMessageContentPart updatePart
      in update.ContentUpdate)
    {
        LetterText += updatePart.Text;
    }
}
```

OpenAI offers several additional services beyond chat-related features. Here are some other popular clients you can use in your app:

- `ImageClient`: This generates images based on a prompt.

- `AudioClient`: This allows you to transcribe audio or convert text to speech.

- `EmbeddingClient`: This creates embeddings from text. An embedding is a numerical representation of the meaning of the text, which helps you find other texts with similar meanings.

OpenAI continually updates its range of services, so you can check out their documentation for the latest information: `https://platform.openai.com/docs/overview`.

Building a chat bot with Ollama deployed to a self-hosted server

Ollama is a platform that lets you run pre-trained AI models on your own machine. What are the benefits? You avoid paying for cloud AI services, you don't need to share your data with other companies, and you can potentially achieve lower latency. While Ollama mainly focuses on language processing models, it also supports models that can process and describe images.

There are many state-of-the-art models optimized for Ollama, so you don't need to be a machine learning expert to use them. You can handle nearly all the tasks you would with OpenAI but run them on your own server. Just install Ollama, select a model, and call the Ollama APIs using a .NET library.

However, Ollama is too resource-intensive to run on mobile devices. Therefore, we'll deploy it to an ASP.NET Core server and access it from a .NET MAUI client application. We'll create a simple chatbot where users can type messages and get responses from the AI model.

Figure 6.5 – Ollama response

Getting ready

In this recipe, we will create both .NET MAUI and ASP.NET Core projects, so make sure that you have the required workloads in Visual Studio to create both project types. Refer to the *Getting ready* section of the *Creating an authentication service with ASP.NET Core Identity* recipe in *Chapter 5* to learn how to install the required workloads. Additionally, we will use a dev tunnel to access an ASP. NET Core service from the .NET MAUI app, so you need to configure it as described in the *There's more…* section of the *Creating an authentication service with ASP.NET Core Identity* recipe in *Chapter 5*.

The code for this recipe is available at `https://github.com/PacktPublishing/.NET-MAUI-Cookbook/tree/main/Chapter06/c6-DeployedAiAssistant`.

How to do it...

This recipe involves three main parts:

1. Installing Ollama.

2. Creating an ASP .NET Core with a single endpoint to provide access to a deployed Ollama service.

3. Creating a .NET MAUI client application with a basic chat UI.

Let's start with setting up Ollama:

1. Visit `https://ollama.com/download` to download Ollama. Run the downloaded installer.

2. Once Ollama is installed and running, a console should open where you can execute an AI model. Type the following command:

   ```
   ollama run llama3.1
   ```

   It may take a few minutes to download the Llama model the first time you run it. Once the model is running, you can test it directly in the console by typing arbitrary messages. Note that the model operates directly on your machine without using cloud services.

3. Create a new ASP.NET Core Web API project. In the project setup wizard, uncheck all options except **Configure for HTTPS** and **Enable OpenAPI support**:

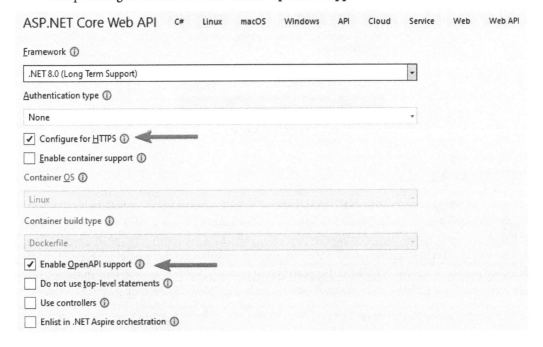

Figure 6.6 – ASP.NET Core Web API project options

4. In the created project, remove the generated `weatherforecast` endpoint and the `WeatherForecast` record definition from the `Program.cs` file.

5. Add the `OllamaSharp` NuGet package to access the Ollama service.

6. Register the `OllamaApiClient` class in the service container so that you can use it in your endpoint methods. Add the following code before the `Build` method call in `Program.cs`:

```
builder.Services.AddSingleton(sp =>
    new OllamaApiClient(new Uri
        ("http://localhost:11434")));
```

Note that `11434` is the default port used by Ollama on your local machine.

7. Next, implement an endpoint that accepts a question as a parameter and uses `OllamaApiClient` to get a response from the AI model deployed on Ollama. In this endpoint, call the `Chat` method and pass a `ChatRequest` object as a parameter. Make sure to specify the model name and include a chat message:

```
app.MapGet("/ask-question", async (string question,
  OllamaApiClient ollamaClient) =>
{
    var chat = await ollamaClient.Chat(new
      ChatRequest()
    {
        Model = "llama3.1",
        Messages = new List<Message>
        {
            new Message(ChatRole.User, question)
        }
    });
    return Results.Content(chat.Message.Content);
});
```

We used the `llama3.1` model, which is the same model we ran in *step 2*. However, you can visit the Ollama site (`https://ollama.com/library`) and choose a different model if you prefer.

8. Now, let's create a .NET MAUI client app. Right-click the solution and select **Add | New Project**. Create a new .NET MAUI project and add the following NuGet packages:

- `CommunityToolkit.Mvvm`: Add this to use auto-generated view models

- `Indiko.Maui.Controls.Markdown`: Add this to display AI model responses in markdown

9. Create a `MainViewModel` class with two string properties to, firstly, hold the user's question and secondly, hold the AI model's response. Also, define a field to store `HttpClient`:

```
public partial class MainViewModel : ObservableObject
{
    HttpClient httpClient = new HttpClient()
    {
        BaseAddress = new Uri("[Your Dev Tunnel Address]/"),
        Timeout = TimeSpan.FromSeconds(30)
    };

    [ObservableProperty]
    string? message;

    [ObservableProperty]
    string? answer;
}
```

In `HttpClient`, set `BaseAddress` to the address of your dev tunnel. To get this address, set the ASP.NET Core project as the startup project, activate the dev tunnel, and run the project. A browser window should open where you can copy the URL and use it as the base address. Make sure to add a slash after the copied URL, so it looks something like this:

```
BaseAddress = new Uri("https://zz4kwazx-7107.asse.devtunnels.
ms/")
```

10. Add the `SendMessage` command to send a message to the ASP.NET Core service:

MainViewModel.cs

```
[RelayCommand]
async Task SendMessageAsync()
{
    var response = await httpClient
      .GetAsync($"ask-question?question=
      '{Uri.EscapeDataString(Message)}'");
    response.EnsureSuccessStatusCode();
    Answer = await response.Content
      .ReadAsStringAsync();
    Message = null;
}
bool CanSendMessage()
    => !string.IsNullOrEmpty(Message);
```

11. Now, let's set up the view. In `MainPage.xaml`, add the following elements:

    - `MarkdownView`: Add this to display the AI model's responses

    - `Entry`: Add this for users to type their questions

    - `Button`: Add this to send questions to the server:

    ```
    xmlns:vm="clr-namespace:c6_AiAssistantClient"
    xmlns:idk="clr-namespace:Indiko.Maui.Controls
        .Markdown; assembly=Indiko.Maui.Controls.Markdown"

    <ContentPage.BindingContext>
        <vm:MainViewModel/>
    </ContentPage.BindingContext>
    <Grid ColumnDefinitions="*,70"
            RowDefinitions="*, 40"
            RowSpacing="20"
            Padding="10">
        <ScrollView Grid.ColumnSpan="2"
                    VerticalOptions="End">
            <idk:MarkdownView MarkdownText="{Binding Answer}" />
        </ScrollView>
        <Entry Text="{Binding Message}"
                Grid.Row="1"/>
        <Button Text="Send"
                Command="{Binding SendMessageCommand}"
                Grid.Row="1"
                Grid.Column="1"/>
    </Grid>
    ```

    You can remove all unnecessary default code from the `MainPage.xaml` and `MainPage.xaml.cs` files.

12. Finally, you can run and test the project. Start by activating the dev tunnel and running the ASP. NET Core application. Then, run the .NET MAUI application. Type any text into the input field and press the **Send** button. Keep in mind that it may take a moment for the model to respond since the API we used generates all the text at once instead of in smaller pieces.

How it works...

Ollama creates an environment for running ready-to-use AI models directly on your machine. You don't need to design or train these models, nor do you need to rely on any third-party online services to build your app – everything runs locally on your computer. Plus, all input and output are typically represented in natural language, so you can use the same prompts you might use in something such as ChatGPT.

When you install Ollama, it doesn't come with any predefined AI models, so the first step is to install one, which we did by executing the run command in the console in *step 2*:

```
ollama run llama3.1
```

We used the `llama3.1` model, but there are many other models available for Ollama.

When Ollama is running, it listens on port `11434` on your machine. We used this port when creating `OllamaApiClient` in the server app:

```
builder.Services.AddSingleton(sp =>
    new OllamaApiClient(new Uri
        ("http://localhost:11434")));
```

Once the connection is configured, all we need to do is send chat requests using `OllamaApiClient`. These chat requests have similar elements to those we used for OpenAI: we pass a collection of messages with different roles (system, user, assistant) and get a response.

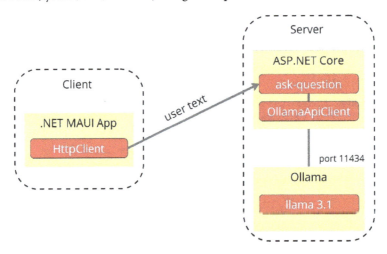

Figure 6.7 – Ollama on the server side

There's more...

Responding to text requests in a chat format isn't the only functionality available with Ollama models. Similar to OpenAI, it supports models that can work with images or generate embeddings to search for similar text. You can explore the supported models in the official Ollama library: `https://ollama.com/library`.

When making a request to a model, you can pass additional parameters beyond just the prompt. For example, you can adjust the `Temperature` parameter to make the model's responses more creative:

```
var chat = await ollamaClient.Chat(new ChatRequest()
{
    Model = "llama3.1",
    Options = new OllamaSharp.Models.RequestOptions()
      { Temperature = 0.5f },
    //...
});
```

Additionally, instead of waiting for the entire reply, you can receive it piece by piece using the streaming feature:

```
ollamaClient.SelectedModel = "llama3.1";
var streamChat = ollamaClient.Chat(streamResponse =>
{
    Console.WriteLine(streamResponse.Message.Content);
});
await streamChat.Send("How are you?");
```

You can learn more about Ollama's capabilities on GitHub: `https://github.com/ollama/ollama/blob/main/docs/README.md`. Note that this document covers Ollama itself. To learn more about `OllamaSharp`, the .NET library for Ollama, check out `https://github.com/awaescher/OllamaSharp`.

Detecting with a local ONNX model deployed on the device

In the previous recipes, we worked with models running in the cloud or on a server. But what if your device isn't always connected to the internet, or if you need faster response times? You can actually run AI models directly on your device – even on a mobile phone. The best part is that you don't need to be a machine learning expert to do this because there are pre-trained AI models available. With **ONNX** models and **ML.NET**, you can achieve all of this right on your device.

ONNX is an open source format designed to represent machine learning models. It allows models to be interoperable across different frameworks.

This essentially means that a model created and trained in other frameworks, such as TensorFlow or PyTorch, can be converted to the ONNX format. ONNX models run in ONNX Runtime, which has libraries available for .NET.

Another important part of the system is ML.NET. This is a machine learning framework for .NET developers, enabling them to build, train, and deploy models using C#.

While ML.NET provides a wide range of advanced features for creating and training AI models, we won't need those in this case. Instead, we'll use a pre-trained ONNX model. ML.NET will serve as the infrastructure that feeds data into ONNX Runtime and retrieves the results. In this recipe, we'll build an app that detects faces in images using the **UltraFace** model, which is optimized for mobile devices.

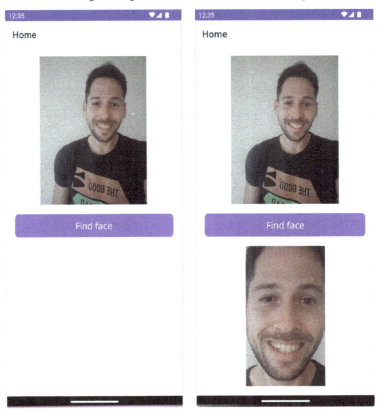

Figure 6.8 – Detecting a face demo

Getting ready

To follow the steps described in this recipe, we just need to create a blank .NET MAUI application.

The code for this recipe is available at `https://github.com/PacktPublishing/.NET-MAUI-Cookbook/tree/main/Chapter06/c6-AIFaceDetection`.

How to do it...

This recipe has three main logical parts:

1. **Preparing the core modules**: We'll download the pre-trained ONNX model and install the necessary NuGet packages.

2. **Preprocessing and postprocessing data**: We'll convert the input image to the format the model expects and handle the model's output.

3. **Implementing the UI**: We'll add visual elements to display the results.

Let's start with setting up the ONNX model.

1. First, let's download the ONNX model we'll use to detect faces in images. You can find various pre-trained ONNX models in this GitHub repository: `https://github.com/onnx/models`. We'll use the UltraFace model, which is available at the following link: `https://github.com/onnx/models/tree/main/validated/vision/body_analysis/ultraface`.

2. Create a .NET MAUI project and add the downloaded model to the `Resources/Raw` folder. Also, add an image with a face to the same folder. Note that while the UltraFace model expects an image with specific dimensions, you can use an image with any width and height, as we will resize it during preprocessing.

3. Create a `FileOperations` class to copy files from the `Raw` folder to a working `AppData` directory. We'll use this class to copy both the model and image files:

```
public static class FileOperations
{
    public static async Task<string> CopyToAppData
      (string assetFileName)
    {
        string targetFile = Path.Combine
          (FileSystem.Current.AppDataDirectory,
          assetFileName);
        if (File.Exists(targetFile))
            return targetFile;
        using Stream inputStream =
          await FileSystem.Current
          .OpenAppPackageFileAsync(assetFileName);
        using FileStream outputStream =
          File.Create(targetFile);
        await inputStream.CopyToAsync(outputStream);
        return targetFile;
    }
}
```

We use the standard `OpenAppPackageFileAsync` method to read the file as a stream and then write this stream to a file using `FileStream.CopyToAsync`.

4. Add the following NuGet packages to run the ONNX model and feed data to it:

    *   `Microsoft.ML.ImageAnalytics`

    *   `Microsoft.ML.OnnxRuntime`

    *   `Microsoft.ML.OnnxTransformer`

5. Additionally, reference MAUI and MVVM Community Toolkit packages to easily implement MVVM:

    *   `CommunityToolkit.Mvvm`

    *   `CommunityToolkit.Maui`

    Don't forget to call `UseMauiCommunityToolkit` in the `MauiProgram.CreateMauiApp` method to activate the features available in the `CommunityToolkit.Mvvm` package.

6. When working with ONNX models, the first step is to prepare the data. Each ONNX model expects data in a specific format. For our case, UltraFace expects a three-dimensional array of float values with the size [320 x 240 x 3], where 320 is the width, 240 is the height, and 3 represents the color channels (RGB). Each value in the array should be normalized to a range from -1 to 1. The exact input format depends on the model's structure and is typically described by the model's author. Let's start by adding a class to store the image path. ML.NET will use this class to load the input image and transform it into data ready for further processing.

    ```
    public class ImageNetData
    {
        public string ImagePath { get; set; }
    }
    ```

7. Define a method to normalize image data. This involves subtracting 127 from each value in the image array and dividing the result by 128. Since each RGB color value originally ranges from 0 to 255, this normalization will scale the values to a range from -1 to 1. This process is known as mean normalization or zero-centered normalization. Create a class named `NormalizationData` with the `Reshape` field and the `MeanAndScaleNormalization` method:

    ```
    public class NormalizationData
    {
        [ColumnName("input")]
        [VectorType(3, 240, 320)]
        public VBuffer<float> Reshape;

        public static void MeanAndScaleNormalization
          (NormalizationData input, NormalizationData output)
    ```

```
        {
            output.Reshape = new VBuffer<float>(
                input.Reshape.Length,
                input.Reshape.GetValues().ToArray()
                .Select(v => (v - 127) / 128).ToArray());
        }
    }
```

The MeanAndScaleNormalization method takes objects with the original and transformed data according to the algorithm described at the beginning of this step. During preprocessing, we use the ColumnName attribute to indicate that the Reshape field holds the data. The VectorType attribute defines the dimensions (or shape) of the array (tensor).

8. Create a MainViewModel class with fields to store information related to the machine learning model, input images, and output images:

```
public partial class MainViewModel : ObservableObject
{
    MLContext mlContext = new MLContext();
    ITransformer mlModel;
    readonly string sourceImageName =
      "test_image.jpg";
    readonly string modelName = "version-RFB-320.onnx";
    string sourceImagePath;

    [ObservableProperty]
    ImageSource? sourceImage;

    [ObservableProperty]
    ImageSource? faceImage;
}
```

The MLContext object is the entry point for ML.NET operations. We'll use it to preprocess data and prepare the ML model. The mlModel field, of type ITransformer, will store the ML model that transforms an input image into a numeric array with potential face bounds.

9. Define the preprocessing flow and prepare the ML model. The MLContext object provides ready-to-use methods for data preprocessing in common scenarios. These methods are generally called transformations and are accessible through the Transforms object. You define the preprocessing flow once using the Append method, and this flow can be applied to multiple objects (such as images in our case):

```
ITransformer LoadModel(string modelLocation)
{
    var data = mlContext.Data.LoadFromEnumerable
      (new List<ImageNetData>());
```

```
       return mlContext.Transforms.LoadImages(
          outputColumnName: "input", imageFolder: "",
          inputColumnName: nameof(ImageNetData
           .ImagePath))
           .Append(mlContext.Transforms.ResizeImages(
                       outputColumnName: "input",
                       imageWidth: 320,
                       imageHeight: 240,
                       inputColumnName: "input",
                       resizing: ResizingKind.Fill))
           .Append(mlContext.Transforms
           .ExtractPixels(outputColumnName: "input"))
           .Append(mlContext.Transforms
           .CustomMapping<NormalizationData,
             NormalizationData>(
               NormalizationData
               .MeanAndScaleNormalization,
               contractName: null))
           .Append(mlContext.Transforms
             .ApplyOnnxModel(
                   modelFile: modelLocation,
                   outputColumnNames: new[] { "scores",
                     "boxes" },
                   inputColumnNames: new[] { "input"}))
                     .Fit(data);
}
```

The ApplyOnnxModel method loads the model we downloaded in *step 1*. The complete sequence of transformations, including the ONNX model itself, is referred to as a **pipeline**. During the pipeline construction, no actual calculations are performed – It's essentially about creating the structure. We use the LoadFromEnumerable method with an empty list of ImageNetData objects to allow the pipeline to adjust to our data schema. This adjustment is done by the Fit method.

10. Prepare the model and input files. Add the InitializeAsync method to copy the image and model files and then call the LoadModel method created in the previous step:

```
[RelayCommand]
async Task InitializeAsync()
{
    sourceImagePath = await FileOperations
       .CopyToAppData(sourceImageName);
    string onnxModelPath = await FileOperations
       .CopyToAppData(modelName);
```

```
        SourceImage = ImageSource
          .FromFile(sourceImagePath);
        mlModel = LoadModel(onnxModelPath);
    }
```

11. Next, create a method to get actual estimations from the model based on the image provided. Call `LoadFromEnumerable` to load the image, and then use `Transform` to get the results from the model:

```
    IDataView GetScoredData(string imagePath)
    {
        IEnumerable<ImageNetData> images = new
          List<ImageNetData>() { new ImageNetData() {
          ImagePath = imagePath } };
        IDataView imageDataView = mlContext.Data
          .LoadFromEnumerable(images);
        return mlModel.Transform(imageDataView);
    }
```

The `Transform` method returns a `DataView` object. Each row in this object corresponds to an input data item. Since we have only one input image in the images list, `DataView` will contain one row. Additionally, `DataView` contains a set of columns determined by the model schema defined in the `LoadModel` method. In our case, the column names are input, scores, and boxes. We are particularly interested in the scores and boxes columns, as they contain the results calculated by the model.

12. Create a method to find the index of the box with the highest probability of containing a human face. AI models processing images typically produce multiple arrays rather than a single value. In our scenario, the UltraFace ONNX model produces two arrays:

- It produces the `boxes` array with a shape of `[4420 x 4]`. This array contains `4420` rectangles that may contain a face, with each rectangle represented by the top, left, right, and bottom coordinates.

- It also produces the `scores` array with a shape of `[4420 x 2]`. This array can be considered as two layers with `4420` elements each. The first layer contains probabilities related to background objects ("not a face" objects), which are not of interest to us. The second layer contains probabilities indicating whether a rectangle with the same index in the `boxes` array contains a face.

To detect a face, we need to find the index of the maximum value in the `scores` array and use this index to access the corresponding value in the `boxes` array. Let's start by finding the index in the `scores` array:

```
int GetFaceBoxIndex(float[] scores)
{
    int objectScoreIndex;
    float maxScore = -1;
    int maxScoreIndex = 0;
    for (int i = 0; i < scores.Length / 2; i++)
    {
        objectScoreIndex = i * 2 + 1;
        if (scores[objectScoreIndex] > maxScore)
        {
            maxScore = scores[objectScoreIndex];
            maxScoreIndex = i;
        }
    }
    return maxScoreIndex;
}
```

Note that while the ONNX model operates with multi-dimensional arrays internally, the result is provided as a linear array. To access the second dimension, multiply each index by 2 and add 1.

13. Combine the model output with the face index finding. Add a `FindFaceAsync` method that calls `GetScoredData` and `GetFaceBoxIndex`, which were created in the previous steps. We'll execute these methods in a task to avoid freezing the UI:

```
[RelayCommand]
async Task FindFaceAsync()
{
    await Task.Run(() =>
    {
        IDataView scoredData = GetScoredData(sourceImagePath);
        float[] boxes = scoredData
          .GetColumn<float[]>("boxes").First();
        float[] scores = scoredData
          .GetColumn<float[]>("scores").First();

        int scoreIndex = GetFaceBoxIndex(scores);
        int boxIndex = scoreIndex * 4;

        CropImage(sourceImagePath,
            left: boxes[boxIndex],
            top: boxes[boxIndex + 1],
```

```
            right: boxes[boxIndex + 2],
            bottom: boxes[boxIndex + 3]);
    });
}
```

Now, the `boxIndex` variable holds the index of the rectangle that likely contains a face. We will use this index in the `CropImage` method, which will be introduced in the next step, to create an image that contains only the detected face.

14. Create a cropped image with the face using `SkiaSharp` to display it below the original image. Create a bitmap from the source stream. Then, use the coordinates passed to the method to create a cropped bitmap, and finally, generate the resulting image from this cropped bitmap:

```
void CropImage(string imagePath, float left, float
  top, float right, float bottom)
{
    using var inputStream = File.OpenRead(imagePath);
    var originalBitmap = SKBitmap.Decode(inputStream);
    var croppedBitmap = CreateCroppedBitmap(
        originalBitmap,
        new SKRectI(
            (int)(left * originalBitmap.Width),
            (int)(top * originalBitmap.Height),
            (int)(right * originalBitmap.Width),
            (int)(bottom * originalBitmap.Height)));
    FaceImage = ImageSource.FromStream(() =>
      BitmapToStream(croppedBitmap));
}
SKBitmap CreateCroppedBitmap(SKBitmap originalBitmap,
  SKRectI cropRect)
{
    var croppedBitmap = new SKBitmap(cropRect.Width,
      cropRect.Height);
    using var canvas = new SKCanvas(croppedBitmap);
    canvas.DrawBitmap(originalBitmap, cropRect, new
      SKRectI(0, 0, cropRect.Width, cropRect.Height));
    return croppedBitmap;
}
Stream BitmapToStream(SKBitmap bitmap)
{
    var memoryStream = new MemoryStream();
    bitmap.Encode(memoryStream,
      SKEncodedImageFormat.Jpeg, 30);
    memoryStream.Seek(0, SeekOrigin.Begin);
```

```
            return memoryStream;
    }
```

These operations aren't directly related to machine learning, so I won't go into detail about each method here.

15. Add a view to display both the original and cropped images. Also, make sure to trigger `InitializeCommand` when the view appears, and `FindFaceCommand` when the **Find Face** button is clicked:

```
xmlns:vm="clr-namespace:c6_AIFaceDetection"
xmlns:tk="http://schemas.microsoft.com/dotnet/2022/maui/toolkit"
<ContentPage.BindingContext>
    <vm:MainViewModel/>
</ContentPage.BindingContext>
<ContentPage.Behaviors>
    <tk:EventToCommandBehavior
        EventName="Appearing"
        Command="{Binding InitializeCommand}"/>
</ContentPage.Behaviors>
<Grid RowDefinitions="*,50, 300"
        RowSpacing="20"
        Padding="20">
    <Image Source="{Binding SourceImage}"/>
    <Button Text="Find face"
            Command="{Binding FindFaceCommand}"
            Grid.Row="1" />
    <Image Source="{Binding FaceImage}"
            Grid.Row="2"/>
</Grid>
```

Finally, you can run and test the project.

How it works...

As you might have noticed, much of the code in this recipe focuses on preparing data for the ONNX model and processing its output. Each ONNX model has a unique structure and expects input data in a specific format. The following figure illustrates the input and output data for the UltraFace model:

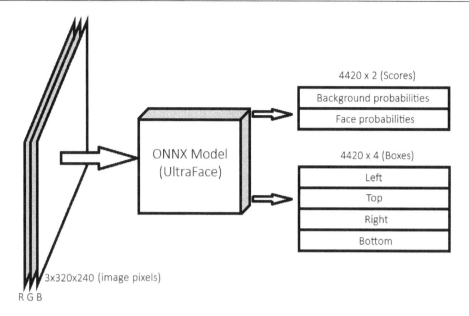

Figure 6.9 – UltraFace input and output

The UltraFace model processes an image as a three-dimensional array of float values with the shape 3 x 320 x 240, where 320 x 240 represents the image dimensions and 3 denotes the RGB color channels. UltraFace produces two outputs: scores and boxes. The scores array contains probabilities indicating whether a face or a background object is present in each corresponding box, while the boxes array holds the rectangle coordinates corresponding to these probabilities.

In the GetFaceBoxIndex method (*step 13*), we locate the index of the highest probability in the scores array (focusing only on the face probabilities) and use that index to retrieve the corresponding rectangle from the boxes array. To handle cases where multiple faces might be detected in an image, consider using non-max suppression to filter out overlapping boxes that represent the same object. You can find an example of this algorithm for the UltraFace model here: https://github.com/onnx/models/blob/main/validated/vision/body_analysis/ultraface/dependencies/box_utils.py.

Normalization is also crucial because the UltraFace model was trained with color values normalized to a range of -1 to 1. Initially, RGB values are between 0 and 255, so we need to normalize these values before processing. This is achieved with the MeanAndScaleNormalization method defined in *step 7*.

The entire data transformation pipeline is set up in the `LoadModel` method (*step 9*). ML.NET provides transformation methods to load, resize, and process the image, converting it into the format expected by the UltraFace model. Each transformation method uses the output of the previous method as its input. Ensure that the column name for the input data matches what the UltraFace model expects. You can check the input requirements of any ONNX model using the **Netron** tool, which allows you to open and visualize ONNX files: `https://netron.app`.

There's more...

We used the UltraFace ONNX model for face detection in this example. However, the world of pre-trained models offers solutions for many other tasks that you might need for your app. For instance, you can find models for object classification, text extraction from images, face and emotion recognition, and more. Some resources for finding these models include the following:

- **ONNX Model Zoo**: `https://onnx.ai/models/`
- **ONNX models' GitHub repository**: `https://github.com/onnx/models`

Not all these models are optimized for mobile devices due to the complexity of the tasks they solve. However, you can always run a model on a server, as demonstrated in the previous recipe with Ollama. While Ollama is a simpler solution for natural language tasks, it may not be as effective for specific tasks compared to other specialized models. ONNX provides a format that allows state-of-the-art models from frameworks such as TensorFlow and PyTorch to be used in your projects. You can take a pre-trained model from TensorFlow, convert it to ONNX, and integrate it into your project.

Sending real-time updates from the server using SignalR

Imagine you have an app that shows information from a server, and this information can be updated by other users. How do you get notified when someone else makes a change so you can update the UI? Periodically polling the server for updates is one approach, but it's not very efficient. This is where **SignalR** can be a game-changer.

> SignalR
>
> **SignalR** is a library in ASP.NET Core that enables bi-directional communication between a server and its connected clients. It allows servers to push updates to clients instantly, rather than requiring the client to poll the server for updates.

In this recipe, we'll create an auction-style app where bids are sent from the server and displayed in a list. Bids can come in at any time, and when a new bid arrives, it should automatically show up in the client app. Users can then accept a bid by clicking the **Accept** button.

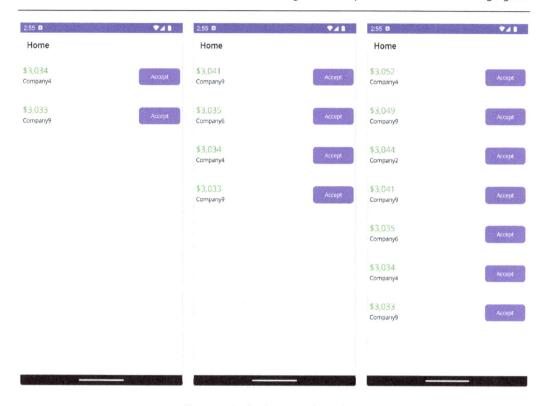

Figure 6.10 – Real-time updates demo

Getting ready

In this recipe, we will create both .NET MAUI and ASP.NET Core projects, so make sure that you have the required workloads in Visual Studio to create both project types. Refer to the *Getting ready* section of the *Creating an authentication service with ASP.NET Core Identity* recipe in *Chapter 5* to learn how to install the required workloads. Additionally, we will use a dev tunnel to access an ASP. NET Core service from the .NET MAUI app, so you need to configure it as described in the *There's more…* section of the *Creating an authentication service with ASP.NET Core Identity* recipe in *Chapter 5*.

The code for this recipe is available at `https://github.com/PacktPublishing/.NET-MAUI-Cookbook/tree/main/Chapter06/c6-SignalRConnection`.

How to do it...

In this recipe, we'll set up both a server and a client project: an ASP.NET Core Web API for the server and a .NET MAUI app for the client. The server will use SignalR to send updates to clients, while the .NET MAUI app will use SignalR's client library to receive updates and refresh the UI:

1. Start by creating a new ASP.NET Core Web API project. In the project creation dialog, uncheck everything except **Configure for HTTPS** and **Enable OpenAPI support**. After the project is set up, remove the default `weatherforecast` endpoint and the `WeatherForecast` record definition from the `Program.cs` file.

2. Next, add a new class named `BidsHub` that inherits from Hub. This class will manage sending and receiving messages. Implement the `AcceptBid` method within this class. The `AcceptBid` method will handle client requests to stop further bids:

    ```
    public class BidsHub : Hub
    {
        public static bool IsAuctionRunning = true;
        public void AcceptBid(string winner)
        {
            IsAuctionRunning = false;
        }
    }
    ```

3. Register SignalR-related services. For this, call the `AddSignalR` method before the `Build` method in the `Program.cs` file:

Program.cs

```
builder.Services.AddSignalR();
```

4. Register a hub endpoint so that client apps can connect to the bids hub. Let's call the endpoint `auction`. To register it, call the `MapHub` method before the `Run` method:

Program.cs

```
app.MapHub<BidsHub>("/auction");
```

5. Set up a cycle to send messages to connected clients using `BidsHub`. Obtain an instance of a hub context with the `GetRequiredService` method and create an async task with a `while` loop that repeatedly calls the `SendAsync` method. Insert the following code before the `Run` method:

    ```
    using (var scope = app.Services.CreateScope())
    {
        var services = scope.ServiceProvider;
    ```

```
var hubContext = services
  .GetRequiredService<IHubContext<BidsHub>>();
_ = Task.Run(async () =>
{
    Random rnd = new Random();
    int price = 1;
    while (BidsHub.IsAuctionRunning)
    {
        price = rnd.Next(price, price + 10);
        await hubContext.Clients.All
          .SendAsync("BidReceived",
            new { Bidder = $"Company{rnd.Next(1, 10)}",
              Price = price });
        await Task.Delay(rnd.Next(500, 3000));
    }
});
}
```

We used the `_ = Task.Run` construction to indicate that we don't need to work with the result of the task, which is a common pattern when you don't need to await the task's completion. The cycle will continue running until `IsAuctionRunning` is set to false in the `AcceptBid` method of `BidsHub`, as introduced in *step 2*. In the `SendAsync` method, we specify the handler name `BidReceived`, which will be created on the client side, and pass the data as a parameter. This data is an anonymous object containing the `Bidder` and `Price` properties.

6. Now, let's move to the client part. Add a new .NET MAUI project to the existing solution and reference the following NuGet packages:

    -   `Microsoft.AspNetCore.SignalR.Client`: Reference this to use client-side SignalR APIs.

    -   `CommunityToolkit.Mvvm`: Reference this to use auto-generated view models.

    -   `CommunityToolkit.Maui`: Reference this to use the `EventToCommand` behavior. Don't forget to call `UseMauiCommunityToolkit` in the `MauiProgram.CreateMauiApp` method to initialize the library.

7. Create a new class named `BidData`. We will use it to deserialize data received from the server:

    ```
    public class BidData(string bidder, decimal price)
    {
        public string Bidder { get; set; } = bidder;
        public decimal Price { get; set; } = price;
    }
    ```

As you may have noticed, we used the same property names as in the object passed to the `SendAsync` method in the previous step.

8. Create a view model named `MainViewModel`. Add fields to keep track of the hub connection, received bids, and whether a client accepted a bid:

```
public partial class MainViewModel : ObservableObject
{
    HubConnection hubConnection;
    bool isBidAccepted;

    [ObservableProperty]
    ObservableCollection<BidData> bids = new
      ObservableCollection<BidData>();
}
```

9. Set up the hub connection by creating an `Initialize` method. Use `HubConnectionBuilder` to configure the connection. Register a message handler with `HubConnection.On` and start the connection using `HubConnection.StartAsync`:

MainViewModel.cs

```
[RelayCommand]
async Task Initialize()
{
    hubConnection = new HubConnectionBuilder()
        .WithUrl("[Your Dev Tunnel Address]/auction")
        .Build();
    hubConnection.On<BidData>("BidReceived", bid =>
    {
        Bids.Insert(0, bid);
    });
    await hubConnection.StartAsync();
}
```

Note that you need to activate your dev tunnel for the ASP.NET Core app and use the tunnel address in the connection URL. The `auction` suffix corresponds to the endpoint registered in *step 4*.

10. Create a command to accept a bid and end the auction. Add an `AcceptBid` method that calls `HubConnection.InvokeAsyncCore`. Also, define the `CanAcceptBid` method to determine if a bid can be accepted based on the `isBidAccepted` field value:

MainViewModel.cs

```
[RelayCommand(CanExecute = nameof(CanAcceptBid))]
async Task AcceptBid(BidData bid)
{
    await hubConnection.InvokeCoreAsync("AcceptBid",
      args: [bid.Bidder]);
    isBidAccepted = true;
}
bool CanAcceptBid() => !isBidAccepted;
```

11. Finally, create a view to display the bids. Trigger the initialization when the page appears and bind the `AcceptBid` command to a button click:

```
xmlns:vm="clr-namespace:c6_SignalRConnection"
xmlns:tk="http://schemas.microsoft.com/dotnet/2022/maui/toolkit"
<ContentPage.BindingContext>
    <vm:MainViewModel/>
</ContentPage.BindingContext>
<ContentPage.Behaviors>
    <tk:EventToCommandBehavior
        EventName="Appearing"
        Command="{Binding InitializeCommand}"/>
</ContentPage.Behaviors>
<ContentPage.Resources>
    <DataTemplate x:Key="bidTemplate"
                  x:DataType="vm:BidData">
        <Grid ColumnDefinitions="*,100"
              RowDefinitions="30,26"
              Padding="6,18">
            <Label Text="{Binding Price, StringFormat='{0:C0}'}"
                   TextColor="Green"
                   FontSize="20"/>
            <Label Text="{Binding Bidder}"
                   Grid.Row="1"/>
            <Button Text="Accept"
                    Command="{Binding Path=BindingContext
                      .AcceptBidCommand,
                      Source={RelativeSource Mode=FindAncestor,
                      AncestorType={x:Type CollectionView}}}"
```

```
                        CommandParameter="{Binding}"
                        HeightRequest="40"
                        Grid.Column="1"
                        Grid.RowSpan="2"/>
            </Grid>
        </DataTemplate>
    </ContentPage.Resources>
    <CollectionView ItemsSource="{Binding Bids}"
                    ItemTemplate="{StaticResource bidTemplate}"/>
```

We're not introducing any new techniques in this step, so we won't go into detail about this view.

Now, you can run and test the application. Make sure to activate the dev tunnel and start the ASP.NET Core project first. Once that's running, launch the .NET MAUI project. Wait for new bids to show up in the collection, and then press the **Accept** button to stop receiving messages.

How it works...

The core object used in SignalR is a **hub**.

> ### Hub
>
> Hub is a central class that handles communication between a server and connected clients. It provides a high-level API for clients and servers to call methods on each other, enabling real-time communication in web applications.

Hubs let you define methods that clients can call on the server, and also methods on the client that the server can call.

On the server side, we used HubContext, which lets you send messages from outside a hub. Since we registered SignalR services in *step 3* with the AddSignalR method, you can access HubContext in any endpoint by adding it as a parameter to the endpoint method. Dependency injection will automatically provide an instance of HubContext.

On the client side, the main class is HubConnection. It allows you to set up handlers for messages from the server and call methods that will be executed on the server.

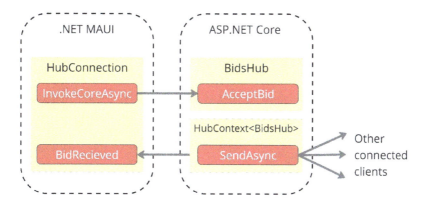

Figure 6.11 – SignalR application structure

The `SendAsync` method sends messages to all connected clients. If you run the application on both an emulator and a physical device, you'll see that both instances of the app receive messages from the server.

There's more...

We sent messages to all clients at once. But what if you need to send a message to just a specific group of users or even a single user? SignalR makes this easy by letting you specify a group name or client ID when sending a message.

To send a message to a group of users, start by adding users to a group. You can do this by calling `Groups.AddToGroupAsync` in your Hub class:

```
public class BidsHub : Hub
{
    //...
    public async Task AddToAuctionGroup(string groupName)
    {
        await Groups.AddToGroupAsync(Context.ConnectionId,
            groupName);
    }
}
```

The `Hub` object automatically receives a `Context` object, which includes details about the connection, such as the `ConnectionId` property.

On the client side, you can join a group by calling the AddToAuctionGroup method we defined earlier:

```
await hubConnection.InvokeCoreAsync("AddToAuctionGroup",
  args: ["SomeGroup"]);
```

Once you've added the user to a group, you can send a message to all users in that group from the server by calling the Group method before SendAsync:

```
await hubContext.Clients.Group("SomeGroup")
  .SendAsync("BidReceived", new { Bidder = "CompanyX",
    Price = 100 });
```

When designing SignalR APIs, it's good practice to use object parameters rather than simple types. This approach helps avoid breaking changes if you need to add more data later. For instance, in the BidsHub.AcceptBid method, we used a simple string parameter for the group name:

```
public void AcceptBid(string winner)
{
    IsAuctionRunning = false;
}
```

While we used it here for demonstration, it's better to use a class with properties, such as a Winner property, as the parameter. This way, if you need to introduce new parameters, you won't break existing client apps. Adding properties to a complex object is more flexible and avoids issues with older clients.

Uploading large files in chunks to a server

When working with documents, images, or videos, uploading files to the server is a common task. While it's possible to upload binary data as part of another entity and store it directly in the database, this approach can become problematic. Large files can quickly bloat your database, and users won't see any visual feedback until the entire entity containing the file is fully uploaded.

A more effective solution is to upload files in chunks using a dedicated endpoint on the server. This way, users can see the progress of their uploads. In this example, we'll create an endpoint in an ASP. NET Core application to handle chunked file uploads and build a .NET MAUI client that allows users to select a file and monitor the upload progress.

Figure 6.12 – File uploading demo

Getting ready

In this recipe, we will create both .NET MAUI and ASP.NET Core projects, so make sure that you have the required workloads in Visual Studio to create both project types. Refer to the *Getting ready* section of the *Creating an authentication service with ASP.NET Core Identity* recipe in *Chapter 5* to learn how to install the required workloads. Additionally, we will use a dev tunnel to access an ASP. NET Core service from the .NET MAUI app, so you need to configure it as described in the *There's more…* section of the *Creating an authentication service with ASP.NET Core Identity* recipe in *Chapter 5*.

The code for this recipe is available at `https://github.com/PacktPublishing/.NET-MAUI-Cookbook/tree/main/Chapter06/c6-FileUploading`.

How to do it...

We'll create two projects for this setup: an ASP.NET Core project to handle the file uploads and a .NET MAUI client application that lets users pick a file from their device to upload. Follow these steps:

1. Start by creating a new ASP.NET Core Web API project. In the project wizard, uncheck all options except **Configure for HTTPS** and **Enable OpenAPI support**. Once the project is created, remove the default `weatherforecast` endpoint and `WeatherForecast` record definition from the `Program.cs` file.

2. Add a new folder to the project named `Uploads`. This is where we'll save the files that are uploaded.

3. Create an endpoint for accepting file chunks and call it `upload`. In this endpoint, extract information about the current chunk number and the total number of chunks from the request headers. We'll include this information in the headers when making a request from the client side. The file bytes will be transferred in the request body. Open a temporary file and write the transferred bytes to it. Once the last chunk is received, move the file from the temporary location to the `Uploads` folder:

```
app.MapPost("/upload", async (HttpRequest request) =>
{
    var chunkNumber = int.Parse(request
      .Headers["Chunk-Number"]);
    var totalChunks = int.Parse(request
      .Headers["Total-Chunks"]);
    var fileName = request.Headers["File-Name"];

    var tempFilePath = Path.Combine(Path
      .GetTempPath(), fileName);
    using (var fileStream = new FileStream
      (tempFilePath, FileMode.Append,
      FileAccess.Write))
```

```
        {
            await request.Body.CopyToAsync(fileStream);
        }

        if (chunkNumber == totalChunks - 1)
        {
            var finalFilePath = Path.Combine(Directory
                .GetCurrentDirectory(), "Uploads",
                fileName);
            if (File.Exists(finalFilePath))
            {
                File.Delete(finalFilePath);
            }
            File.Move(tempFilePath, finalFilePath);
        }
        return Results.Ok();
    });
```

4. Add a new .NET MAUI project to the existing solution. Then, include the `CommunityToolkit.Mvvm` NuGet package in this project to leverage auto-generated view models.

5. Create a view model with properties to store the uploaded file name, numeric progress, and text progress of the upload operation. Additionally, create and initialize a field to store `HttpClient` for accessing the service:

```
public partial class MainViewModel : ObservableObject
{
    [ObservableProperty]
    string fileName;

    [ObservableProperty]
    string textProgress;

    [ObservableProperty]
    double uploadProgress;

    HttpClient httpClient = new HttpClient()
    {
        BaseAddress = new Uri("[Dev Tunnel Address]/")
    };
}
```

6. In the view model, create a method that uploads a single file chunk. In this method, create a `ByteArrayContent` object to represent the request body with the file bytes. Set the `Chunk-Number`, `Total-Chunks`, and `File-Name` request headers. Finally, call the `PostAsync` method to send the chunk to the server:

```
async Task<HttpResponseMessage> SendChunkAsync(byte[]
chunkBuffer, int bytesRead, int chunkNumber, int totalChunks)
{
    var content = new ByteArrayContent(chunkBuffer, 0,
      bytesRead);
    content.Headers.Add("Chunk-Number",
      chunkNumber.ToString());
    content.Headers.Add("Total-Chunks",
      totalChunks.ToString());
    content.Headers.Add("File-Name", FileName);

    var response = await httpClient
      .PostAsync("upload", content);
    response.EnsureSuccessStatusCode();
    return response;
}
```

7. Create a method to pick a file and split it into chunks. Use the default `PickAsync` method to select a file. After that, read the file into an array and split the array into chunks of 2 MB each. In a loop, call the `SendChunkAsync` method created in the previous step to send each chunk to the server:

```
[RelayCommand]
async Task UploadFileAsync()
{
    var result = await FilePicker.Default.PickAsync();
    if (result == null)
    {
        return;
    }
    FileName = result.FileName;

    const int chunkSize = 2 * 1024 * 1024;
    var fileStream = new FileStream(result.FullPath,
      FileMode.Open, FileAccess.Read);
    var fileLength = fileStream.Length;
    var totalChunks = (int)Math.Ceiling(
      (double)fileLength / chunkSize);
    TextProgress = "Starting...";
    for (int chunkNumber = 0;
```

```
        chunkNumber < totalChunks; chunkNumber++)
    {
        var chunkBuffer = new byte[chunkSize];
        var bytesRead = await fileStream
          .ReadAsync(chunkBuffer, 0, chunkSize);
        await SendChunkAsync(chunkBuffer, bytesRead,
          chunkNumber, totalChunks);
        UploadProgress = (double)(chunkNumber + 1) /
          totalChunks;
        TextProgress = $"{chunkNumber + 1} / {totalChunks}";
    }
    TextProgress = "Uploaded";
}
```

8. Implement a view with a button to upload a file and display the file name and upload progress:

```
xmlns:vm="clr-namespace:c6_FileUploadingClient"
<ContentPage.BindingContext>
    <vm:MainViewModel/>
</ContentPage.BindingContext>
<VerticalStackLayout VerticalOptions="Center"
                     Spacing="10"
                     Padding="10">
    <Button Text="Upload file"
            Command="{Binding UploadFileCommand}"/>
    <Label Text="{Binding FileName}"/>
    <ProgressBar Progress="{Binding UploadProgress}"/>
    <Label Text="{Binding TextProgress}"/>
</VerticalStackLayout>
```

Now, you can run and test the project. First, activate a dev tunnel. Then, start the server project followed by the client .NET MAUI app. If you're using an emulator, make sure to upload a test file. You can either download a file using a browser on the emulator or drag and drop a file from your desktop machine to the emulator.

How it works...

We used a straightforward approach to handle file uploads. On the client side, we read the file from the device into a stream and process a predefined number of bytes at a time:

```
var bytesRead = await fileStream.ReadAsync(chunkBuffer, 0,
  chunkSize);
```

We sent the bytes to the server using a POST request, including headers that specified the current chunk number, the total number of chunks, and the file name.

On the server side, we set up an endpoint to accept these file chunks. We read the bytes from the request body and appended them to a temporary file:

```
using (var fileStream = new FileStream(tempFilePath,
  FileMode.Append, FileAccess.Write))
{
   await request.Body.CopyToAsync(fileStream);
}
```

We used a temporary file to handle incomplete transfers due to connection issues or client-side errors. Once the server receives the final chunk (as indicated by the header information), we move the file from the temporary location to the `Uploads` directory.

There's more...

Uploading files in chunks offers several benefits:

- **Progress reporting**: You can provide users with real-time updates on the upload progress, which is crucial for large files or users with unstable internet connections.

- **Performance**: Chunked uploading allows the server to start processing the file before the entire upload is complete. While one chunk is being processed, the next chunk is being transferred, improving overall efficiency.

- **Reduced memory usage**: Since the server processes each chunk separately, it doesn't need to load the entire file into memory, thus lowering memory consumption.

Once a file is transferred, you need to decide how to store it on the server. Here are some common alternatives when considering solutions for file storage:

- **Filesystem**: Save files directly to the filesystem, with database objects storing only metadata, such as file path, name, type, size, and checksum.

- **Database binary large objects (BLOBs)**: Store files as binary data directly in the database. This method can be convenient for small files but is generally less suitable for large files due to increased database size and complexity in backups. It can also be costly with cloud databases.

- **Cloud storage services**: Use services such as Amazon S3, Azure Blob Storage, or Google Cloud Storage. These services offer scalability, resilience, access control, and encryption, though they come with associated costs.

- **Content delivery network (CDN)**: Store files in cloud storage and use a CDN to serve them. This method speeds up access and reduces latency, and while it is commonly used for web assets such as images and CSS, it can also be applied in mobile and desktop apps for audio or video streaming.

Sending local push notifications

Alerts, reminders, and updates for ongoing in-app processes are great use cases for local push notifications. It's important to understand the difference between local and remote notifications. Local notifications are scheduled or triggered from within your app and do not come from a server. While local notifications can appear even if your app isn't running, they must be scheduled in advance to achieve this.

In .NET MAUI, creating a local push notification is straightforward with the `Plugin.LocalNotification` library. By calling a few methods, you can send and manage notifications. In this recipe, we'll build a basic app that sends a custom local push notification.

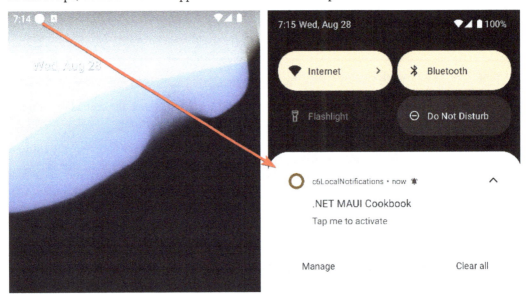

Figure 6.13 – Local push notifications demo

> **Important**
> The `Plugin.LocalNotification` library supports only Android and iOS. You can't show notifications using it in Windows or macOS.

Getting ready

To follow the steps described in this recipe, we just need to create a blank .NET MAUI application.

The code for this recipe is available at `https://github.com/PacktPublishing/.NET-MAUI-Cookbook/tree/main/Chapter06/c6-LocalNotifications`.

How to do it...

We will create a very simple application with minimal modifications from the default .NET MAUI template project. Essentially, we'll need to add a NuGet package with a library that manages notifications, use the library to create a notification request, and request user permission for notifications. Follow these steps:

1. Let's start by creating a new .NET MAUI project. In this project, add the `Plugin.LocalNotification` NuGet package, which provides functionality for local notifications.

2. Next, create a notification request and send a notification. To do this, replace the content of the default `OnCounterClicked` method with the following code:

```
private void OnCounterClicked(object sender,
   EventArgs e) {
     var request = new NotificationRequest
     {
         NotificationId = 123,
         Title = ".NET MAUI Cookbook",
         Description = "Tap me to activate",
         BadgeNumber = 2,
         Schedule = new NotificationRequestSchedule
         {
             NotifyTime = DateTime.Now.AddSeconds(7),
         },
     };
     LocalNotificationCenter.Current.Show(request);
}
```

The `NotificationRequest` object holds details about the notification. In the preceding code snippet, we set up a notification to appear seven seconds after clicking the button. The `BadgeNumber` property specifies the number displayed with the notification. Keep in mind that the display format of notifications can vary depending on the platform and OS version. `NotificationId` can be any unique number and helps identify notifications when they are triggered.

3. Subscribe to the `NotificationActionTapped` event in the `MainPage.xaml.cs` file to handle user interactions with the notification:

```
public MainPage()
{
    InitializeComponent();
    LocalNotificationCenter.Current
       .NotificationActionTapped +=
       OnNotificationActionTapped;
}
```

```
private async void OnNotificationActionTapped
  (NotificationActionEventArgs e)
{
    if (e.IsTapped)
    {
        //...
        return;
    }
    if (e.IsDismissed)
    {
        //...
        return;
    }
}
```

4. Define the required permissions for Android. Navigate to the `Platforms/Android/`
    `AndroidManifest.xml` file, right-click it, and select **Open With | XML (Text) Editor**.
    Add the following user permission tags:

```
<uses-permission android:name="android.permission.POST_
  NOTIFICATIONS" />
<uses-permission android:name="android.permission.RECEIVE_BOOT_
  COMPLETED" />
<uses-permission android:name="android.permission.VIBRATE" />
```

5. To add permissions on iOS, navigate to `Platforms/iOS/Info.plist`, right-click this
    file, and select **Open With | XML (Text) Editor**. After that, add the following tags to the
    dictionary with other keys:

```
<key>UIBackgroundModes</key>
<array>

<string>fetch</string>

<string>remote-notification</string>
</array>
```

6. To request user permission when the application starts, subscribe to the Loaded event of the main page and call RequestNotificationPermission if permission hasn't been granted before. To check if notifications are already enabled, use the AreNotificationsEnabled method:

```
private async void OnLoaded(object sender,
  EventArgs e)
{
    if (await LocalNotificationCenter.Current
      .AreNotificationsEnabled() == false)
    {
        await LocalNotificationCenter.Current
          .RequestNotificationPermission();
    }
}
```

Note that it's necessary to add the async keyword to the Loaded handler because we are calling asynchronous methods.

Now, you can run the project and click the button. After seven seconds, you should see a notification icon at the top of the screen. Swipe down to view the notification content.

How it works...

The main class for managing notifications is LocalNotificationCenter. This class lets you show notifications, handle notification events, and request permission to display notifications to users.

You define notifications using the NotificationRequest object, which includes all the details that will be presented to the user:

- Title
- Subtitle
- Description
- Badge
- Icon
- Sound
- Platform-specific elements (such as action buttons for Android)

Keep in mind that the appearance of notifications can vary depending on the platform and OS version. So, some of these properties might not always affect how the notification looks when you test it on your device.

There's more...

As mentioned in the *How it works...* section, the `Plugin.LocalNotification` library has more features than those covered in this recipe. The library is continually evolving, so the API might change over time. For the latest details, code snippets, and sample projects, check out the repository wiki here: `https://github.com/thudugala/Plugin.LocalNotification/wiki`.

Synchronizing data between offline and online databases

In today's world, we're so used to having internet access all the time that being offline, even for a few hours, feels uncomfortable. But it's common for mobile devices to occasionally lose connection or change the IP address, causing mid-stream disconnections. Even then, we still expect our apps to keep working – at least in offline mode. Take WhatsApp, for instance. You can open the app, read messages that were already loaded, write a new one, and have it added to a queue to send later. This is all thanks to syncing data between offline and online modes.

Another reason to consider offline data storage is performance. With local data storage, you can avoid network delays and offer a smoother experience for your users.

Syncing data can be a bit challenging since both the server and the client might update the same data at the same time, leading to conflicts that need to be handled. Plus, you usually don't want to copy the entire server database to the client, so the local data may need some restructuring. To simplify this process, we'll use the `CommunityToolkit.Datasync` library, which is built to sync data between client and server apps.

In this recipe, we'll create a .NET MAUI app that functions in both online and offline modes. The app will allow users to add new items and display them in a list. When the app is online, it will automatically sync local and remote data. While offline, it will rely solely on the local SQLite database, and any changes will be stored locally without being uploaded to the server. Once the connection is restored, the data will sync again.

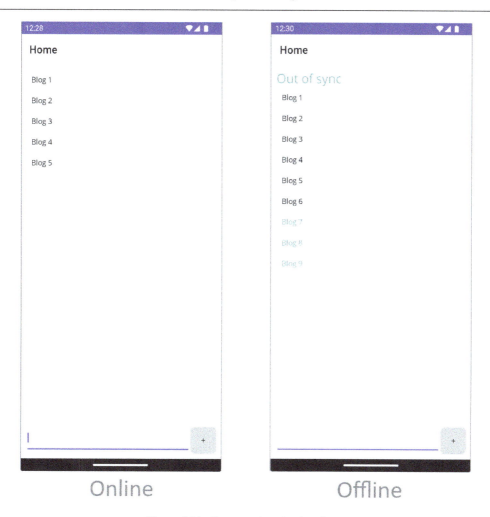

Figure 6.14 – Data synchronization demo

Getting ready

In this recipe, we will create both .NET MAUI and ASP.NET Core projects, so make sure that you have the required workloads in Visual Studio to create both project types. Refer to the *Getting ready* section of the *Creating an authentication service with ASP.NET Core Identity* recipe in *Chapter 5* to learn how to install the required workloads. Additionally, we will use a dev tunnel to access an ASP. NET Core service from the .NET MAUI app, so you need to configure it as described in the *There's more...* section of the *Creating an authentication service with ASP.NET Core Identity* recipe in *Chapter 5*.

We will use SQL Server on the server side, so if you don't have it, download and install the free *Developer* edition available at this link: `https://www.microsoft.com/en-za/sql-server/sql-server-downloads`.

For macOS users, you can either run SQL Server in a Docker container or use an alternative database, such as LiteDB, as described in the Datasync documentation: `https://communitytoolkit.github.io/Datasync/index.html`.

You can download the code for this recipe at `https://github.com/PacktPublishing/.NET-MAUI-Cookbook/tree/main/Chapter06/c6-OfflineDataSync`.

How to do it...

In this recipe, we'll begin by setting up and configuring a service. To handle data synchronization, we'll use a standard ASP.NET Core Web API application along with a few NuGet packages and some adjustments. Then, we'll create a .NET MAUI app that uses the **Datasync** client library to sync data between the app and the server. Follow these steps:

1. Let's create a new ASP.NET Core Web API project in Visual Studio. In the project wizard, uncheck all options except **Configure for HTTPS** and **Enable OpenAPI support**. Once the project is created, remove the default `weatherforecast` endpoint and the `WeatherForecast` record definition from the `Program.cs` file.

2. Install the following NuGet packages:

   - `CommunityToolkit.Datasync.Server`: Install this to access core data synchronization functionality

   - `CommunityToolkit.Datasync.Server.EntityFrameworkCore`: Install this to use **Entity Framework** (**EF**) when working with a database

   - `Microsoft.EntityFrameworkCore.SqlServer`: Install this to use SQL Server for data storing and management

3. Add a `Blog` class with a single `Title` property. Inherit this class from `EntityTableData`, which includes basic properties required for the synchronization engine (such as `Id`, `UpdatedAt`, `Version`, and `Deleted`):

   ```
   public class Blog : EntityTableData
   {
       [Required, MinLength(2)]
       public string Title { get; set; } = string.Empty;
   }
   ```

   We've added the `Required` and `MinLength` attributes to avoid blogs with empty titles.

4. Create an `AppDbContext` class inherited from `DbContext`. Define a public `InitializeDatabaseAsync` method so that we can call it during database initialization:

```
public class AppDbContext(DbContextOptions
  <AppDbContext> options) : DbContext(options)
{
    public DbSet<Blog> Blogs => Set<Blog>();
    public async Task InitializeDatabaseAsync()
    {
        await Database.EnsureCreatedAsync();
    }
}
```

Just like in any EF Core project, `AppDbContext` handles the connection between your app and the database.

5. Create a `Controllers` folder and add the `BlogController` class inherited from `TableController` included in the Datasync library. `TableController` contains data synchronization endpoints that will be used by the client app:

```
using Microsoft.AspNetCore.Mvc;

namespace c6_OfflineDataSyncServer
{
    [Route("tables/[controller]")]
    public class BlogController (AppDbContext
      context) : TableController<Blog>(new
        EntityTableRepository<Blog>(context))
    {   }
}
```

While we won't use the `BlogController` class explicitly, the ASP.NET Core engine will automatically discover and register it when we call `AddControllers` in the next step.

6. Register `AppDbContext`, Datasync services, and controllers in the dependency injection container:

Program.cs

```
var connectionString = @"Server=(localdb)\
    mssqllocaldb; Database=MyDatabase;
    Trusted_Connection=True;
    MultipleActiveResultSets=true";
builder.Services.AddDbContext<AppDbContext>(options =>
  options.UseSqlServer(connectionString));
builder.Services.AddDatasyncServices();
builder.Services.AddControllers();
```

Note that we've configured `AppDbContext` to work with SQL Server, so you'll need to have it installed on your machine, as mentioned in the *Getting ready* section. For macOS users, you can either run SQL Server in a Docker container or use an alternative database, such as LiteDB, as described in the Datasync documentation: `https://communitytoolkit.github.io/Datasync/index.html`.

7. Call `MapControllers` to map controllers to endpoints:

Program.cs

```
app.MapControllers();
```

8. Our service is set up, so now we can shift our focus to the client. Create a new .NET MAUI application. You can remove all the default controls from the `MainPage.xaml` file, leaving just the page constructor in `MainPage.xaml.cs`.

9. Add the following NuGet packages:

   - `CommunityToolkit.Datasync.Client`: Add this to access the client data synchronization API.

   - `CommunityToolkit.Mvvm`: Add this to build a view model with auto-generated members.

   - `CommunityToolkit.Maui`: Add this to use the `HideKeyboardAsync` method, which will allow us to hide the keyboard after entering a new blog title. To use this library, don't forget to call `UseMauiCommunityToolkit` in the `MauiProgram.CreateMauiApp` method.

10. Create an `OfflineClientEntity` class with the basic properties that the Datasync library will use for synchronization:

```
public abstract class OfflineClientEntity
{
    [Key]
    public string Id { get; set; } =
      Guid.NewGuid().ToString("N");
    public DateTimeOffset? UpdatedAt { get; set; }
    public string? Version { get; set; }
    public bool Deleted { get; set; }
}
```

11. Next, create a `Blog` class inherited from `OfflineClientEntity`. Add the `Title` property just like we did in the server project. Additionally, define an `InSync` property to indicate whether a blog is synchronized with the server. Since we won't be storing this property in the database, mark it with the `NotMapped` attribute:

```
public class Blog : OfflineClientEntity
{
    public string Title { get; set; } = string.Empty;
    [NotMapped]
    public bool InSync { get; set; } = true;
}
```

12. Create a `LocalAppDbContext` class inherited from `OfflineDbContext`. Define the `Blogs` property so that EF Core creates a local `Blogs` table for us. Additionally, override the `OnConfiguring` method to set up the local database connection string:

LocalAppDbContext.cs

```
public class LocalAppDbContext : OfflineDbContext
{
    public DbSet<Blog> Blogs => Set<Blog>();
    protected override void OnConfiguring
        (DbContextOptionsBuilder optionsBuilder){
            string dbPath = Path.Combine(FileSystem
                .AppDataDirectory, "local.db");
            optionsBuilder.UseSqlite($"Filename=
{dbPath}");
            base.OnConfiguring(optionsBuilder);
        }
}
```

The `OfflineDbContext` class is available in the `CommunityToolkit.Datasync.Client` library and extends it with additional capabilities for data synchronization.

13. In the `LocalAppDbContext` class, override the `OnDatasyncInitialization` method to specify the service endpoint:

LocalAppDbContext.cs

```
protected override void OnDatasyncInitialization
    (DatasyncOfflineOptionsBuilder optionsBuilder) {
        HttpClientOptions clientOptions = new()
        {
            Endpoint = new Uri("[YOUR DEV TUNNEL URL]/"),
        };
```

```
            _ = optionsBuilder.UseHttpClientOptions
                (clientOptions);
        }
```

As in the previous chapters, to obtain your dev tunnel address, select the service application as the startup project, activate the dev tunnel, and run it. You'll see the address in the browser's URL. Copy the text that appears before the /swagger part of the URL.

14. Define a SynchronizeAsync method that will be used to synchronize data. To do this, first call PushAsync to upload any changed items to the server. Then, call PullAsync to retrieve fresh data:

LocalAppDbContext.cs

```
public async Task SynchronizeAsync(
    CancellationToken cancellationToken = default) {
    PushResult pushResult = await this.PushAsync(
        cancellationToken );
    if (!pushResult.IsSuccessful)  {
        throw new ApplicationException($"Push failed:
            {pushResult.FailedRequests.FirstOrDefault()
                .Value.ReasonPhrase}" );
    }
    PullResult pullResult = await this.PullAsync(
        cancellationToken );
    if (!pullResult.IsSuccessful)   {
        throw new ApplicationException($"Pull failed:
            {pullResult.FailedRequests.FirstOrDefault()
                .Value.ReasonPhrase}" );
    }
}
```

15. Create a view model with properties to store the following information:

- A collection of blogs

- New item text

- A Boolean indicating whether the app is synchronized with the service

- A Boolean indicating whether the data is currently refreshing

MainViewModel.cs

```
public partial class MainViewModel : ObservableObject
{
```

```
        [ObservableProperty]
        ConcurrentObservableCollection<Blog> items = [];

        [ObservableProperty]
        [NotifyCanExecuteChangedFor(nameof(AddBlogCommand))]
        string newItemText = string.Empty;

        [ObservableProperty]
        bool outOfSync;

        [ObservableProperty]
        bool isRefreshing = true;
}
```

16. Add a `Refresh` command that will be invoked when the view appears and when a user requests a refresh. In this command, set `OutOfSync` to `true` if the synchronization doesn't succeed. Additionally, create a `SetNonSyncedItems` method that sets `InSync` to false for all unsynchronized items. To do this, iterate through `OfflineDbContext.DatasyncOperationsQueue`, which contains all pending items:

MainViewModel.cs

```
    [RelayCommand]
    async Task RefreshAsync() {
        IsRefreshing = true;
        using var context = new LocalAppDbContext();
        SetNonSyncedItems(context);
        Items = new ConcurrentObservableCollection
          <Blog>(context.Blogs);
        try {
            await context.SynchronizeAsync();
            Items = new ConcurrentObservableCollection
              <Blog>(context. Blogs);
            OutOfSync = false;
        }
        catch {
            OutOfSync = true;
        }
        finally {
            IsRefreshing = false;
        }
    }
    void SetNonSyncedItems(LocalAppDbContext context)
```

```
    {
        var queuedBlogs = context.DatasyncOperationsQueue
          .Where(x => x.EntityType == typeof(Blog)
          .FullName);
        foreach (var blog in queuedBlogs)
        {
            if (blog.State != OperationState.Completed)
            {
                var item = context.Blogs.Find(blog
                  .ItemId);
                item.InSync = false;
            }
        }
    }
```

The Datasync client library creates a table with an operations queue
(DatasyncOperationsQueue). To determine if an item is synchronized, we search for
ItemId in this table and check the OperationState value, which can be Pending,
Completed, or Failed.

17. Add an AddBlog command to add a new blog:

```
[RelayCommand(CanExecute = nameof(CanAddBlog))]
void AddBlog() {
    var newBlog = new Blog()
    {
        Title = NewItemText,
        InSync = false,
    };
    Items.Add(newBlog);
    NewItemText = string.Empty;
    SaveChangedItem(newBlog);
}
bool CanAddBlog() =>
    !string.IsNullOrEmpty(NewItemText);
```

18. Implement the SaveChangedItem method to save the added blog to the local database
(SaveChanges) and push it to the server (PushAsync). Additionally, update the local
collection (Items) to reflect changes in the UI:

```
void SaveChangedItem(Blog newBlog) {
    Task.Run(async () =>
    {
        using var context = new LocalAppDbContext();
        context.Blogs.Add(newBlog);
```

```
            context.SaveChanges();
            PushResult pushResult = await context
              .PushAsync();
            if (pushResult.IsSuccessful)
            {
                UpdateCollectionItem(newBlog.Id);
            }
        });
    }
    void UpdateCollectionItem(string itemId) {
        using var context = new LocalAppDbContext();
        var freshItem = context.Blogs.Find(itemId);
        Shell.Current.Dispatcher.Dispatch(() =>
        {
            Items.ReplaceIf(item => item.Id == itemId,
              freshItem);
        });
    }
```

Note that while `OfflineDbContext` has the `SaveChangesAsync` method, SQLite data providers don't support asynchronous operations. To execute all operations without freezing the UI, we create a new task using `Task.Run`. In the `UpdateCollectionItem` method, we use `Dispatcher.Dispatch` to update the `Items` collection on the UI thread. This is necessary because the `CollectionView` that handles the `Items` collection changes operates in the UI thread, and .NET MAUI doesn't allow visual controls to function in background threads.

19. Now, let's implement a view with the following elements:

- `CollectionView`: This is for displaying blogs.

- `Entry`: This is for typing in a new blog title.

- `Button`: This is to invoke the `Add` command.

- `RefreshView`: This is to enable the pull-to-refresh gesture for data refresh.

- `label`: This is to display the `Out of sync` text when the `OutOfSync` property is `true`.

- `DataTemplate`: This is to represent blogs. In the template, add a trigger that changes the blog title color when `InSync` is `false`:

MainPage.xaml

```
xmlns:model="clr-namespace:c6_OfflineDataSyncClient.Model"
xmlns:vm="clr-namespace:c6_OfflineDataSyncClient"

<ContentPage.BindingContext>
```

```xml
        <vm:MainViewModel/>
    </ContentPage.BindingContext>
    <ContentPage.Resources>
        <DataTemplate x:Key="blogTemplate"
                      x:DataType="model:Blog">
            <Label Text="{Binding Title}"
                   Margin="10">
                <Label.Triggers>
                    <DataTrigger Binding="{Binding InSync}"
                                         Value="False"
                                         TargetType="Label">
                        <Setter Property="TextColor"
Value="CadetBlue"/>
                    </DataTrigger>
                </Label.Triggers>
            </Label>
        </DataTemplate>
    </ContentPage.Resources>
    <Grid RowDefinitions="Auto, *,50"
          ColumnDefinitions="*,50"
          Padding="10">
        <Label Text="Out of sync"
               IsVisible="{Binding OutOfSync}"
               FontSize="24"
               TextColor="CadetBlue"/>
        <RefreshView Command="{Binding RefreshCommand}"
                     IsRefreshing="{Binding IsRefreshing}"
                     Grid.Row="1"
                     Grid.ColumnSpan="2">
            <CollectionView ItemsSource="{Binding Items}"
                     ItemTemplate="{StaticResource blogTemplate}"
                     Grid.Row="1"/>
        </RefreshView>
        <Entry x:Name="newBlogEntry"
               Text="{Binding NewItemText}"
               Grid.Row="2"/>
        <Button Text="+"
                Command="{Binding AddBlogCommand}"
                Clicked="OnAddClicked"
                Grid.Row="2"
                Grid.Column="1"/>
    </Grid>
```

We subscribed to the `Button.Clicked` event to hide the keyboard when the **Add** button is tapped.

20. Call `HideKeyboardAsync` available in the `CommunityToolkit.Maui` to hide the keyboard when the **Add** button is tapped:

MainPage.xaml.cs

```
using CommunityToolkit.Maui.Core.Platform;
//...
private void OnAddClicked(object sender, EventArgs e) {
    newBlogEntry.HideKeyboardAsync(CancellationToken
        .None);
}
```

Now you can run and test the project:

1. Activate your dev tunnel.

2. Run the ASP.NET Core project.

3. Run the .NET MAUI project.

4. In the running .NET MAUI app, add a few blogs by typing their title and pressing the plus button.

5. Stop the service app without stopping the client.

6. Add a few more items to the collection. These items should be displayed in a different color to indicate that they are not synchronized.

7. Pull the collection down to invoke the pull-to-refresh action. Alternatively, re-run the .NET MAUI app. You should see the `Out of sync` label.

How it works...

When building an app that uses the Datasync library for data synchronization, there are a few key components to keep in mind:

- `TableController`: This server-side class sets up endpoints for retrieving and modifying data. It's built on OData and creates a RESTful API that supports RFC-9110-compliant operations such as `Create` (via POST), `Replace` (via PUT), and `Delete` (via DELETE), along with OData-compatible `List` and `Get` functionalities. As a result, `TableController<T>` is one of the ways to construct RESTful APIs with full authentication and authorization even without Datasync capabilities.

- **Server database**: In this recipe, we used SQL Server, but other databases can also be used. You can find more details here: `https://communitytoolkit.github.io/Datasync/in-depth/server/databases/index.html`. The database stores properties defined in your model class, along with service information, such as entity IDs, timestamps, and versioning.

- `OfflineDbContext`: This client-side class handles the storing, retrieving, and syncing of data. It has the `PushAsync` and `PullAsync` methods to upload data to the server and fetch the latest updates. When setting up `OfflineDbContext`, you'll specify the service base address, so it knows where to get the data.

- **Client database**: We used SQLite since it's commonly used on mobile devices. The client database typically includes three tables: data entities (e.g., Blogs), synchronization timestamps (`DatasyncDeltaTokens`), and pending sync operations (`DatasyncOperationsQueue`). Most of the time, you'll only interact with the data entities. However, sometimes, you might need to access the pending operations (`DatasyncOperationsQueue`), like in our recipe, where we marked items that hadn't been synced yet. You generally don't need to interact with the `DatasyncDeltaTokens` table – it's managed by the system to track when a table was last synced, so it only pulls the changes. If you ever need a full data refresh, though, you'll need to clear both the `DatasyncOperationsQueue` and `DatasyncDeltaTokens` tables.

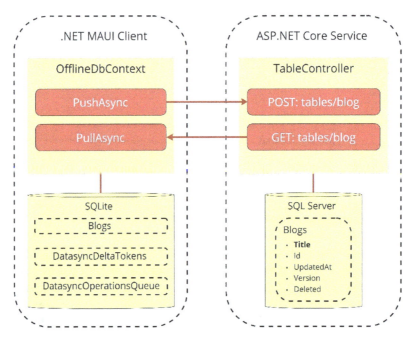

Figure 6.15 – Datasync key components

The Datasync library adds the following properties to data entities for correct synchronization:

- `Id`: An identifier that must be globally unique. While a common choice for `Id` for this purpose is v4 UUID, you can use any globally unique string (such as snowflake IDs). A globally unique `Id` helps avoid conflicts if two clients push data to the server at the same time.

- `UpdatedAt`: This indicates the last time the entity was updated on the server. It's crucial for incremental synchronization, as it ensures that only entities modified since the last sync are downloaded to the client. Notably, this timestamp is accurate to the millisecond, and it's expected that each record on the server side will have a unique `UpdatedAt` value, which helps with paging.

- `Version`: This acts as an opaque concurrency token. It's used by the client (and in the protocol defined by RFC 9110) to ensure that a change is only made on the server if the server's version matches the one provided by the client. This mechanism is essential for conflict resolution.

- `Deleted`: This is a Boolean flag that indicates the entity stored on the server should be deleted on the client. This property is crucial for implementing a soft delete mechanism, where a record is marked as deleted instead of being permanently removed. Using soft deletes in production systems helps ensure that deletions are properly propagated to all clients.

There's more...

Here's a quick look at some additional features offered by the Datasync library:

- **Selective synchronization**: You can control which entities are synced using LINQ-based conditions or by excluding entire tables.

- **Online operations**: Not all data needs to be stored locally. For certain information, you can opt for an online-only mode.

- **Authentication integration**: Datasync can be used alongside authentication and authorization mechanisms to restrict access to service data.

- **Configuring access permissions**: You can set up rules to control which data a specific user has access to.

- **Database flexibility**: The library supports various databases, including SQL Server, PostgreSQL, LiteDB, and more.

- **Custom actions**: You can inject actions to run before or after data is modified on the service. For instance, you could analyze newly added data or broadcast it to other users via SignalR.

- **Logging integration**: You can log requests sent to the server, which is helpful for error tracking, auditing, and other monitoring tasks.

- **OpenAPI support**: This feature lets you view the available service APIs right in the browser.

For more details on how to take advantage of these features, check out the official documentation: `https://communitytoolkit.github.io/Datasync`.

Alternatives to the Datasync framework include Realm and Firebase, which require you to use specific online services. You can also build your own by using CQRS.

7

Understanding Platform-Specific APIs and Custom Handlers

Even though .NET MAUI is designed to allow a single code base for all supported platforms, there are still compelling reasons to write platform-specific code:

- **Platform-specific settings**: Each platform may have its own unique settings. For instance, iOS uses a different address to access the host machine compared to Android.

- **User interface differences**: In the first chapter (*Crafting the Page Layout*), we built UIs tailored to each platform using primarily XAML techniques. However, for more complex scenarios, you might need to implement custom logic in C# to meet specific platform requirements.

- **Platform view customization**: .NET MAUI wraps native views for each platform, providing customization options through its APIs. However, many underlying platform capabilities are not directly exposed through these wrappers. For instance, in our next chapter, dedicated to performance, we'll explore how to measure view loading speed by tapping into these hidden platform features.

In this chapter, we'll dive into various techniques for implementing platform-specific behavior and leveraging the full potential of native platform views. We'll cover how to compile code based on the current platform, create a custom class with a cross-platform API, and customize existing controls with handlers.

In this chapter, we'll be covering the following recipes:

- Compiling code based on the target platform
- Implementing a cross-platform API
- Customizing a platform view with an existing control handler
- Creating a custom handler

Technical requirements

There are no specific requirements for the recipes in this chapter. All of them start with a basic .NET MAUI application created by the default Visual Studio template.

You can download all the projects created in this chapter from GitHub: `https://github.com/PacktPublishing/.NET-MAUI-Cookbook/tree/main/Chapter07`.

Compiling code based on the target platform

.NET offers a powerful mechanism that lets you compile code based on specific conditions and parameters. This feature is known as **preprocessor directives**, and more specifically, **conditional compilation directives**.

> **Preprocessor directives**
>
> Preprocessor directives are instructions processed by the compiler before the actual compilation of the code begins.

Preprocessor directives have a wide range of applications, and we're focusing on them here because they enable us to include specific code sections in the compilation process based on the target platform

In this recipe, we'll create a simple example that displays the current platform name on a label. However, platform-based compilation is a versatile tool that can be utilized in various scenarios, such as the following:

- **Calling platform APIs**: Access APIs that are available only on specific platforms, for instance, getting the custom accent color that is available only on Android and Windows but not on iOS
- **Specifying settings based on the platform**: For example, you might specify different base addresses for `HttpClient` to access the host machine – one for iOS and another for Android

Getting ready

To follow the steps described in this recipe, we just need to create a blank .NET MAUI application.

The code for this recipe is available at `https://github.com/PacktPublishing/.NET-MAUI-Cookbook/tree/main/Chapter07/c7-ConditionalCompilation`.

How to do it...

To see preprocessor directives in action, let's create a simple application that uses a `Label` element to display the name of the current platform:

1. Create a new .NET MAUI project.

2. Replace the default code from `MainPage.xaml` with a label:

   ```
   <Label x:Name="label"/>
   ```

3. In the `MainPage` constructor, set the `Label.Text` property for each platform. Use the `#if` and `#elif` directives with the platform names as parameters like this:

   ```
   public partial class MainPage : ContentPage
   {
       public MainPage()
       {
           InitializeComponent();
   #if ANDROID
           label.Text = "Android";
   #elif IOS
           label.Text = "iOS";
   #elif WINDOWS
           label.Text = "Windows";
   #elif MACCATALYST
           label.Text = "Mac";
   #endif
       }
   }
   ```

Now, you can run and test the project. You should see the name of the platform on which you're running the application.

How it works...

Preprocessor directives let you control the compilation process based on specified conditions. The directives are marked with the # symbol. We used them to include separate code blocks in compilation for specific platforms. In our example, we set the Label.Text property four times, but when this code was compiled for each platform, only code blocks that correspond to the current platform were included in the resulting package.

It's important to note that preprocessor directives are not evaluated at runtime like normal if/else statements. This means you cannot include or exclude code dynamically during program execution.

There's more...

Conditional compilation symbols are useful beyond just writing platform-specific code. For instance, you can include specific code blocks only when your app is built in a debug configuration:

```
#if DEBUG
    label.Text = "Debugging";
#else
```

You can also create custom conditional compilation symbols to implement simple feature flags, allowing you to create separate builds where a feature is either enabled or disabled:

```
#if MY_SYMBOL
    label.Text = "Custom feature is enabled";
#else
```

You can use the following techniques to define a custom symbol:

- Use the #define directive directly in the code:

    ```
    #define MY_SYMBOL

    namespace c7_ConditionalCompilation
    {
        //...
    }
    ```

- Add the DefineConstants tag to the *.csproj file:

    ```
    <PropertyGroup>
      <DefineConstants>$(DefineConstants);
        MY_SYMBOL</DefineConstants>
    </PropertyGroup>
    ```

- Right-click your project in Visual Studio, select **Properties**, type `conditional compilation` in the search box at the top, and enter a custom symbol name in the corresponding textbox:

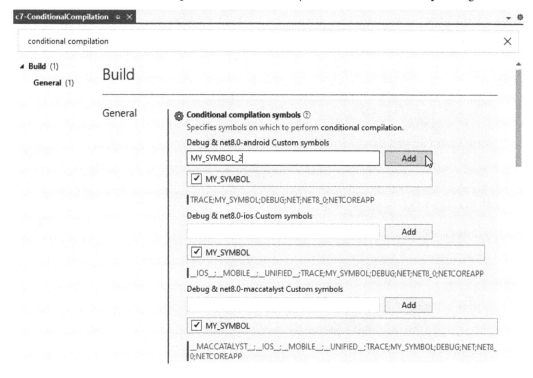

Figure 7.1 – Adding a custom conditional compilation symbol

Implementing a cross-platform API

The preprocessor directives described in the previous recipe are easy to use but can become difficult to read and maintain. A better way to write platform-specific code while keeping things clear is to implement a common cross-platform class with platform-specific implementations.

In this recipe, we'll create a class where the cross-platform logic is defined in the main project, while the platform-specific code is implemented in the `Platforms/ Android/iOS/Windows` folders.

Getting ready

To follow the steps described in this recipe, simply create a blank .NET MAUI application.

The code for this recipe is available at `https://github.com/PacktPublishing/.NET-MAUI-Cookbook/tree/main/Chapter07/c7-CrossPlatformApi`.

How to do it...

Let's modify the project from the previous recipe so that the platform name is returned by a method implemented in platform-specific code. Although .NET MAUI already provides APIs to access the current platform, we'll use this task as a simple example:

1. In a new .NET MAUI project, create a partial class named `PlatformInfo` with a partial method named `GetPlatform`:

```
public partial class PlatformInfo
{
    public static partial string GetPlatform();
}
```

2. In the `Platforms/Android` folder, create a file named `PlatformInfo` and add a partial class with the same name. Implement the `GetPlatform` method to return the `"Android"` string:

```
namespace c7_CrossPlatformApi.Platforms.Android
{
    public partial class PlatformInfo
    {
        public static partial string GetPlatform()
        {
            return "Android";
        }
    }
}
```

Here's an image showing where to place the class:

Figure 7.2 – Android implementation location

3. Remove the `Platforms.Android` suffix from the namespace so that the `PlatformInfo` class in the `Android` folder has the same namespace as the `PlatformInfo` class defined in *step 1*:

```
//namespace c7_CrossPlatformApi.Platforms.Android
namespace c7_CrossPlatformApi
{
    //...
}
```

4. Repeat *steps 2* and *3* for the `Platforms/iOS` and `Platforms/Windows` folders as well, but return `"iOS"` and `"Windows"`, respectively, in the `GetPlatform` method for each. Keep in mind that you need to implement a partial class for every platform listed in the `TargetFrameworks` tag of the `.csproj` file, Otherwise, Visual Studio may display this compilation error: `Partial method 'PlatformInfo.GetPlatform()' must have an implementation part because it has accessibility modifiers.`

Here are the settings in the `.csproj` file that specify the target platforms:

```
<TargetFrameworks>net8.0-android;net8.0-ios</TargetFrameworks>
<TargetFrameworks Condition="$([MSBuild]::IsOSPlatform('wi
ndows'))">$(TargetFrameworks);net8.0-windows10.0.19041.0</
TargetFrameworks>
```

For simplicity, we've removed Mac Catalyst and Tizen from the `.csproj` file, but feel free to keep them if you're targeting either platform.

5. In the `MainPage` constructor, set `Label.Text` to the string returned by the `PlatformInfo.GetPlatform` method:

```
public MainPage()
{
    InitializeComponent();
    label.Text = PlatformInfo.GetPlatform();
}
```

Now, you can run and test the project. The label should display the name of the current platform.

How it works...

The .NET MAUI compilation system automatically includes files from the `Android`, `iOS`, `Windows`, and `MacCatalyst` folders based on the platform you're building the project for. While we've defined multiple versions of the `PlatformInfo` class, the final output will only contain two: the cross-platform version and the platform-specific version.

This approach allows us to define cross-platform APIs while, behind the scenes, these APIs rely on platform-specific code:

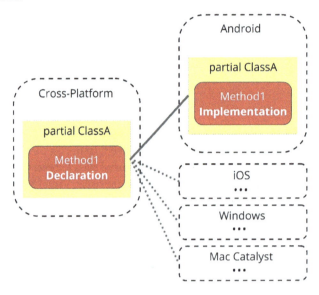

Figure 7.3 – Cross-platform API class with platform-specific implementation

There's more...

In this recipe, we added platform-specific code to their respective folders (Android, iOS, Windows, etc.). The code in these folders is compiled only when you build the project for the corresponding platform. However, you can organize the project structure differently by placing all platform-specific files in the same directory. To determine when to include a file in the compilation process, you can use the filename:

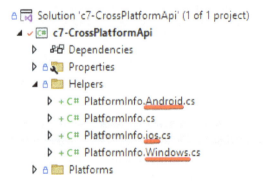

Figure 7.4 – Platform code in a single folder

To modify the compilation rules based on this structure, use a combination of `<ItemGroup>`, `<Compile>`, and `<None>` tags in your `.csproj` file. For example, to adjust the rules for Android, you can use the following code:

```
<ItemGroup Condition="$(TargetFramework.StartsWith
  ('net8.0-android')) != true">
  <Compile Remove="**\Android\**\*.cs" />
  <None Include="**\Android\**\*.cs"
Exclude="$(DefaultItemExcludes);$(DefaultExcludesInProjectFolder)" />
</ItemGroup>
```

Customizing a platform view with an existing control handler

.NET MAUI is built on multiple layers, with the top .NET layer abstracting the platform implementations for each platform. However, native platform controls have unique APIs that can't always be simplified into a single cross-platform API. As a result, MAUI controls may not expose all the APIs available in their native counterparts. This is why we sometimes may need to interact with platform controls through .NET MAUI handlers.

> **Handlers**
>
> A control handler in .NET MAUI is an object that connects a cross-platform UI control with its native platform-specific counterpart. It serves as a bridge between the shared properties defined in .NET MAUI controls and the native platform elements.

UI components in .NET MAUI already come with handlers, allowing us to access and customize the native controls used under the hood. In this recipe, we'll utilize an existing handler of the `Entry` element to customize its selection color for each platform.

Getting ready

To follow the steps described in this recipe, simply create a blank .NET MAUI application.

The code for this recipe is available at `https://github.com/PacktPublishing/.NET-MAUI-Cookbook/tree/main/Chapter07/c7-PlatformViewCustomization`.

How to do it...

Let's create a simple application using the Entry element. We'll access the platform controls behind the Entry element to set the text selection color. Although the Entry element doesn't provide a property to set the selection color directly, such properties do exist in the native controls for Android, iOS, and Windows. We can access these properties through handlers:

1. Create a new project and add a new partial class named PlatformCustomizer. In the class, define a partial CustomizeEntry method:

    ```
    public static partial class PlatformCustomizer
    {
        public static partial void CustomizeEntry(object
          platformView);
    }
    ```

    We will implement the CustomizeEntry method for each platform separately, just as we did in the previous recipe for the GetPlatform method.

2. In the Platforms/Android folder, create a similar PlatformCustomizer class and implement CustomizeEntry in the following manner:

    ```
    using AndroidX.AppCompat.Widget;
    namespace c7_CustomizeHandler
    {
        public static partial class PlatformCustomizer
        {
            public static partial void CustomizeEntry
              (object platformView)
            {
                AppCompatEditText editor =
                  (AppCompatEditText)platformView;
                editor.SetHighlightColor(Android
                  .Graphics.Color.Argb(255, 0, 255, 209));
            }
        }
    }
    ```

    AppCompatEditText is the native control that gets created behind the scenes when the Entry MAUI element is used on Android devices. Keep in mind that the *namespace for all partial classes should match*.

3. For iOS, create `PlatformCustomizer` in the `Platforms/iOS` folder:

```
using UIKit;
public static partial class PlatformCustomizer
{
    public static partial void CustomizeEntry(object
      platformView)
    {
        UITextField editor = (UITextField)
          platformView;
        editor.TintColor = UIColor.FromRGBA(0, 255,
          209, 255);
    }
}
```

4. Repeat *step 2* for Windows, but in the `Platforms/Windows` folder:

```
public static partial class PlatformCustomizer
{
    public static partial void CustomizeEntry(object
      platformView)
    {
        TextBox editor = (TextBox)platformView;
        editor.SelectionHighlightColor = new
          Microsoft.UI.Xaml.Media.SolidColorBrush
          (Windows.UI.Color.FromArgb(255, 0, 255,
          209));
    }
}
```

5. In the `MainPage.xaml` file, replace the default content with a single `Entry`. Subscribe to the `HandlerChanged` event so that we can customize the handler:

```
<Entry Text="Select this text"
       HandlerChanged="OnEntryHandlerChanged"/>
```

6. In the `OnEntryHandlerChanged` method, access the platform control using the `Handler.PlatformView` property and pass it to the `CustomizeEntry` method we created earlier:

```
void OnEntryHandlerChanged(object sender, EventArgs e)
{
    Entry entry = (Entry)sender;
    PlatformCustomizer.CustomizeEntry(entry
     .Handler.PlatformView);
}
```

Since we implemented `CustomizeEntry` for each platform, a corresponding method implementation will be called based on the platform you are using.

Now, you can run and test the project. When you select text in the `Entry` element, it should be highlighted with a light green color.

How it works...

In .NET MAUI, controls utilize handlers to connect the cross-platform API with native platform elements. Handlers include the `PlatformView` property, which contains the native control that corresponds to the platform on which your application is currently running.

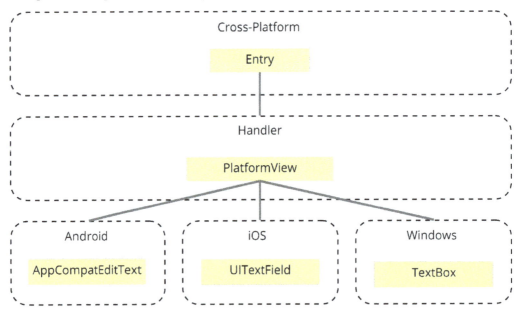

Figure 7.5 – Handler and platform views

It's important to note that when you create a new control instance, a handler isn't assigned immediately. That's why we use the `HandlerChanged` event to capture the moment when the handler is initialized.

There's more...

As we discussed in this recipe, each platform uses its own classes to create native controls. These classes are typically not covered in Microsoft documentation because they are based on native components implemented in other frameworks.

So, how can we determine which properties are available in native components? C# wrappers usually mimic the API of the native controls they wrap. Here's an approach to find out what APIs are available:

1. **Identify the native control type**: Subscribe to the `HandlerChanged` event and check the object stored in the `Handler.PlatformView` property during debugging.

2. **Check the type name**: If the type name of the object in `PlatformView` starts with `Maui`, you'll want to check its base class.

3. **Consult native documentation**: Look up the native documentation for the class in the previous step. For example, here are the help topics for the native classes used in this recipe:

   - `AppCompactEditText`: https://developer.android.com/reference/androidx/appcompat/widget/AppCompatEditText

   - `UITextField`: https://developer.apple.com/documentation/uikit/uitextfield

   - `TextBox`: https://learn.microsoft.com/en-us/uwp/api/windows.ui.xaml.controls.textbox

You may notice that even though these controls are implemented using different technologies, all the similar APIs are available in their .NET counterparts.

Creating a custom handler

In the previous recipe, we set the selection color for an editor in the `HandlerChanged` event, which is typically raised only once for a control. But what if we want to make the selection color dynamic, for instance, when a user selects a new theme? Since `HandlerChanged` won't be raised again, we wouldn't be able to set the native property responsible for the selection color. We will achieve our goal with a custom handler and a **property mapper**.

> Property mapper
>
> A property mapper is an object that maps properties from a cross-platform control to platform-specific views.

Property mappers are called each time a cross-platform property is changed – this will allow us to dynamically update the platform view when a cross-platform property changes.

In this recipe, we'll achieve the same effect of changing the selection color as in the previous recipe, but this time, using a custom handler and mapper.

Getting ready

To follow the steps described in this recipe, simply create a blank .NET MAUI application.

The code for this recipe is available at `https://github.com/PacktPublishing/.NET-MAUI-Cookbook/tree/main/Chapter07/c7-DerivedHandler`.

How to do it...

Let's create a custom `Entry` class with a property responsible for the selection color and customize its handler:

1. Create a new `CustomEntry` class inherited from `Entry` and add a `SelectionColor` bindable property:

    ```
    public class CustomEntry : Entry
    {
        public static readonly BindableProperty
        SelectionColorProperty = BindableProperty.Create(
            nameof(SelectionColor),
            typeof(Color),
            typeof(CustomEntry),
            Colors.Gray);

        public Color SelectionColor
        {
            get => (Color)GetValue
                    (SelectionColorProperty);
            set => SetValue(SelectionColorProperty,
              value);
        }
    }
    ```

2. Create a partial `CustomEntryHandler` class inherited from `EntryHandler`. Add a static `PropertyMapper` property to this class. Additionally, define a partial `MapSelectionColor` method, as shown here:

```
public partial class CustomEntryHandler : EntryHandler
{
    public CustomEntryHandler() : base(PropertyMapper,
      CommandMapper) { }

    public static IPropertyMapper<CustomEntry,
      CustomEntryHandler> PropertyMapper = new
        PropertyMapper<CustomEntry,
        CustomEntryHandler>(EntryHandler.Mapper)
    {

        [nameof(CustomEntry.SelectionColor)] =
          MapSelectionColor
    };

    static partial void MapSelectionColor
      (CustomEntryHandler handler, CustomEntry entry);
}
```

A mapper is essentially a dictionary where the key represents a cross-platform property name (such as `SelectionColor`), and the value is an action (such as `MapSelectionColor`) that gets executed when the corresponding property changes. We defined `MapSelectionColor` as a partial method so that we can implement it separately for each platform. When creating the mapper, we pass the default `Entry` mapper as a constructor parameter, which saves us from having to re-implement mappings for all default properties.

3. In the `Platforms/Android` folder, create a partial `CustomEntryHandler` class and adjust its namespace to match the namespace defined in the cross-platform `CustomEntryHandler`. Use the following code for the Android implementation:

```
namespace c7_DerivedHandler
{
    public partial class CustomEntryHandler
    {
        static partial void MapSelectionColor
          (CustomEntryHandler handler,
            CustomEntry entry)
        {
            handler.PlatformView?.SetHighlightColor
              (entry.SelectionColor.ToAndroid());
```

```
        }
      }
    }
```

In the `MapSelectionColor` method implementation, we call `SetHighlightColor` for the native Android platform view, as we did in the previous recipe.

4.   Repeat the same step for iOS but use this code for the handler:

```
public partial class CustomEntryHandler
{
    static partial void MapSelectionColor
      (CustomEntryHandler handler, CustomEntry entry)
    {
        if (handler.PlatformView != null)
        {
            handler.PlatformView.TintColor = entry
              .SelectionColor.ToUIColor();
        }
    }
}
```

5.   Now, let's implement a handler for Windows using the same technique:

```
public partial class CustomEntryHandler
{
    static partial void MapSelectionColor
      (CustomEntryHandler handler, CustomEntry entry)
    {
        if (handler.PlatformView != null)
        {
            handler.PlatformView.SelectionHighlightColor = new
    Microsoft.UI.Xaml.Media.SolidColorBrush
    (entry.SelectionColor.ToWindowsColor());
        }
    }
}
```

6.   To inform `CustomEntry` that it should use our custom handler, we need to register the handler in `MauiAppBuilder` configured within the `MauiProgram.CreateMauiApp` method. Let's create an extension method where we'll call `ConfigureMauiHandlers` to register the handler for the `CustomEntry` class:

```
public static class CustomBuilderExtensions
{
    public static MauiAppBuilder UseCustomEntry(this
```

```
        MauiAppBuilder builder)
    {
        builder.ConfigureMauiHandlers(handlers =>
        {
            handlers.AddHandler<CustomEntry,
                CustomEntryHandler>();
        });
        return builder;
    }
}
```

7. Call `UseCustomEntry` in the `MauiProgram.CreateMauiApp` method to execute the logic we implemented in the previous step:

```
public static MauiApp CreateMauiApp()
{
    var builder = MauiApp.CreateBuilder();
    builder
        .UseMauiApp<App>()
        .UseCustomEntry()
        //...
}
```

8. Add `CustomEntry` to the view and set the `SelectionColor` property to Red:

```
<local:CustomEntry Text="Select this text"
    SelectionColor="Red"/>
```

Now, you can run the project and select text to see a custom selection color.

How it works...

The key component in this recipe is the property mapper we defined in our custom handler:

```
public static IPropertyMapper<CustomEntry,
    CustomEntryHandler> PropertyMapper = new PropertyMapper
        <CustomEntry, CustomEntryHandler>(EntryHandler.Mapper)
{
    [nameof(CustomEntry.SelectionColor)] =
        MapSelectionColor
};
```

The mapper enables us to specify which actions (such as `MapSelectionColor`) should be executed when the `SelectionColor` property changes. While we've defined just one mapping, you can easily add more as needed.

Another important technique we employed is the partial declaration of the `MapSelectionColor` method. By implementing this method separately for each platform, we can leverage platform-specific APIs to change the selection color. When the application compiles for a specific platform, the resulting binary will include only the cross-platform part and the code from the corresponding platform folder.

To ensure that the platform uses our custom handler for the `CustomEntry` class, we called `MauiAppBuilder.ConfigureMauiHandlers`:

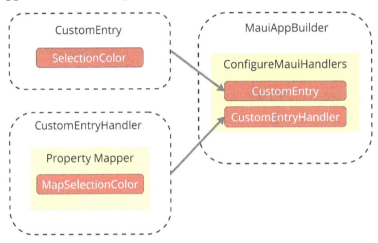

Figure 7.6 – Custom handler and mapper

There's more...

You can customize an existing control mapper without needing to create a new handler. By using the `AppendToMapping` method, you can easily add a new mapping to an existing mapper:

```
#if ANDROID
using Microsoft.Maui.Controls.Compatibility.Platform.Android;
#endif
//…
Microsoft.Maui.Handlers.EntryHandler.Mapper.AppendToMapping
    ("EntryCustomization", (handler, view) =>
{
    if (view is CustomEntry entry)
    {
#if ANDROID
        handler.PlatformView?.SetHighlightColor(entry
            .SelectionColor.ToAndroid());
#elif IOS
        //..
```

```
#elif WINDOWS
        //..
#endif
    }
});
```

This technique requires creating fewer classes; however, if you need to implement custom logic, reading and maintaining your code may become much more challenging.

8

Optimizing Performance

Have you ever used Windows Vista? While some people were okay with it, most didn't enjoy the experience - largely due to poor performance. This brings us to a key takeaway: application speed and responsiveness are crucial for delivering high-quality user experience.

In this chapter, we'll explore techniques to optimize the performance of your .NET MAUI applications. You'll not only learn how to boost speed and efficiency but also how to measure the impact of these optimizations. We'll dive into powerful tools for performance and memory profiling using VS Code and wrap up by mastering how to prevent memory leaks that can slow down your app over time.

In this chapter, we'll be covering the following recipes:

- Comparing performance in debug and release configurations
- Simplifying a collection item template
- Using images with an optimal size
- Using compiled bindings
- Loading data in asynchronous methods
- Profiling the application
- Detecting memory leaks
- Getting rid of memory leaks

Technical requirements

There are no specific requirements for the recipes in this chapter. All of them start with a basic .NET MAUI application created by the default Visual Studio template.

You can download all the projects created in this chapter from GitHub: `https://github.com/PacktPublishing/.NET-MAUI-Cookbook/tree/main/Chapter08`

Comparing performance in debug and release configurations

Many developers new to .NET MAUI often feel disappointed by the performance, especially when even a simple page can take a second to load in debug mode. The good news is that you can reduce this loading time by 30-60% just by switching to release mode.

It's no secret that release mode outperforms debug mode, but the difference in .NET MAUI can be particularly striking. In this recipe, we'll not only switch from debug to release mode but also measure the performance boost this change provides. This measurement technique will serve as a foundation for future recipes, where we'll assess the effectiveness of our optimizations.

Getting ready

To follow the steps described in this recipe, we just need to create a blank .NET MAUI application.

The code for this recipe is available at `https://github.com/PacktPublishing/.NET-MAUI-Cookbook/tree/main/Chapter08/c8-DebugVsRelease`.

How to do it...

In this recipe, we'll create a page with `CollectionView` to evaluate how quickly it opens in both debug and release modes. To accurately capture the moment when the page is fully displayed to the user, we'll implement a custom handler and utilize platform APIs. This approach is necessary because the standard `Loaded` and `Appearing` events are triggered before the content is actually drawn, preventing us from measuring the full loading time.

1. Start by creating a new .NET MAUI project. Next, add a class called `LoadingTimePage` that inherits from `ContentPage`. Inside this class, define a static field to hold a `Stopwatch` object, which we'll use to measure the loading time. Additionally, create a partial handler class that inherits from `PageHandler`:

```
public class LoadingTimePage : ContentPage
{
    static Stopwatch LoadingStopwatch = new
      Stopwatch();
    public static void StartTimer() =>
      LoadingStopwatch.Restart ();
    public static void ShowTimeElapsed()
    {
        LoadingStopwatch.Stop();
        Shell.Current.DisplayAlert("Elapsed
          miliseconds",LoadingStopwatch
          .ElapsedMilliseconds.ToString(), "OK");
```

```
        }
    }
    public partial class LoadingTimePageHandler :
        PageHandler { }
```

2. In the Platforms/Android folder, add a partial class named LoadingTimePageHandler. Override the CreatePlatformView method and use the AddOnGlobalLayoutListener method to detect when the native view has fully loaded. This method takes an instance that implements IOnGlobalLayoutListener, which includes a single OnGlobalLayout method:

```
public partial class LoadingTimePageHandler {
    protected override ContentViewGroup
      CreatePlatformView()
    {
        var platformView = base.CreatePlatformView();
        platformView.ViewTreeObserver!
          .AddOnGlobalLayoutListener(new
          MyGlobalLayoutListener(platformView));
        return platformView;
    }
}

class MyGlobalLayoutListener(ContentViewGroup
  platformView) : Java.Lang.Object,
  ViewTreeObserver.IonGlobalLayoutListener {
    ContentViewGroup PlatformView = platformView;
    public void OnGlobalLayout()
    {
        LoadingTimePage.ShowTimeElapsed();
        PlatformView.ViewTreeObserver!
          .RemoveOnGlobalLayoutListener(this);
    }
}
```

In Android, OnGlobalLayoutListener allows you to detect a native view's layout changes, for example, when the view becomes visible. In the OnGlobalLayout method, stop the timer and display the elapsed milliseconds in an alert. Make sure that all partial LoadingTimePageHandler classes share the same namespace.

3. Next, let's create a custom page handler for iOS. In the `Platforms/iOS` folder, add a class named `LoadingTimePageHandler` and include the following code:

```
public partial class LoadingTimePageHandler
{
    class CustomViewController (IView page,
      IMauiContext mauiContext) :
      PageViewController(page, mauiContext)
    {
        public override void ViewDidAppear(bool
          animated)
        {
            base.ViewDidAppear(animated);
            LoadingTimePage.ShowTimeElapsed();
        }
    }
    protected override Microsoft.Maui.Platform
      .ContentView CreatePlatformView()
    {
        if (ViewController == null)
            ViewController = new CustomViewController
              (VirtualView, MauiContext);
        if (ViewController is PageViewController pc
          && pc.CurrentPlatformView is Microsoft.Maui
          .Platform.ContentView pv)
            return pv;
        if (ViewController.View is Microsoft.Maui
          .Platform.ContentView cv)
            return cv;
        throw new InvalidOperationException
            ($"PageViewController.View must be a
{nameof(Microsoft.Maui.Platform.ContentView)}");
    }
}
```

The main goal of overriding `CreatePlatformView` is to replace the default page controller with `CustomViewController`. In iOS, view controllers are responsible for handling such tasks as navigation, layout, and life cycle. In `CustomViewController`, we override `ViewDidAppear` to identify when the page is fully displayed.

4. For Windows, follow a similar process in the `Platforms/Windows` folder, and include the following code:

```
public partial class LoadingTimePageHandler {
    protected override void ConnectHandler
```

```
   (ContentPanel platformView)
{
    base.ConnectHandler(platformView);
    if (platformView is ContentPanel contentPanel)
    {
        contentPanel.Loaded += (s,e) =>
            LoadingTimePage.ShowTimeElapsed();
    }
}
}
```

5. In the MauiProgram.CreateMauiApp method, register LoadingTimePageHandler for LoadingTimePage by using ConfigureMauiHandlers:

MauiProgram.cs

```
var builder = MauiApp.CreateBuilder();
builder
    .UseMauiApp<App>()
    .ConfigureMauiHandlers(handlers => handlers
      .AddHandler(typeof(LoadingTimePage),
      typeof(LoadingTimePageHandler)));
```

6. Create a new page and set its base class to LoadingTimePage in both C# and XAML:

TestPage.xaml.cs

```
public partial class TestPage : LoadingTimePage
{
    //...
}
```

TestPage.xaml

```
<local:LoadingTimePage
    xmlns:local="clr-namespace:c8_DebugVsRelease">
  ...
</local:LoadingTimePage>
```

7. Add a CollectionView with a simple ItemTemplate to the newly created page:

```
<CollectionView x:Name="collectionView">
    <CollectionView.ItemTemplate>
        <DataTemplate>
            <Border>
```

```
                    <HorizontalStackLayout Spacing="10">
                        <Button Text="{Binding Id}"/>
                        <Label Text="{Binding Name}"/>
                    </HorizontalStackLayout>
                </Border>
            </DataTemplate>
        </CollectionView.ItemTemplate>
    </CollectionView>
```

8. Populate the `CollectionView` with sample data items in the page constructor. Let's add 30 items to the source collection:

```
public TestPage()
{
    InitializeComponent();

    ObservableCollection<Item> items = new
      ObservableCollection<Item>();
    for (int i = 1; i < 30; i++)
    {
        items.Add(new Item(i, $"Item{i}"));
    }
    collectionView.ItemsSource = items;
}
public class Item(int id, string name)
{
    public int Id { get; set; } = id;
    public string Name { get; set; } = name;
}
```

9. In `MainPage`, add a button to navigate to `TestPage`:

MainPage.xaml

```
<Button Text="Open TestPage"
        Clicked="OnOpenTestPageClicked"
        HorizontalOptions="Center"
        VerticalOptions="Center"/>
```

MainPage.cs

```
async void OnOpenTestPageClicked(object sender,
  EventArgs e)
{
    LoadingTimePage.StartTimer();
    await Shell.Current.GoToAsync(nameof(TestPage),
      false);
}
```

10. In the `AppShell` constructor, register a route for `TestPage`:

```
Routing.RegisterRoute(nameof(TestPage),
  typeof(TestPage));
```

Now you can run the project to see how long it takes to load `TestPage`. Try running the app in debug mode, then switch to release mode to compare the loading times.

Figure 8.1 – Switching to release mode

Building the project in release mode may take anywhere from 5 to 15 minutes, depending on your machine's capabilities and the project's complexity. This is why debug mode is the default configuration – it's much more convenient for development.

To get more accurate results, consider opening `TestPage` multiple times to calculate an average value. Keep in mind that, to test a cold start, you should close the application and run it again instead of just pressing the back button. Views load faster if they were opened previously, so for cleaner results, close the app after each opening.

Here's a diagram illustrating the opening time of `TestPage` on my Android emulator:

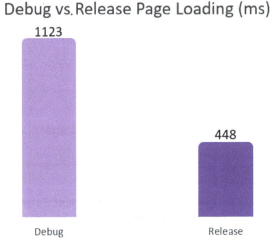

Figure 8.2 – Debug versus release page loading

Note that results may vary significantly depending on the platform and device you use.

How it works...

Several factors contribute to improved performance when you run the application in release mode:

- **Ahead-of-time** (AOT) compilation is enabled, which means native code is generated upfront. This reduces or even eliminates the need for **just-in-time** (JIT) compilation.

- The Visual Studio debugger is detached, so you won't see any logs in the **Output** window during app execution. This detachment helps reduce the overhead caused by communication between the app and the tracing mechanism.

- The trimming mechanism is enabled, which reduces the size of deployed assemblies. It inspects the source code and removes any unused branches from the assemblies.

When you build your application, the C# code is first transformed into **Microsoft Intermediate Language** (MSIL) in both release and debug modes. However, the subsequent stages differ. In release mode, MSIL is trimmed and converted to native code using AOT compilation.

In debug mode, MSIL is deployed to the device and converted to specific commands at runtime. On iOS, MSIL is executed by an interpreter, which directly executes each MSIL instruction. On Android and Windows, JIT compilation is used.

Here's a simplified diagram illustrating the difference between the process of code transformation and deployment in release and debug modes:

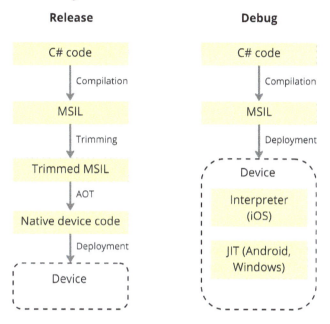

Figure 8.3 – Release and debug process

In the preceding figure, the interpreter and JIT compilation are omitted from the release process for simplicity, as most code is translated to native code using AOT compilation. However, certain dynamic code sections can still be interpreted or JIT-compiled on the fly. This often occurs with `Reflection` and `Emit` calls, where generating native code in advance is challenging.

There's more...

iOS and Android utilize different mechanisms for AOT and MSIL-to-native code translation due to architectural and security policy differences.

On iOS, .NET MAUI does not use JIT compilation because Apple prohibits generating code on the fly; all code must be vetted and signed before the application is published. The interpreter meets this requirement by executing MSIL instructions directly rather than generating and saving native code in memory.

While the interpreter is not enabled by default for iOS devices in release mode, you can activate it for the entire application or for specific assemblies. This may be necessary if certain libraries cannot be fully compiled to native code during AOT compilation. For instance, EF Core uses `Emit` to dynamically generate classes, which cannot be AOT-compiled. Therefore, you may need to enable the interpreter for EF Core by using the `UseInterpreter` and `MtouchInterpreter` tags in the `*.csproj` file:

```
<PropertyGroup>
    <UseInterpreter Condition="$(TargetFramework
        .Contains('-ios')) AND '$(Configuration)' ==
        'Release'">true</UseInterpreter>
    <MtouchInterpreter Condition="$(TargetFramework
        .Contains('-ios')) AND '$(Configuration)' ==
        'Release'">-all,AssemblyName </MtouchInterpreter>
</PropertyGroup>
```

In the preceding code snippet, `-all` excludes all assemblies, while `AssemblyName` specifies one particular assembly to include. Both `UseInterpreter` and `MtouchInterpreter` control the same interpreter, but `UseInterpreter` enables or disables it, whereas `MtouchInterpreter` allows you to include or exclude specific assemblies. Note that `MtouchInterpreter` has no effect when `UseInterpreter` is set to `false`.

It's also important to recognize that iOS and Android use different AOT mechanisms. For Android, .NET MAUI relies on **Mono AOT**. In contrast, iOS utilizes a compiler and toolchain known as **Low Level Virtual Machine** (**LLVM**) for AOT. LLVM performs additional optimizations to enhance runtime performance. These factors can impact the differences you observe between debug and release configurations when testing the app on various devices.

Simplifying a collection item template

For complex tasks, users may need to read and compare information from multiple fields within a collection item. Our initial instinct might be to present all this information to the user at once. While this comes from a good place, it can harm user experience and significantly impact performance.

It may seem obvious but displaying fewer controls on a page results in faster loading and scrolling. To minimize the number of elements shown on a page, we should carefully consider what task users are trying to accomplish. For instance, if you have a collection of items, do users really need to see all the specific information for each item? Or, do they simply want to locate a specific item and access detailed information or additional options on a separate page?

Controls such as `CollectionView` are designed to optimize performance by reusing elements as you scroll, rather than creating new ones. However, even with this optimization, you will likely run into performance issues if your item templates are too complex. In this recipe, we will create a collection with a relatively complex item template and then apply various design techniques to simplify the template, enhancing both performance and user experience. We will also utilize the technique from the first recipe to measure performance improvements after the optimizations.

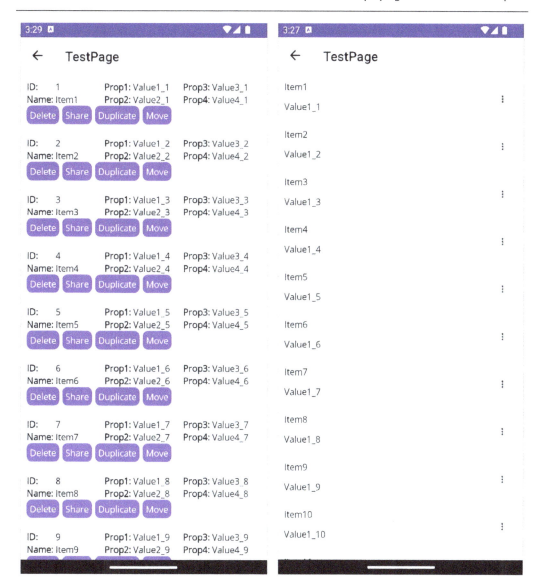

Figure 8.4 – Original and redesigned item template

While the design on the left might seem cluttered, it illustrates the common tendency among developers to incorporate too much information and too many actions into a single displayed item.

Getting ready

Start with the project from the first recipe of this chapter: *Comparing performance in debug and release configurations*. This project is available at `https://github.com/PacktPublishing/.NET-MAUI-Cookbook/tree/main/Chapter08/c8-DebugVsRelease`.

The code for this recipe is available at `https://github.com/PacktPublishing/.NET-MAUI-Cookbook/tree/main/Chapter08/c8-SimplifiedItemTemplate`.

How to do it...

We'll start by creating a collection that features an item template with six properties and four buttons. Next, we'll apply design optimization techniques to enhance the original template and evaluate the performance impact of our changes.

1. In the project from the previous recipe, add four more properties that will be displayed in the `CollectionView`:

```
public class Item(int id,
        string name,
        string prop1,
        string prop2,
        string prop3,
        string prop4)
{
    public int Id { get; set; } = id;
    public string Name { get; set; } = name;
    public string Prop1 { get; set; } = prop1;
    public string Prop2 { get; set; } = prop2;
    public string Prop3 { get; set; } = prop3;
    public string Prop4 { get; set; } = prop4;
}
```

2. In the constructor of `TestPage`, update the code that generates items to include the new properties you just added:

TestPage.xaml.cs

```
ObservableCollection<Item> items = new
ObservableCollection<Item>();
for (int i = 1; i < 30; i++)
{
    items.Add(new Item(i,
        $"Item{i}",
        $"Value1_{i}",
```

```
        $"Value2_{i}",
        $"Value3_{i}",
        $"Value4_{i}"));
    }
    collectionView.ItemsSource = items;
```

3. Update `ItemTemplate` in `CollectionView` to show multiple properties along with the action buttons:

TestPage.xaml

```xml
<DataTemplate>
    <Grid Padding="10"
          ColumnDefinitions="Auto, *, Auto, *,
            Auto, *"
          RowDefinitions="Auto,Auto,Auto">
        <Label Text="ID: " FontAttributes="Bold"/>
        <Label Text="Name: " FontAttributes="Bold"
            Grid.Row="1"/>
        <Label Text="Prop1: " FontAttributes="Bold"
            Grid.Column="2"/>
        <Label Text="Prop2: " FontAttributes="Bold"
            Grid.Row="1" Grid.Column="2"/>
        <Label Text="Prop3: " FontAttributes="Bold"
            Grid.Column="4"/>
        <Label Text="Prop4: " FontAttributes="Bold"
            Grid.Column="4" Grid.Row="1"/>
        <Label Text="{Binding Id}"
            Grid.Row="0" Grid.Column="1"/>
        <Label Text="{Binding Name}"
            Grid.Row="1" Grid.Column="1"/>
        <Label Text="{Binding Prop1}"
            Grid.Row="0" Grid.Column="3"/>
        <Label Text="{Binding Prop2}"
            Grid.Row="1" Grid.Column="3"/>
        <Label Text="{Binding Prop3}"
            Grid.Row="0" Grid.Column="5"/>
        <Label Text="{Binding Prop4}"
            Grid.Row="1" Grid.Column="5"/>
        <HorizontalStackLayout Grid.Row="6"
                               Grid.ColumnSpan="6"
                               Spacing="5"
                               HeightRequest="28">
            <Button Text="Delete" Padding="5"/>
```

```xml
                <Button Text="Share" Padding="5"/>
                <Button Text="Duplicate" Padding="5"/>
                <Button Text="Move" Padding="5"/>
            </HorizontalStackLayout>
        </Grid>
    </DataTemplate>
```

4. Run the project and open TestPage. Take note of the displayed time it takes to load the page.

5. Adjust ItemTemplate in CollectionView to reduce the number of displayed elements:

```xml
    <DataTemplate >
        <Grid Padding="10" ColumnDefinitions="*, 50"
            RowDefinitions="*,*" RowSpacing="8">
            <Label Text="{Binding Name}" />
            <Label Text="{Binding Prop1}"
                Grid.Row="1"/>
            <Button BackgroundColor="Transparent"
                Text="&#x22EE;"
                FontAttributes="Bold"
                TextColor="Black"
                FontSize="18"
                Grid.Column="1"
                Grid.RowSpan="2"/>
        </Grid>
    </DataTemplate>
```

⋮ represents the symbol for three vertical dots. In the *How it works…* section, we'll go over the design techniques we've applied.

6. Run the project again and compare the numbers with those from the original item template. You can also check the differences between debug and release modes. Here are the numbers I obtained on my Android emulator:

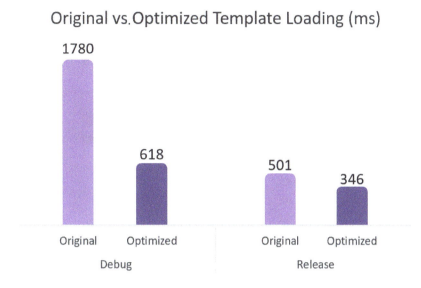

Figure 8.5 – Loading time in milliseconds of the original and optimized item templates

How it works...

In this recipe, we applied the following design optimization techniques:

- **Removed labels with property names**: In mobile apps, it's often beneficial to eliminate obvious labels. For instance, if the text shows "Apr 12," it's clear that it represents a date, so there's no need to add a "Date" label in front of it.

- **Used one dropdown button instead of multiple buttons**: When multiple actions are related to an item, consolidate them into a single button that opens a dropdown menu. You can use a popup or a bottom sheet to display these options.

- **Focused on essential information**: Consider what users need most frequently when they open a page. Keep only the key information in `ItemTemplate` and move other properties to a detail view that opens when an item is tapped. This detail view can be displayed on a separate page or a bottom sheet.

- **Increased the space between elements**: Utilize the `Margins`, `Padding`, and `Spacing` properties to create a balanced item density. Taller items mean fewer can fit on the screen at once, which can improve performance and make it easier for users to read the information.

When it comes to performance, keeping the UI simple is crucial because each visual element needs to be measured and arranged. Subsequently, the native controls created behind the scenes are also measured and drawn. Additionally, interaction between .NET and native elements involves interop mechanisms, which can often affect performance.

If you don't have a professional designer on your team, it might be challenging to consider all design aspects. The good news is that you can reuse design ideas and apply best practices from guidelines such as Material Design 3. For instance, you can find various item templates on this page: `https://m3.material.io/components/lists`.

There's more...

There are a couple of basic elements that can surprisingly impact your layout performance:

- Borders
- Shadows

While you can still use borders and shadows and maintain good performance, it's generally best to avoid them in item templates whenever possible. Below is a chart illustrating how adding a border and shadow to the optimized template we created in this recipe affects loading time in release mode:

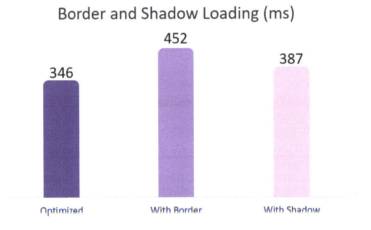

Figure 8.6 – Effect of border and shadow on page loading time

Using images with an optimal size

Applications often use a variety of images (user avatars, icons, and backgrounds) to enhance the user experience. However, like many other elements, excessive use of images can lead to performance issues.

When using an image, it's important to remember that we usually don't need high-quality images if they will be displayed in a 50 x 50 box. A sensible approach is to reduce the size of the original images based on the dimensions they will be shown in. Even when you use SVG images in .NET MAUI, they're automatically converted to raster images at the size set by the `MauiImage.BaseSize` attribute in the `*.csproj` file. This conversion happens because not all target platforms support native SVG rendering. So, it's important to specify a size that meets your app's requirements, even when working with SVGs.

In this recipe, we'll implement image picking and resizing using the **SkiaSharp** library. Afterward, we'll compare how using a resized image affects the loading speed of the test page.

Getting ready

Start with the project from the first recipe of this chapter: *Comparing performance in debug and release configurations*. This project is available at `https://github.com/PacktPublishing/`. `NET-MAUI-Cookbook/tree/main/Chapter08/c8-DebugVsRelease`.

The code for this recipe is available at `https://github.com/PacktPublishing/.NET-MAUI-Cookbook/tree/main/Chapter08/c8-OptimizedImages`.

How to do it...

We'll implement an image picker and dynamically resize the selected image using SkiaSharp. Afterward, you'll navigate to another page that displays a collection of images and compare how reducing the image size impacts the page loading time.

1. Begin with the project from the *Comparing performance in debug and release configurations* recipe. Add the `SkiaSharp.Views.Maui.Controls` NuGet package to your project to enable image resizing with SkiaSharp.

2. In the `MainPage` class, create a `ResizeImage` method that takes an image and desired dimensions and then returns a resized image. Within this method, use the following Skia APIs:

   - `SKBitmap.Decode`: This is used to decode the original image.

   - `SKCanvas.DrawBitmap`: This is used to draw the image with the new dimensions on the Skia canvas.

   - `SKBitmap.Encode`: This is used to encode the resized image and write its data to a stream. When encoding, you can additionally reduce the final image size by adjusting the `quality` parameter – in the following code snippet, we've set it to `100`, which will preserve the original quality:

```
public Stream ResizeImage(Stream inputStream,
  int width, int height)
{
    using var originalBitmap = SKBitmap
      .Decode(inputStream);
    using var resizedBitmap = new SKBitmap(width,
      height);
    using var canvas = new SKCanvas(resizedBitmap);
    canvas.Clear(SKColors.Transparent);

    var scale = Math.Min((float)width / originalBitmap
```

```
      .Width, (float)height / originalBitmap.Height);
    var destRect = new SKRect(0, 0, originalBitmap
      .Width * scale, originalBitmap.Height * scale);
    canvas.DrawBitmap(originalBitmap, destRect);

    var outputStream = new MemoryStream();
    resizedBitmap.Encode(outputStream,
      SKEncodedImageFormat.Png, 100);
    outputStream.Seek(0, SeekOrigin.Begin);
    return outputStream;
}
```

3. In `MainPage.xaml`, add a button to select an image and include an `Image` element to display the selected image:

```xml
<VerticalStackLayout Spacing="10"
                     VerticalOptions="Center"
                     Padding="10">
    <Button Text="Select Image"
            Clicked="OnSelectImageClick"/>
    <Button Text="Open TestPage"
            Clicked="OnOpenTestPageClicked"/>
    <Image x:Name="imageControl"
           WidthRequest="100"
           HeightRequest="100"
           HorizontalOptions="Center"/>
</VerticalStackLayout>
```

4. Implement the `OnSelectImageClick` method to select an image from the device. Then, resize the selected image using the `ResizeImage` method and save it to `AppDataDirectory` so that we can simulate loading an image from a file in `TestPage`:

```csharp
async void OnSelectImageClick(object sender,
  EventArgs e)
{
    PickOptions options = new()
    {
        PickerTitle = "Select an image",
        FileTypes = FilePickerFileType.Images
    };
    var result = await FilePicker.Default
      .PickAsync(options);
    if (result != null)
    {
        var imageStream = await result
```

```
                    .OpenReadAsync();
                imageStream = ResizeImage(imageStream, 40,
                    40);
                imageControl.Source = ImageSource
                    .FromStream(() => imageStream);

                using FileStream fileStream = File.Create(Path
                    .Combine(FileSystem.Current
                        .AppDataDirectory, "test.png"));
                await imageStream.CopyToAsync(fileStream);
                imageStream.Seek(0, SeekOrigin.Begin);
        }
    }
```

5. Update the `Item` class to accept a single `ImageSource` parameter:

```
public class Item(ImageSource icon)
{
    public ImageSource Icon { get; set; } = icon;
}
```

6. In the `TestPage` constructor, update the item generation logic so that each item reads an image from a file, simulating a scenario where all the images are different (even though we only have one image in this test project):

TestPage.xaml.cs

```
ObservableCollection<Item> items = new
    ObservableCollection<Item>();
for (int i = 1; i < 30; i++)
{
    items.Add(new Item(ImageSource.FromFile(Path
        .Combine(FileSystem.Current.AppDataDirectory,
            "test.png"))));
}
collectionView.ItemsSource = items;
```

7. Update `ItemTemplate` in `CollectionView` to display the image:

TestPage.xaml

```
<CollectionView.ItemTemplate>
    <DataTemplate>
        <Image Source="{Binding Icon}"
```

```
                WidthRequest="50"
                HeightRequest="50"/>
        </DataTemplate>
    </CollectionView.ItemTemplate>
```

8. Run the project in release mode. If you're testing the app on an emulator, you can add an image by using drag and drop or by opening a browser on the emulator to download a large image from the internet (5–10 MB). In the app, tap the **Select Image** button, then navigate to `TestPage`. Reopen the app and repeat the process to see how long it takes on average to display `TestPage`.

9. Modify the `OnSelectImageClick` method so that a non-resized image is used. You can simply comment out the following line:

TestPage.xaml.cs

```
//imageStream = ResizeImage(imageStream, 40, 40);
```

10. Run the project in release mode and repeat *step 8* to compare the loading speed of `TestPage`. Here are the numbers I obtained on my Android emulator:

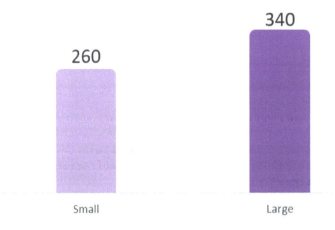

Figure 8.7 – Small and large image loading time

How it works...

Images typically use CPU resources for decoding and require memory to store the decoded image. It's inefficient to decode a high-resolution image into memory if it will be scaled down for display. In this recipe, we used SkiaSharp to resize an image selected from the device's image gallery. Here are the key points in the resizing code:

1. **Decoding the original image**: We passed the input memory stream to the `SKBitmap.Decode` method to create a bitmap representation of the original image.

2. **Creating a resized bitmap**: We created a new `SKBitmap` object with the desired width and height.

3. **Maintaining aspect ratio**: To avoid distortion, we calculated the appropriate scale factor using the original image's dimensions.

4. **Drawing the image**: We used the `SKCanvas` class to render the original bitmap onto the new resized canvas.

5. **Encoding the resized image**: We used the `SKBitmap.Encode` method to save the resized image in PNG format.

This technique is useful when users select images from their device but you don't need to store high-resolution images. You can resize the image on the fly before saving it to a database. Sometimes, you might need to store two versions of the same image – one with the original quality and another as a thumbnail for smaller areas, like user avatars displayed in `CollectionView`.

Using compiled bindings

Default bindings let you get values from an object even if its type isn't known beforehand. They just need to know the name of the property to bind to, and this is done using reflection, which pulls public properties from the object at runtime. As you may know, reflection isn't the fastest process.

However, in most cases, we already know what object type will be used in `BindingContext`. When we provide this type to .NET MAUI, it can get rid of reflection by creating a binding at compile time. For this, it's sufficient to specify `x:DataType` in your view or `DataTemplate`:

```
<DataTemplate x:DataType="local:Item">
    ...
</DataTemplate>
```

We've used this technique in previous recipes, so why revisit it in this one? Sometimes, you might not be able to use compiled bindings because the object in `BindingContext` is unknown in advance or contains nested properties with unknown types. Understanding the performance benefits of compiled bindings can help you decide whether you need to rethink your architecture to enable them.

Additionally, some developers suggest completely eliminating bindings and creating a custom control to set property values in C#. While this approach may seem logical, let's explore the performance impact of standard bindings and determine whether we should avoid them.

In this recipe, we will enable compiled bindings and measure how they impact loading speed. Additionally, we will find out whether it makes sense to avoid bindings at all to achieve better performance.

Getting ready

Start with the project from the following recipe: *Simplifying a collection item template*. This project is available at `https://github.com/PacktPublishing/.NET-MAUI-Cookbook/tree/main/Chapter08/c8-SimplifiedItemTemplate`.

The code for the current recipe is available at `https://github.com/PacktPublishing/.NET-MAUI-Cookbook/tree/main/Chapter08/c8-CompiledBindings`.

How to do it...

To create a performance test for bindings, let's create a collection where each item displays six labels. After that, we will compare the loading speed of this page with usual bindings, compiled bindings, and without bindings:

1. Begin with the project from the *Simplifying a collection item template* recipe, as it already has the necessary infrastructure in place. Modify the collection item template to display six horizontally arranged labels in each row:

    ```
    <CollectionView.ItemTemplate>
        <DataTemplate>
            <HorizontalStackLayout>
                <Label Text="{Binding Id}"/>
                <Label Text="{Binding Name}"/>
                <Label Text="{Binding Prop1}"/>
                <Label Text="{Binding Prop2}"/>
                <Label Text="{Binding Prop3}"/>
                <Label Text="{Binding Prop4}"/>
            </HorizontalStackLayout>
        </DataTemplate>
    </CollectionView.ItemTemplate>
    ```

2. Run the project in release mode and navigate to `TestPage` to check the loading time.

3. Set the `x:DataType` attribute in `DataTemplate` to enable compiled bindings:

    ```
    <CollectionView.ItemTemplate>
        <DataTemplate x:DataType="local:Item">
            ...
    ```

```
        </DataTemplate>
    </CollectionView.ItemTemplate>
```

4. Run the project again in release mode to compare the page loading time.

5. Now let's replace all the bindings with static strings:

```
<CollectionView.ItemTemplate>
    <DataTemplate>
        <HorizontalStackLayout>
            <Label Text="Id10"/>
            <Label Text="Name10"/>
            <Label Text="Value10_10"/>
            <Label Text="Value20_20"/>
            <Label Text="Value30_30"/>
            <Label Text="Value40_40"/>
        </HorizontalStackLayout>
    </DataTemplate>
</CollectionView.ItemTemplate>
```

6. Run the project in release mode once more to check the page loading time. The results may vary, but here's the loading time I observed on my Android emulator:

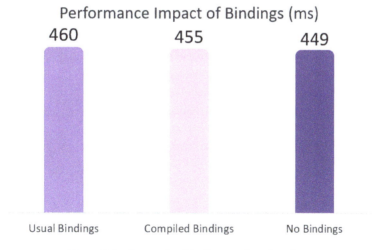

Figure 8.8 – Comparing bindings and static strings

As you can see, the difference isn't significant and falls within the margin of fluctuation error. This indicates that, generally, bindings perform quite well, and there's usually no need to avoid them. However, using compiled bindings whenever possible is considered best practice because this approach helps you catch errors at compile time.

How it works...

Here are the key things about compiled bindings in .NET MAUI:

- Compiled bindings are activated only when you specify the `x:DataType` attribute.

- They are strongly typed, meaning that binding expressions are validated during compilation. This ensures that property names, types, and data types used in bindings are accurate and exist in the view model.

- Traditional data bindings in XAML use reflection to resolve property names and types at runtime, while compiled bindings generate the necessary code during compilation. This can lead to slight performance improvements. However, element creation, measurement, and arrangement usually consume much more time than bindings. As a result, you're unlikely to notice a significant performance boost simply by enabling compiled bindings or even by eliminating bindings.

Loading data in asynchronous methods

While we've explored asynchronous data loading techniques in earlier recipes, it's difficult to ignore this topic in this chapter on performance. Data loading operations often have one of the most significant impacts in real applications.

The concept of this recipe is straightforward: instead of loading data in the view model (or view) constructor, we will load it asynchronously when the view is displayed. We'll create a simple view model that initiates the data-loading process as the page becomes visible.

Getting ready

To follow the steps described in this recipe, we just need to create a blank .NET MAUI application.

The code for this recipe is available at `https://github.com/PacktPublishing/.NET-MAUI-Cookbook/tree/main/Chapter08/c8-AsyncLoading`.

How to do it...

Let's create a simple view that displays a couple of properties from a view model and apply a technique we've used in several earlier recipes: converting the view's `Appearing` event into an asynchronous command. We'll achieve this using the `EventToCommand` behavior from the `CommunityToolkit.Maui` package.

1. Create a new .NET MAUI project and add the following NuGet packages:

    - `CommunityToolkit.Mvvm`: Add this to use an auto-generate view model.

    - `CommunityToolkit.Maui`: Add this to use the `EventToCommand` behavior.

As usual, don't forget to call `UseMauiCommunityToolkit` in the `MauiProgram.`
`CreateMauiApp` method to initialize the library.

2. Create a view model class with an `async` command that imitates data loading for two properties:

MainViewModel.cs

```
public partial class MainViewModel : ObservableObject
{
    [ObservableProperty]
    string productName;

    [ObservableProperty]
    string description;

    [RelayCommand]
    async Task LoadDataAsync()
    {
        await Task.Delay(2000);
        ProductName = "Some product";
        Description = "Product description";
    }
}
```

3. In `MainPage`, define a simple view that triggers `LoadDataCommand` when the `Appearing`
    event is raised. Use the `EventToCommand` behavior for this purpose. Additionally, use the
    `ActivityIndicator` element to inform a user that loading is in progress:

```
<ContentPage.BindingContext>
    <local:MainViewModel/>
</ContentPage.BindingContext>
<ContentPage.Behaviors>
    <tk:EventToCommandBehavior EventName="Appearing"
      Command="{Binding LoadDataCommand}"/>
</ContentPage.Behaviors>
<VerticalStackLayout>
    <ActivityIndicator IsRunning="{Binding
      LoadDataCommand.IsRunning}"/>
    <Label Text="{Binding ProductName}"/>
    <Label Text="{Binding Description}"/>
</VerticalStackLayout>
```

That's it – you can run and test the project. You should see a spinning activity indicator when the view
is shown, and then actual data will appear.

How it works...

Let's review the key points covered in this recipe:

1. When the view is displayed, the `EventToCommand` behavior triggers `LoadDataCommand`.

2. Since `LoadDataCommand` is asynchronous, it awaits other async methods (such as `Task.Delay` in our example) without blocking the UI thread.

3. During the execution of `LoadDataCommand`, the `IsRunning` flag is set to `true`, allowing us to bind it to `ActivityIndicator.IsRunning` and display a loading indicator.

4. Once the `async` methods in the command finish, the execution returns to the UI thread where we set the `ProductName` and `Description` properties.

Profiling the application

When you've optimized the obvious things but the app still feels slow, it's time to use a performance profiler. A profiler can help identify which methods are consuming the most execution time.

While Visual Studio doesn't provide built-in tools to profile .NET MAUI apps on all supported platforms, there are other tools that can assist us. In this recipe, we'll profile a .NET MAUI application using VS Code, powered by two extensions: **.NET Meteor** and **speedscope**.

Getting ready

You can use any test project and profile it. For example, you can take the project from the *Comparing performance in debug and release configurations recipe*: `https://github.com/PacktPublishing/.NET-MAUI-Cookbook/tree/main/Chapter08/c8-DebugVsRelease`.

How to do it...

In this recipe, we will install the .NET Meteor and speedscope extensions in VS Code to collect and analyze profiling data. These tools will help us understand which parts of the application are impacting performance and guide us in making optimizations.

1. Install the tooling:

    - **VS Code**: A cross-platform code editor that can serve as a fully functional IDE with the right extensions for development. You can download it here: `https://code.visualstudio.com/download`

    - **.NET Meteor**: A VS Code extension that lets you debug .NET MAUI projects and collect profiling snapshots. You can find it here: `https://marketplace.visualstudio.com/items?itemName=nromanov.dotnet-meteor`

- **speedscope**: A VS Code extension for visualizing profiling snapshots. Download it here: `https://marketplace.visualstudio.com/items?itemName=sransara.speedscope-in-vscode`

2. Run VS Code and open the folder containing your test project. To do this, click **File** | **Open Folder**, then navigate to your project folder with the `*.csproj` file.

3. Navigate to the **Run and Debug** tab in VS Code and click on **create a launch.json file**. This file is used by .NET Meteor to determine how to run the project in the desired configuration.

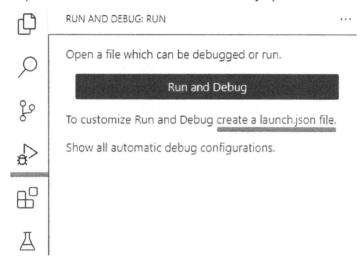

Figure 8.9 – Creating a launch.json file

4. Update the generated JSON file by adding a profiling configuration to it:

```
{
    "version": "0.2.0",
    "configurations": [
        {
            "name": ".NET Meteor Debugger",
            "type": "dotnet-meteor.debugger",
            "request": "launch",
            "preLaunchTask": "dotnet-meteor: Build"
        },
        {
            "name": ".NET Meteor Profiler",
            "type": "dotnet-meteor.debugger",
            "request": "launch",
            "profilerMode": "trace",
            "preLaunchTask": "dotnet-meteor: Build"
```

```
        }
    ]
}
```

In the newly created `launch.json` file, make sure to set `profilerMode` to `trace`. This enables snapshot collection during profiling, allowing .NET Meteor to gather performance data.

5. Save the updated JSON file, and select the **.NET Meteor Profiler** configuration from the dropdown menu next to the **Run** button.

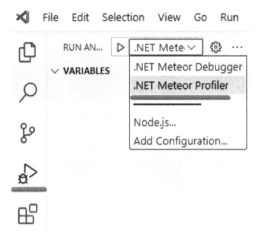

Figure 8.10 – Selecting the configuration

6. After that, select the device to run the application. For this, click the current device name in the status bar and then click the required device in the drop-down menu at the top:

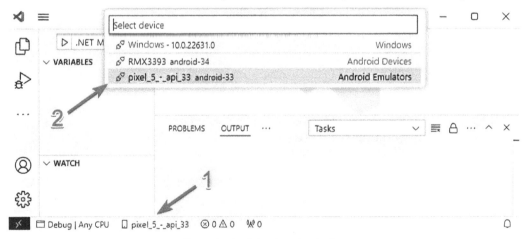

Figure 8.11 – Selecting the device

7. Now we can start the app. Delete the `bin` and `obj` folders located in your project folder, click **Run**, and choose **Run Without Debugging**:

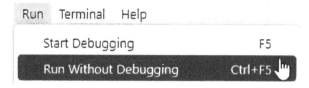

Figure 8.12 – Running without debugging

8. Interact with your test app to run the functions you want to investigate. For instance, if you started with the project from the *Comparing performance in debug and release configurations* recipe, open `TestPage`.

9. When you're ready, click **Stop** in VS Code to halt the application and generate a profiling snapshot.

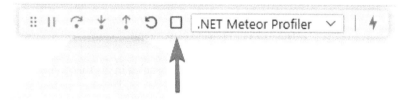

Figure 8.13 – Stop button in VS Code

This snapshot will be saved in your project folder and will have a name format of `*.speedscope.json`, where `*` will be replaced by your project name and the company ID specified in the `*.csproj` file.

10. Right-click the snapshot file and open it with speedscope. You'll see a snapshot visualization presented as a flame graph.

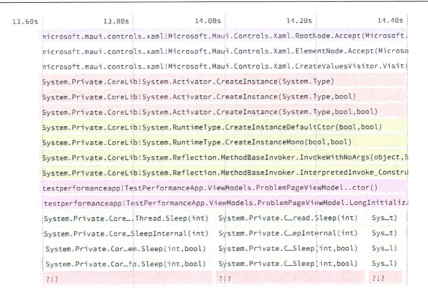

Figure 8.14 – Profiling flame graph

Now we can analyze the performance data. This process is detailed in the following section.

How it works...

While a flame graph generated by speedscope may seem complex at first glance, the principle is quite simple: each row section corresponds to a function, and the longer the section, the more time it took for that function to execute.

Function calls with a similar call stack are grouped together into one section.

Figure 8.15 – Simplified flame graph

In this example, method F1 calls F2, which then calls F3. After that, a new instance of F3 starts and calls F4. When F4 finishes, both F3 and F1 complete as well. At this point, a new F3 function begins. Since this last F3 has a different call stack, it isn't merged with the earlier F3 functions.

If you suspect that a method may be causing a performance issue, you can easily find it in the flame graph by pressing *Ctrl + F*. This will allow you to see how long the method took to execute and what other functions it calls.

There's more...

My team and I recorded a video on profiling with .NET Meteor. If you encounter any issues with the process described, you can watch it here: `https://www.youtube.com/watch?v=-4VWRt_-PKw`

Detecting memory leaks

A memory leak is a condition when the memory used by an object isn't released when that object is no longer needed. Memory leaks can lead to significant performance issues and faster battery drain.

Identifying objects that remain in memory can be challenging without the right tools. Similar to performance profiling, Visual Studio doesn't provide functionality to diagnose memory leaks on Android and iOS. However, we can utilize nearly the same set of tools as in the previous recipe: VS Code, the .NET Meteor extension, and an additional extension called **Heapview**.

Before diving into memory profiling, let's briefly discuss the basics of memory management in .NET. Managed memory is handled by the **garbage collector** (**GC**), which takes care of both memory allocation and deallocation when objects are no longer in use. Memory allocated to an object can only be reclaimed if no strong references to it exist from other active objects. For example, if `ObjectA` has a property that references `ObjectB`, then `ObjectB` won't be released.

In this recipe, we'll set up the necessary profiling tools, obtain a memory dump, and learn how to analyze it to find memory leaks and their cause.

Getting ready

We will profile a test project with intentionally introduced memory leaks. The project is available here: `https://github.com/PacktPublishing/.NET-MAUI-Cookbook/tree/main/Chapter08/c8-TypicalMemoryLeaks`.

How to do it...

Like performance profiling, the memory profiling process includes setting up the necessary tools, collecting the snapshot (memory dump), and then analyzing it.

1. Prepare the tooling:

    -   **VS Code**: This will serve as the IDE.

    -   **.NET Meteor**: We will use this to run the project and collect the memory dump.

    -   **Heapview**: We will use this extension to visualize the memory dump. You can download it here: `https://github.com/1hub/dotnet-heapview`:

        ```
        dotnet tool install -g dotnet-heapview
        ```

2. In VS Code, open a folder with our test project (`https://github.com/ PacktPublishing/.NET-MAUI-Cookbook/tree/main/Chapter08/ c8-TypicalMemoryLeaks`). Click on **File**, then select **Open Folder**, and choose the folder that contains the `*.csproj` file.

3. Open the **Run and Debug** tab, then click on **create a launch.json file**. Modify the generated JSON file as shown here and save your changes:

    ```
    {
        "version": "0.2.0",
        "configurations": [
            {
                "name": ".NET Meteor Debugger",
                "type": "dotnet-meteor.debugger",
                "request": "launch",
                "preLaunchTask": "dotnet-meteor: Build"
            },
            {
                "name": ".NET Meteor Profiler",
                "type": "dotnet-meteor.debugger",
                "request": "launch",
                "profilerMode": "gcdump",
                "preLaunchTask": "dotnet-meteor: Build"
            }
        ]
    }
    ```

Note that, this time, `profilerMode` should be set to `gcdump`, not `trace` like in the previous recipe.

4. Save the updated JSON file, and select the .NET Meteor Profiler configuration from the dropdown menu next to the **Run** button.

5. After that, select the device to run the application. For this, click the current device name in the status bar and then click the required device in the dropdown menu at the top.

6. Now we can start the application. Remove the bin and obj folders, click **Run**, and select **Run Without Debugging**. Open different pages in the test app, and then tap the **Check Instances** button. This button triggers the GC using the following code:

    ```
    GC.Collect();
    GC.WaitForPendingFinalizers();
    ```

    Keep in mind that it's a good idea to tap the button *multiple times*. The GC releases memory in several cycles with delays, and its algorithm can't be directly controlled by simply calling Collect and WaitForPendingFinalizers (even if you call them multiple times in a row).

7. Obtain the memory dump by opening the **Debug Console** panel in VS Code and typing the /dump command. You should see a message similar to this:

    ```
    Writing gcdump to
      '...\com.companyname.MyApp.gcdump'...
    command handled by DotNet.Meteor.Debug
      .GCDumpLaunchAgent
    Finished writing 672119 bytes.
    ```

    The dump file should appear in the project folder.

8. Open the dump file in Heapview. To do this, click on **Terminal**, then select **New Terminal** in VS Code, and type the following command:

    ```
    dotnet-heapview [YOUR DUMP FILE NAME]
    ```

    Alternatively, you can type the dotnet heapview command without any parameters. This will launch the Heapview tool, allowing you to click on **File | Open**, and then select the memory dump file.

Now you can analyze the snapshot. Let's discuss this in the *How it works...* section.

How it works...

After completing *step 8*, you should see a window that looks like this:

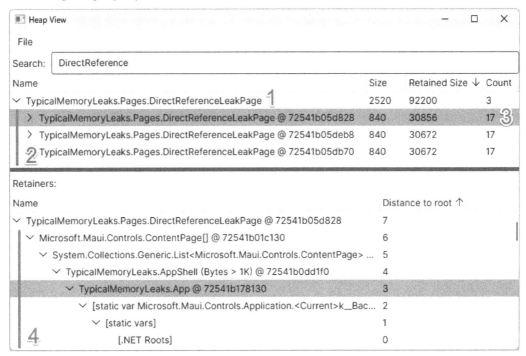

Figure 8.16 – Memory dump in Heapview

Here are the key elements:

1. A list of types still present in memory.

2. A list of instances remaining in memory.

3. The number of child objects held by a specific type or object instance.

4. The chain of references that holds a specific object instance.

The main indicator of a memory leak is the presence of multiple instances of the same page. This typically happens when you navigate back and forth between pages, creating a new page instance each time without destroying the previous one. To check if an object still exists in memory, enter its type in the search field to see if any instances are found.

The area labeled with the number *4* is crucial for identifying the cause of the leak. It shows you which objects have a reference to the selected object. To release the object, we need to eliminate the references that are holding onto it. We'll discuss techniques to help you with this process in the next recipe.

There's more...

If you encounter any issues with this recipe, take a moment to check out the video we recorded at DevExpress about memory profiling: `https://www.youtube.com/watch?v=faUljIKIulc`

It's worth mentioning that there's another straightforward way to detect memory leaks using the `MemoryToolkit.Maui` library. This library helps catch common memory leaks related to UI controls by setting the `LeakMonitorBehavior.Cascade` attached property at the page level:

```
<ContentPage …
xmlns:mtk="clr-namespace:MemoryToolkit
  .Maui;assembly=MemoryToolkit.Maui"
           mtk:LeakMonitorBehavior.Cascade="True">
```

Once configured, the `MemoryToolkit.Maui` library will automatically display a warning if it detects a memory leak. For more information on how to use the library, refer to the following GitHub repository: `https://github.com/AdamEssenmacher/MemoryToolkit.Maui`.

Getting rid of memory leaks

All memory leaks share a common root cause: an object isn't released from memory because another object holds a strong reference to it. The GC checks if this object is still in use and, as a result, doesn't remove it from memory.

Here are some of the most frequent scenarios that lead to memory leaks:

- **Reference from a long-lived object**: For example, `AppShell` exists for the entire duration of the application. If you create a property in `AppShell` and store a reference to another page, that page will never be released.

- **Reference from a static property or field**: Static properties maintain their values for the life of the application. If you pass an object to a static property, that reference will persist until you explicitly remove it or stop the application.

- **Event handlers or function delegates**: When you subscribe to an event, the instance containing the event handler is stored in the class that raises the event, creating a strong reference. For instance, if you subscribe to the `Button.Click` event on a page, the button will hold a reference to the page. It's important to note that a memory leak will only occur if you subscribe to an event of a long-lived object or static class. In the case of a button, there won't be any memory leaks because both the button and the page exist in the same scope; they reference each other, and the GC can remove both when they are no longer used by external objects.

- **Controls with memory leaks**: If a page contains a control that remains in memory due to external references, the entire page will also be retained in memory. This happens because each control holds a reference to its parent logical element through the `Parent` property.

In this recipe, we will explore several techniques for eliminating common memory leaks.

Getting ready

To follow this recipe, download the project with intentionally introduced memory leaks: `https://github.com/PacktPublishing/.NET-MAUI-Cookbook/tree/main/Chapter08/c8-TypicalMemoryLeaks`

How to do it...

We'll begin with an application that intentionally includes memory leaks on each separate page. This application has multiple buttons that open pages with these leaks. The **Check Instances** button triggers the GC and calculates how many pages are still held in memory.

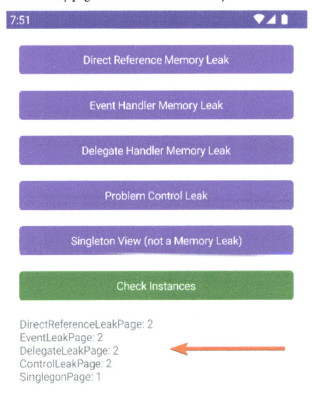

Figure 8.17 – Test app with memory leaks

1. Open and run the following project from the GitHub repository: `https://github.com/PacktPublishing/.NET-MAUI-Cookbook/tree/main/Chapter08/c8-TypicalMemoryLeaks`.

Navigate to each page twice, and then click **Check Instances** three or four times. As you'll see in the text at the bottom, even though we've navigated away from all the pages, they are still held in memory. Now, let's fix this.

2. We'll begin by addressing the delegate handler memory leak. This leak is caused by the following code in `DelegateLeakPage`:

```
Dispatcher.StartTimer(TimeSpan.FromSeconds(1),
    TimerTick);

//...

bool TimerTick() {
    //...
}
```

In this code, we use `TimerTick` as a delegate, and `Dispatcher` holds a reference to the entire `DelegateLeakPage` to call `TimerTick`. Since `Dispatcher` lives for the entire lifetime of the application, `DelegateLeakPage` won't be released from memory due to this existing reference.

3. The best solution is to replace `Dispatcher.StartTimer` with `Dispatcher.CreateTimer` and subscribe to the `Tick` event in the `Appearing` event handler. Additionally, we'll make sure to unsubscribe from the event in the `Disappearing` event handler:

```
IDispatcherTimer timer;
public DelegateLeakPage()
{
    //...
    timer = Dispatcher.CreateTimer();
    timer.Interval = TimeSpan.FromSeconds(1);
    Appearing += OnAppearing;
    Disappearing += OnDisappearing;
}

bool TimerTick()
{
    //...
}
private void TickEventHandler(object sender,
    EventArgs e) => TimerTick();

private void OnAppearing(object sender, EventArgs e)
{
    timer.Tick += TickEventHandler;
    timer.Start();
```

```
    }
    private void OnDisappearing(object sender,
      EventArgs e)
    {
      timer.Stop();
      timer.Tick -= TickEventHandler;
    }
```

`DelegateLeakPage` should now be released from memory.

4. For `EventLeakPage`, let's try another technique using `WeakEventManager`. The leak in `EventLeakPage` happens because we subscribe to `CustomEvent` of the `App` object. Since the `App` object lives for the entire duration of the program, it will always hold a reference to `EventLeakPage`, preventing it from being released. The following are the code snippets that cause a memory leak in the test application:

EventLeakPage.xaml.cs

```
public EventLeakPage()
{
  InitializeComponent();
  ((App)App.Current).CustomEvent +=
    EventLeakPage_CustomEvent;
}
```

App.xaml.cs

```
public partial class App : Application {
//...
    public event EventHandler<EventArgs> CustomEvent;
}
```

5. To fix the leak, update the `CustomEvent` definition so that it uses `WeakEventManager`:

```
public partial class App : Application
{
    readonly WeakEventManager _weakEventManager = new
      WeakEventManager();
    public event EventHandler<EventArgs> CustomEvent
    {
        add => _weakEventManager
          .AddEventHandler(value);
        remove => _weakEventManager
          .RemoveEventHandler(value);
```

```
        }
    }
```

The WeakEventManager class maintains only a weak reference to the subscriber. Weak references don't prevent the target object from being released. In other words, if only a weak reference exists to an object, the GC can destroy that object.

6. Next, we'll address the memory leak in DirectReferenceLeakPage. This leak occurs because we're adding the page instance to the App.OpenedChildPages collection:

App.xaml.cs

```
public partial class App : Application
{
    public List<ContentPage> OpenedChildPages = new
      List<ContentPage>();
    //...
}
```

DirectReferenceLeakPage.xaml.cs

```
public DirectReferenceLeakPage() {
    InitializeComponent();
    ((App)App.Current).OpenedChildPages.Add(this);
}
```

7. While the best approach is to remove DirectReferenceLeakPage from the OpenedChildPages collection (for example, in the Disappearing event handler, as mentioned in *step 3*), let's use a technique with weak references for learning purposes. Modify the type of the App.OpenedChildPages collection to List<WeakReference>:

App.xaml.cs

```
public List<WeakReference> OpenedChildPages = new
  List<WeakReference>();
```

When adding the DirectReferenceLeakPage instance to OpenedChildPages, wrap it in WeakReference:

DirectReferenceLeakPage.xaml.cs

```
((App)App.Current).OpenedChildPages.Add(new
  WeakReference(this));
```

Similar to the previous step, since only a weak reference now exists to the page, it can be successfully reclaimed by the GC when there are no other strong references to it.

8. Now, let's take a look at `ControlLeakPage`. This page contains a `Label` descendant that subscribes to the `DeviceDisplay.MainDisplayInfoChanged` event:

```
public class CustomLabel : Label {
    public CustomLabel() {
      DeviceDisplay.Current.MainDisplayInfoChanged +=
        Current_MainDisplayInfoChanged;
    }

    //...
}
```

ControlLeakPage.xaml

```
<ContentPage ...>
    <Grid x:Name="rootGrid">
        <local:CustomLabel x:Name="customLabel"... />
    </Grid>
</ContentPage>
```

9. While, ideally, we should address the issue within `CustomLabel`, this isn't always straightforward, especially if the control comes from a third-party library. In such cases, the simplest solution is to remove the problematic control from the page in the `Disappearing` event handler:

ControlLeakPage.xaml.cs

```
private void ControlLeakPage_Disappearing(object
  sender, EventArgs e)
{
    rootGrid.Children.Remove(customLabel);
}
```

While this won't release `CustomLabel` from memory, it will at least prevent the entire page from being retained due to `CustomLabel`.

10. The last one is `SingletonPage`. If you run the application, open `SingletonPage` twice, and tap the **Check Instances** button, you'll notice that only one instance of `SingletonPage` is held in memory. This isn't a memory leak, as the number of retained instances doesn't increase. So, why is this single instance of `SingletonPage` still in memory? The reason is that `SingletonPage` is registered as a singleton instance in the `MauiProgram`. `RegisterViews` method:

MauiProgram.cs

```
public static class MauiProgram {
    //...
    public static MauiAppBuilder RegisterViews(this
      MauiAppBuilder mauiAppBuilder) {
        mauiAppBuilder.Services
            .AddSingleton<SingletonPage>();
        return mauiAppBuilder;
    }
}
```

11. You can think of this technique as caching since the same `SingletonPage` instance is consistently used, which significantly speeds up subsequent page openings. This approach is beneficial for frequently used pages. However, if you don't want a page to persist in memory, opt for the `AddTransient` method instead of `AddSingleton`:

```
mauiAppBuilder.Services.AddTransient<SingletonPage>();
```

We've successfully addressed all the memory leaks in our app! Now you can run it, navigate through all the pages, and click the **Check Instances** button multiple times to confirm that the memory usage is as expected.

How it works...

If you haven't delved into memory management before, it can be challenging to grasp what situations cause memory leaks and which don't.

The simplest case of a memory leak occurs when an object is directly referenced by another long-lived object or a static property:

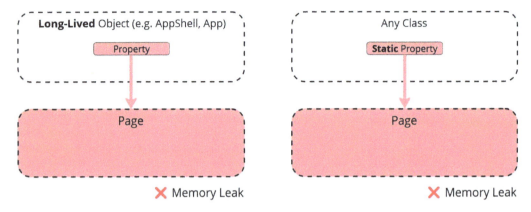

Figure 8.18 – Direct reference memory leak

A less obvious scenario arises when an object subscribes to an event of another object. Since the event emitter retains a reference to the subscriber, this can also lead to a memory leak, preventing the subscriber from being released. For instance, if the App class has an event and we subscribe to it in ContentPage, the App class will hold a reference to ContentPage.

It's also crucial to understand that if both the emitter and subscriber exist within the same scope, there will be no memory leak because the GC will detect the cyclical reference and destroy both objects simultaneously.

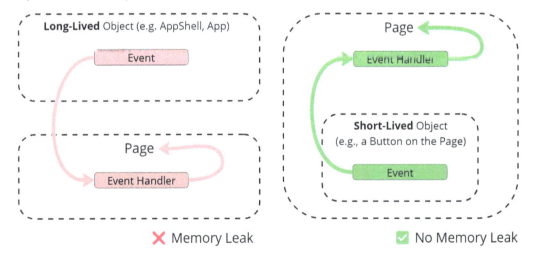

Figure 8.19 – Event handler memory leak

When dealing with a leaking control (like in `ControlLeakPage`), this control can prevent the entire page from being released. Each control retains a reference to its parent element in the `Parent` property, creating a chain of references that ultimately leads back to the page as the root element.

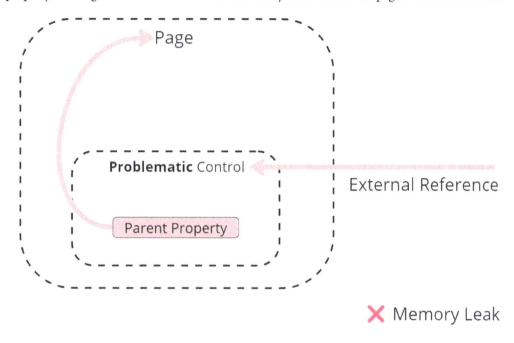

Figure 8.20 – Problematic control memory leak

There's more...

The GC is responsible for managing only managed objects, which encompass most of the entities we typically work with, such as pages, controls, view models, lists, strings, and more. These objects are automatically removed from memory by the GC when there are no strong references to them.

However, applications often utilize unmanaged resources that the .NET GC cannot directly handle. Examples of these resources include file streams, database connections, and network connections. For such objects, you must either explicitly call the `Dispose` method when the object is no longer needed or use a `using` statement in the variable definition to ensure proper resource management:

```
using var fileStream = new FileStream(filePath,
  FileMode.Open, FileAccess.Read)
//or
var fileStream = new FileStream(filePath,
  FileMode.Open, FileAccess.Read)
fileStream.Dispose()
```

The `using` statement ensures that the compiler automatically generates code to call `Dispose` when a variable goes out of scope, effectively managing resources.

Another important consideration is circular references in iOS native objects. While you don't need to worry about circular references when using only cross-platform APIs, customizing handlers and platform views may occasionally result in memory leaks. These leaks can occur when two objects hold references to each other. As we learned in the *Customizing a platform view with an existing control handler* recipe, platform .NET views are essentially wrappers around native objects that live outside the scope managed by .NET. One such native object in iOS is the `UIView` class, which serves as the base class for other views. When you add a child view to `UIView`, this internally creates a reference that .NET does not manage. As a result, if two `UIView` objects create references to each other, they will persist in memory unless you explicitly remove the references or dispose of the objects.

In most cases, you don't need to worry about circular references unless you're building custom iOS views. However, understanding this behavior can save you significant debugging time if you encounter such issues.

Index

`packtpub.com`

Subscribe to our online digital library for full access to over 7,000 books and videos, as well as industry leading tools to help you plan your personal development and advance your career. For more information, please visit our website.

Why subscribe?

- Spend less time learning and more time coding with practical eBooks and Videos from over 4,000 industry professionals

- Improve your learning with Skill Plans built especially for you

- Get a free eBook or video every month

- Fully searchable for easy access to vital information

- Copy and paste, print, and bookmark content

Did you know that Packt offers eBook versions of every book published, with PDF and ePub files available? You can upgrade to the eBook version at `packtpub.com` and as a print book customer, you are entitled to a discount on the eBook copy. Get in touch with us at `customercare@packtpub.com` for more details.

At `www.packtpub.com`, you can also read a collection of free technical articles, sign up for a range of free newsletters, and receive exclusive discounts and offers on Packt books and eBooks.

Other Books You May Enjoy

If you enjoyed this book, you may be interested in these other books by Packt:

.NET MAUI Projects - Third Edition

Michael Cummings, Daniel Hindrikes, Johan Karlsson

ISBN: 978-1-83763-491-0

- Set up .NET MAUI to build native apps for multiple platforms using its single project capabilities
- Understand the core aspects of developing a mobile app, such as layout, UX, and rendering
- Use custom handlers for platform-specific access
- Discover how to create custom layouts for your apps with .NET MAUI Shell
- Implement serverless services in your .NET MAUI apps using Azure SignalR
- Create a .NET MAUI Blazor application leveraging the power of web technologies
- Build and train machine learning models using ML.NET and Azure Cognitive Services

.NET MAUI Cross-Platform Application Development

Roger Ye

ISBN: 978-1-83508-059-7

- Develop high-performance apps with logical user interfaces
- Improve the maintainability of apps using the MVVM design pattern
- Understand the progression from Xamarin.Forms and how to migrate to .NET
- Delve into templated components and Razor class libraries for crafting Blazor UI elements
- Publish your creations to major app stores with guidance on preparation and processes
- Extend your testing repertoire with bUnit for Razor components for reliable unit testing

Packt is searching for authors like you

If you're interested in becoming an author for Packt, please visit `authors.packtpub.com` and apply today. We have worked with thousands of developers and tech professionals, just like you, to help them share their insight with the global tech community. You can make a general application, apply for a specific hot topic that we are recruiting an author for, or submit your own idea.

Share Your Thoughts

Now you've finished *.NET MAUI Cookbook*, we'd love to hear your thoughts! Scan the QR code below to go straight to the Amazon review page for this book and share your feedback or leave a review on the site that you purchased it from.

`https://packt.link/r/1-835-46112-3`

Your review is important to us and the tech community and will help us make sure we're delivering excellent quality content.

Download a free PDF copy of this book

Thanks for purchasing this book!

Do you like to read on the go but are unable to carry your print books everywhere?

Is your eBook purchase not compatible with the device of your choice?

Don't worry, now with every Packt book you get a DRM-free PDF version of that book at no cost.

Read anywhere, any place, on any device. Search, copy, and paste code from your favorite technical books directly into your application.

The perks don't stop there, you can get exclusive access to discounts, newsletters, and great free content in your inbox daily

Follow these simple steps to get the benefits:

1. Scan the QR code or visit the link below

https://packt.link/free-ebook/978-1-83546-112-9

2. Submit your proof of purchase

3. That's it! We'll send your free PDF and other benefits to your email directly

www.ingramcontent.com/pod-product-compliance
Lightning Source LLC
Chambersburg PA
CBHW080610060326
40690CB00021B/4645